Following in Footsteps or Marching Alone?

Following in Footsteps or Marching Alone?

How Institutional Differences Influence Renewable Energy Policy

Srinivas C. Parinandi

University of Michigan Press
Ann Arbor

For questions or permissions, please contact um.press.perms@umich.edu

Published in the United States of America by the
University of Michigan Press
Manufactured in the United States of America
Printed on acid-free paper
First published February 2023

A CIP catalog record for this book is available from the British Library.

Library of Congress Cataloging-in-Publication data has been applied for.

ISBN 978-0-472-07582-9 (hardcover : alk. paper)
ISBN 978-0-472-05582-1 (paper : alk. paper)
ISBN 978-0-472-90315-3 (open access ebook)

DOI: https://doi.org/10.3998/mpub.11764131

This book is freely available in an open access edition thanks to TOME
(Toward an Open Monograph Ecosystem)—a collaboration of the Association
of American Universities, the Association of University Presses, and the
Association of Research Libraries—and the generous support of the University
of Colorado Boulder Libraries. Learn more at the TOME website, available at:
openmonographs.org

The University of Michigan Press's open access publishing program is made
possible thanks to additional funding from the University of Michigan Office
of the Provost and the generous support of contributing libraries.

Cover: *Zauberlehrling*, by the German Art Collective Inges Idee.
Photograph by Tuxyso / Wikimedia Commons / CC-BY-SA-3.0

Contents

Digital materials related to this title can be found on
the Fulcrum platform via the following citable URL:
https://doi.org/10.3998/mpub.11764131

Tables

Figures

Figures

Acknowledgments

I am profoundly thankful for all of the help I have had throughout the intellectual journey of this project. My dissertation co-chairs at the University of Michigan, Charles Shipan and Jenna Bednar, stand out as individuals who helped me throughout various stages of this project. I must also include Elisabeth Gerber and Rob Franzese, who also served on my dissertation committee and whom I am grateful to have as friends and mentors. At my home at the University of Colorado, I am grateful to Jenny Wolak, Andy Baker, Anand Sokhey, Scott Adler, Andy Philips, David Bearce, Ken Bickers, and Sarah Wilson Sokhey, all of whom have been useful sounding boards during this project. I also want to thank Jack Nickelson, Ken Stallman, and Joe Zamadics for research assistance. Within the wider profession, I am thankful to Fred Boehmke, Graeme Boushey, Sanya Carley, David Fortunato, Jeff Harden, Matt Hitt, Andy Karch, Thad Kousser, Rebecca Kreitzer, Chris Mooney, Rachel Potter, Barry Rabe, Molly Reynolds, Leah Stokes, and Craig Volden for providing valuable guidance at critical junctures of the project.

Research specialists at the North Carolina Clean Energy Technology Center were extremely helpful in demystifying the DSIRE renewable energy database. So too were individuals at the National Association of Public Utilities Regulators, who helped explain the internal logic of the public utilities commission world. Institutional support has been provided for this research in the form of a Gerald Ford Fellowship to complete dissertation work at the University of Michigan and then at the University of Colorado, where a conference was organized to discuss the project.

I want to thank reviewers for the University of Michigan Press as well as the editorial staff at the University of Michigan Press (and particularly Elizabeth Demers) for strengthening this project and making it a possibility. Parts of chapter 5 and the appendix appear in similar form in my article "Policy Inventing and Borrowing among State Legislatures," *American Journal of Political Science* 64 (4): 852–68, and I want to thank reviewers for that journal article for helping this project as well.

Finally, I must thank my family. My wife, Carrie, has been an inspiration to me as well as my best friend ever since we met nearly two decades ago, and she has helped me along every step of this endeavor. My children, Grier and Graley, have also been guiding lights to me throughout this time and continue to be great teachers to me. The Schrader family has always been there to provide good cheer and laughter. My brother, Gunnu, also served as a sounding board. Lastly, my parents, Nagamani and Narasimham, have been foundational in my life and taught me about hard work, never giving up, and helping others whenever possible.

CHAPTER I

Introduction

In recent years, much ink has been spilled about the dysfunction of the American federal government. Writing in the news journal *The Hill*, an observer commented that "the United States government has become dysfunctional to the point that gridlock is almost a cliché" (Nye 2019). Similarly, in describing the sorry state of the federal government as a problem solver, a writer in *Governing* magazine alluded to an argument that "drift and dysfunction of the national government" is fueling an absence of federal help to other governments in the American political system (Harkness 2018). A third example comes from the venerable *Atlantic*, where a somewhat recent piece alleges that the national governmental "system isn't working" and that "the dysfunction of the government" is "growing" (Appelbaum 2015).

The sentiment expressed by the comments referenced above is not just confined to public intellectuals and those in the media. Everyday Americans also seem to subscribe to the opinion that the federal government is ineffectual. For example, a Gallup poll in 2013 listed government dysfunction as the nation's most pressing issue (Newport 2013). A 2017 poll authored by the *Washington Post* in collaboration with the University of Maryland showed that respondents have "widespread distrust of the nation's political leaders" as well as an "erosion of pride in the way democracy works in America" (Wagner and Clement 2017). These authors' description of poll results is remarkably chilling in summarizing respondents' view about the state of America's body politic: "Seven in ten Americans say the nation's politics have reached a dangerous low point, and a majority of those believe the situation is a 'new normal' rather than temporary, according to the poll" (Wagner and Clement 2017).

A manifestation of the federal government's dysfunction, and arguably a driver of further plummeting faith among the public in the ability of the federal government to perform even basic tasks, is the increasing inability of the federal government to even adopt a semblance of meaningful policy. Afflicted by party polarization (McCarty 2019) and enmeshed in a culture of brinkmanship, the federal government is unable to effectively produce policy. One key area where such federal government inability has been exhibited is with respect to green energy policy. Although the planet's changing climate is largely acknowledged by the scientific community (Gross 2018) and by major transnational institutions (United Nations 2021), and although a warming climate could wreak economic, ecological, and political havoc on the United States (Overpeck and Udall 2020; Koubi 2019), the federal government has not been able to substantially commit to policies that favor the emergence of cleaner sources of energy over traditional fossil fuels, especially in the electricity sector where fossil fuels and particularly dirtier coal retain significant utilization (Allison and Parinandi 2020).[1] Given that the United States accounts for much of the global production of carbon dioxide emissions (Hickel 2020), the American federal government's inaction regarding fostering the use of green or clean energy has been recognized as a pressing international problem (Vigilone 2020).

One solution that has been put forth to deal with the issue of federal government inaction has been to circumvent the American federal government and advocate for policy-making within the individual U.S. states. The American federal system, with the substantial autonomy and freedom of maneuver that it affords individual states (Riker 1964; Bednar 2008; Boushey 2010; and Karch 2007), creates the possibility that the states could serve as leaders of green energy policy-making. And the very idea that the states *should* lead in policy-making, both with respect to green energy as well as other policy issues, has resonance among politicians, the media, and even the public. Writing about the views of President Ronald

---

1. Possible scenarios in the United States range from sizeable drying out of some of the nation's most valuable farmland (Overpeck and Udall 2020) to the potential evacuation of large metropolitan areas such as Miami and New Orleans (Scott et al. 2020). In 2014, the nation's electricity sector accounted for 30% of America's greenhouse gas emissions, with 67% of the nation's electricity being derived from fossil fuels (United States Environmental Protection Agency 2014).

Reagan in *The Nation*, the Reverend Jesse Jackson remarked that "what was consistent about [Reagan] was his belief that each state has a sovereign right to control its own laws" (Jackson 2004). The idea that each state should control its own policy-making destiny is akin to believing that the states should lead on policy-making, as federal government leadership may imply a loss of state control.

Cutting across the ideological spectrum, journalists also invoke state leadership on policy-making as an antidote to federal inaction or even disagreement with the stated federal position on policy. An author in *Vox*, a news and analysis website, suggested that policy-making autonomy at the state level could be marshalled to dilute the Trump administration's immigration agenda (Gerken 2017). Commenting from a decidedly dissimilar ideological perspective in the newsmagazine *Reason*, a different author claimed that Obamacare stifled state-level autonomy and thus "undermines a core principle of American federalism" (Staley 2010). The ability of the concept of state-level policy-making autonomy to gain adherents from different ideological dispositions speaks to the existence of a widespread faith in the power of the states to solve pressing challenges and is arguably an antidote to the paralysis of federal polarization insofar as the individual state governments are more likely to be ideologically homogenous compared to the federal government.[2] This faith is mirrored in differences in reported public sentiment in the competence of federal versus state governments to handle problems. Plotting the percentage of respondents in 10 years of Gallup polls who signal that they have a "great deal" of trust in the ability of the federal government to handle domestic problems alongside the percentage of respondents who signal that they have a "great deal" of trust in the ability of state governments to handle state problems gives a rough measure of how some of the public ranks the relative competence of federal versus state governments.[3] In figure 1, I provide this plotted comparison using Gallup poll results collected in the 2010–2020 interval (Gallup 2020).

As figure 1 reveals, a higher number of respondents believe that state governments exhibit a great deal of competence compared to the federal

---

2. State-level invention in the areas analyzed is largely driven by ideological extremism. This suggests that novel policies might have difficulty gaining acceptance across a polarized entity.

3. Of course, "domestic problems" asked in the federal question may not be identical to "state problems" asked in the state question. However, I assume there is enough overlap in the two categories for a comparison to be made. Gallup does not provide concrete examples of each.

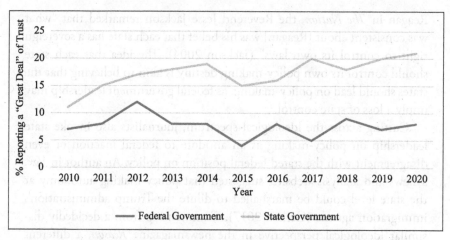

Fig. 1. Respondents Reporting a "Great Deal" of Trust in Government Solving Domestic Problems
Source: Public opinion data come from Gallup.

government. This gives heft to the notion that much of the public believes in letting states take the initiative in solving problems based on a belief in greater state-level competence. Public belief in state-level policy-making complements a famous statement made by Justice Louis Brandeis in the 1932 case *New State Ice Company v. Liebmann.* Commenting about one of the virtues of American federalism in his dissenting opinion, Brandeis argued that "it is one of the happy incidents of the federal system that a single courageous State may, if its citizens choose, serve as a laboratory; and try novel social and economic experiments without risk to the rest of the country" (285 U.S. 262). Meant to articulate one of the benefits of allowing for state autonomy in policy-making, Brandeis's comment has become canonical advice invoked to justify state control over policy-making. From welfare to tax policy to agricultural policy, the thinking goes, letting states take the lead in spearheading policy-making can engender systemwide (e.g., across the 50 U.S. states) benefits in terms of creating unique solutions to problems that may be faced across several states. To use an analogy from gardening, giving the states policy autonomy allows for different kinds of flowers to be grown in 50 different garden plots, which presumably increases the diversity of cultivation compared to if only one garden plot (the federal or national one) were utilized.[4] By this logic and given federal governmental inaction with respect to green energy policy, one might expect that state-level leadership in this area could precipitate an explosion of experimentation in the states, with the possibility that some state-developed policies could diffuse and serve as the basis for similar policy-making in other states and even the federal government (Rabe 2004, 2007, 2008; Volden 2006). In short, the states could illustrate paths forward where the federal government has failed to do so.

The idea that the states can go it alone and find novel policy solutions is alluring and oft-mentioned in policy circles.[5] Moreover, I am highly confident that states adopt novel policies: a 2014 article from the *Washington Post* revealed that state legislatures ushered in over 24,000 laws that year (Wilson 2014); some of the components of these 24,000 laws were almost certainly unique to the states adopting them and not borrowed from other states' policy-making.[6] However, even though policymakers, pundits, and the public believe in the capacity of the states to deliver novel solutions to pressing problems, and even though instances exist of where states adopt novel solutions, we know very little about what factors motivate states to adopt novel policy in the first place. Political science scholarship on policy adoption, which is dominated by work on the U.S. states (Mooney 2020), has conceptualized experimentation in state policy adoption through the lens of a state adopting a policy that is new to it regardless of whether that policy is actually new across the system of all states (Mooney 2020; and Walker 1969). This choice of how to conceptualize experimentation in

---

4. This does not mean that state governments will automatically act in every imaginable policy area; it does suggest, however, that some states will experiment to provide other governments with valuable templates. Take COVID-19 as an example: not every state (for instance, South Dakota) crafted their own stay-at-home responses, but enough states did to provide some diversity in policy templates. In the COVID case, notice that the national government under President Donald Trump abdicated much of its policy responsibility to the states.

5. Writing in affiliation with the American Enterprise Institute, for example, the libertarian scholar Michael Greve commented that "popular appeal aside, one can make a powerful theoretical case for the experimental, decentralized politics that the laboratory metaphor suggests. Political institutions should be capable of adapting to changing economic circumstances and social values" (Greve 2001).

6. Further, there are plenty of instances of state-level novel policy adoption with respect to renewable portfolio standards, the main policy area analyzed in this book.

state policy adoption, along with a heavy emphasis being placed on the diffusion or spread of policy from state to state (Walker 1969; Gray 1973; Berry and Berry 1990; Shipan and Volden 2006; Karch 2007; Shipan and Volden 2008; Boushey 2010; Parinandi et al. 2020), means that scholarship has largely skipped the issue of when states are likely to adopt policy that has never been tested in other states.[7]

Ignoring the influences driving a state to go it alone and inaugurate its own novel policy solutions is problematic, especially since we invoke the states as a potential cure for federal dysfunction. If we view something as a cure but do not understand the motivations behind that cure, then we fail to properly respect the medicine we are prescribing and also fail to anticipate possible side effects that could emanate from that medicine. At a more granular level, investigating novel policy adoption entails doing justice to the part of Brandeis's comment where he speaks about the uniqueness of a given state's policy. If a key virtue within American federalism is that the individual states, facing federal inaction, have the opportunity to enact novel solutions to problems, and if a key expectation among proponents of American federalism is that some novel state-devised solutions will become common best practices utilized across the federation, then exploring the antecedents of novel state-level policy-making is the sine qua non to unpacking what many observers believe to be a major selling point of American federalism. What does state-level novel policy adoption, which I refer to throughout this book and elsewhere (Parinandi 2020) as *invention*, look like, and how can it be distinguished from state adoption of a policy that has already been adopted in another or other state(s), an action that I refer to as *borrowing*? Are the factors motivating state-level invention and borrowing different, and, if so, how are they different? And can we identify explanations that primarily or even uniquely account for when

---

7. This is not to say that political scientists have not recognized that investigating novel policy adoption—where states adopt policy that has *not* been tried by other states—is a worthwhile endeavor. Over a generation ago, scholars like Clark (1985) and Glick and Hays (1991) understood that states can amend policy in unique ways, something they referred to as "reinvention" (Clark 1985; Glick and Hays 1991). More recently, Karch (2007) described how states can "customize" their own solutions to problems. However, even though scholars know that novel policy adoption can occur, a systematic way to identify novel policy adoption along with a thorough exploration of the phenomenon has not been developed. I offer a treatment here. In chapters 3 and 5, I offer a detailed description of relevant literature along with a discussion of how I separate novel policy adoption (invention) from borrowing.

states inject novel policy into the shared cross-state library of attempted policy-making?[8]

Working toward and deciphering answers to the questions above matters for any area where the states try to go it alone and devise their own policy solutions to problems, but it arguably matters urgently with respect to green or renewable energy policy. Due to challenges brought about by a warming climate, the United States faces a great imperative to build its renewable energy infrastructure (Allison and Parinandi 2020). Much of that imperative pertains to the country's retail electricity sector, which has historically been a key source of fossil fuel emissions and has been primarily subject to state-level regulation.[9] The individual states possess the authority to determine how their own retail electricity markets function, and the federal government has not been able to tell the individual states how they should accommodate renewable energy development within their respective retail electricity markets—the inability of the federal Obama-era Clean Power Plan to materialize is one example of the federal government's failure to force state governments to commit to pursuing renewable energy development in designing their own retail electricity markets (United States Environmental Protection Agency 2015). Therefore, seeing how individual states choose to incorporate attempts to foster renewable energy development in their retail electricity markets and specifically seeing how individual states adopt novel policy to foster such renewable energy development provides a window into how the states are spearheading policy in such an important area absent strong federal direction. What are the characteristics of the states that take the lead and adopt novel policy pertaining to renewable energy in their retail electricity markets, and to which states should we look in hopes of finding invention today that may become tomorrow's best practices? Do the factors influencing invention differ based on what actor within state government is doing the inventing?

---

8. Lest some readers think otherwise, my spotlighting of Brandeis's focus on novel state-level policy adoption is not meant to disparage borrowing. Being able to adopt policy that has been vetted by other state(s) is a sizeable benefit. However, this is predicated upon novel policies being adopted by the states in the first place.

9. The retail electricity sector deals with electric utility companies providing and selling electricity to end users and has historically been and is under the purview of state-level regulation (Troesken 2006). The wholesale electricity sector deals with electricity generators and providers selling electricity to each other, often includes transactions crossing state lines, and is under the purview of the Federal Energy Regulatory Commission (Allison and Parinandi 2020).

And, lastly, how can the invention experiences of states in this one important area potentially inform state attempts in other areas where federal
government inaction has arguably resulted in individual states claiming
much of the mantle of policy-making?

In this book, I answer the above questions by delving into a meticulous
study of state-level inventing and borrowing with respect to renewable
portfolio standards, or RPS. An RPS generally specifies that electricity utility companies operating in a given state procure some of the electricity they
provide to end-use consumers in that state from renewable sources. Appearing on the scene in the last quarter of the twentieth century and dissemi-
nating through a wide swath of states, RPSs have become the preeminent
way in which the states have tried to spark renewable energy development
(Rabe 2004, 2007; Carley and Miller 2012; Carley, Nicholson-Crotty, and
Miller 2017; Parinandi 2020; Parinandi et al. 2020; and Stokes 2020).
Unlike policies such as carbon taxes that have been shown to have limited
appeal across the states, RPSs have been described as "climate policy that
can actually win" and have been described by energy economist Michael
Greenstone as "the biggest [carbon policy] we have in this country" (Meyer
2019). RPSs have also been a state-level rather than federal phenomenon,
meaning that we can study and distinguish state inventing and borrowing in the absence of strong federal impulses that may distort when such
inventing and borrowing occurs.[10] Lastly, RPSs have been the site of tremendous state-level diversity in policy adoption, meaning that we actually
observe instances of state invention and borrowing that can be dissected
and analyzed.[11] Simply put, focusing on the RPS area permits us to study
state responses to federal inaction in Brandeis's mold—that is, inventing
by adopting novel policy or borrowing by adopting policy that has been
tested in other states—in what is possibly one of the most important problems facing humanity in the twenty-first century.

The RPS area is also beneficial in that it captures state-level invention

10. A close read of Brandeis's comment suggests that federal-level action might manipulate
state-level proclivities to invent and borrow. Thus, if one wants to examine how states navigate
invention and borrowing given federal inaction, one would be well advised to study an area such
as RPS featuring a scarcity of federal action. Seeing how state-level invention and borrowing
could change given federal action is a second order issue dependent on first establishing what
state-level invention and borrowing look like absent federal action. I take up this second order
issue in the conclusion of the book.

11. In chapters 2 and 3 and, to a lesser extent, in chapters 5 and 6, I describe much of the
diversity that exists across the states with respect to RPS policy adoption.

and borrowing across a multiplicity of institutional actors. Political science research on state experimentation and diffusion typically considers adoption from a legislative perspective (Kousser 2005; Boehmke and Skinner 2012; Graham, Shipan, and Volden 2013). While state legislatures understandably command significant attention with respect to policy adoption given their role as lawmakers, the legislative branch is not the only branch at the state level that adopts policy. Similar to what has transpired at the federal level (Potter 2019), the states depend on an array of regulatory agencies to execute various programs (Parinandi 2013; Boushey and McGrath 2017). These regulatory agencies not only administer policy but often adopt policy in the name of upholding their administrative responsibilities. States' public utilities commissions, which are the regulatory agencies responsible for governing state-level electricity retail sectors, also administer RPS programs in states with such programs and have invoked their authority as overseers of state grid safety and reliability to not only launch RPS programs but to add policy to existing RPS programs. Being able to assess the motivations behind novel policy adoption and borrowing across legislative and regulatory institutional venues is important, not only because regulatory agencies also play a key role in policy adoption but also because many observers may view regulatory policy-making as a backstop against legislative dysfunction (Meier et al. 2019). If state legislatures start to mimic the federal government in terms of exhibiting dysfunction, then it would be worthwhile to know when regulatory agencies are more likely to invent by adopting novel policy.

Ultimately, in the book, I devise a way to identify invention and distinguish it from borrowing in policy adoption data so as to more fully explore Brandeis's evocative vision about the virtues of state-led policy-making, and I also interrogate Brandeis's vision across different institutions to shed light on when various state-level actors will work toward that vision. Lessons gleaned here from studying RPS help elucidate where advances in American renewable and sustainable energy policy-making are likely to come from, especially if current federal-level dysfunction continues unabated. And there is good reason to think that current federal governmental dysfunction may continue: writing in the esteemed journal *Nature*, authors have pointed out that "the [United States] has proved itself to be . . . dysfunctional," no doubt focusing on the inability of the federal government to respond to crises (Maxmen and Tollefson 2020). By focusing on the states, which are increasingly being viewed as a substitute for the federal government, this book resonates with the level of government that many observers believe represents America's best chance to address challenges. And since so many studies tout the preponderance of the states' borrowing from each other—scholars Graham, Shipan, and Volden (2013) identify hundreds of articles focused on the theme of policy diffusion—this book explores how states might populate policy tools potentially slated for diffusion. The framework established in this book may also help the scholarly community investigate the inventive capacity of the states in a host of different areas moving forward.

Roadmap of the Book

I now offer a roadmap of the book featuring synopses of each of the chapters, with theoretical and empirical highlights interwoven into the synopses.

Chapter 2. Given that the RPS area plays such a central role in the book, it is important to delve into some background about RPS programs. What are RPS programs, what do they try to do, why have they emerged over other kinds of pro-renewable-energy policies, and whom are they levied upon? I provide a historical genesis of the RPS policy tool, giving special attention to how the U.S. states have taken the lead in promulgating RPS policy. I also discuss how state legislatures and state public utilities commissions conceivably had the jurisdictional authority to adopt RPS policy, and I detail how both institutional actors have adopted RPS policy across various U.S. states.

Chapter 3. Here, I take up how to identify and measure invention by state governments. In the chapter, I discuss why we should look to subpolicies or policy features rather than a policy regime or program writ large (as is traditionally done in political science) to identify novel adoption. I also introduce and expound upon the definition of invention that I use in the book, and I discuss how the definition of invention (and by extension, borrowing) is agnostic about the institutional source doing the adopting; this matters so that we can analyze and investigate invention coming from different institutional sources.

I give concrete examples from RPS adoption about what counts as invention or borrowing. I then discuss how identified instances of invention and borrowing are used in conjunction with the statistical workhorse employed to examine adoption, event history analysis (Berry and Berry 1990; Box-Steffensmeier and Jones 1997, 2004) and specifically, *pooled* event history analysis (Boehmke 2009; Boushey 2016; Parinandi 2020), to empirically examine potential drivers of invention as well as borrowing in legislative and regulatory settings.

Chapter 4. In this chapter, I talk about how legislatures and public utilities commissions may respond to different motivations in deciding when to invent with respect to RPS. Starting with the observation that state legislatures invented more than state public utilities commissions, I contend that perceptions about the core mission or responsibility of an institution should influence how members of that institution approach novel policy adoption. The legislative branch is considered the chief policy-making branch, and legislatures have broad legitimacy to adopt policy. On the other hand, while public utilities commissions sometimes adopt policy, they are chiefly considered to be filling the role of an executor. This difference in the core responsibilities of each institution arguably impacted how much each institution invented with respect to RPS: the institution with broad legitimacy to adopt policy (the legislative) might have felt more "courage" (to use Brandeis's word) inventing compared to the institution worried about being seen as overstepping its bounds (the regulators).

The same difference in the core responsibility of each institution helps provide clues as to when each institution is more likely to invent. A big part of legislating involves embracing and articulating a worldview and using that worldview to make sense of the policy options that one should pursue. Greater extremism in one's worldview can cause lawmakers to overlook evidence or a track record in advocating for policies that fit their worldview, suggesting that ideological extremism among legislatures might correspond with increased inventing. Given that RPS is a left-leaning area, the expectation is that increased liberalism among legislatures leads to more RPS invention. Public utilities regulators, on the other hand, strive to appear as neutral arbiters and may base invention on when the threat of pushback from key regulated entities—entrenched electric utility companies—is reduced. I believe that such a threat is reduced when states have ushered in deregulated electricity sectors, since entrenched electric utility companies want to hold on to the position that they still have and are more likely to accommodate regulatory dictates. In this chapter, I also discuss how other factors (particularly electoral pressure) could potentially influence legislative as well as public utilities commission inventing, and I use this discussion as a motivator to begin the subsequent analyses of legislative and regulatory RPS adoption.

Chapter 5. Here, I delve into legislative RPS invention in detail and more fully espouse the argument linking increased ideological liberalism among legislatures to a greater likelihood of inventing RPS policy. I also test this argument using a pooled event history dataset of legislative instances of RPS invention and find evidence for the argument. One naturally may wonder whether the same pattern extends to legislative RPS borrowing, and I test for this possibility using pooled event history data on legislative instances of RPS borrowing. The findings here are valuable, as they show that with respect to legislative RPS adoption, Brandeis's courageous inventors are ideologically extreme (on the liberal side) while those borrowing the fruits of others' invention are more ideologically diverse relative to the inventors. Given that state legislatures have been such prodigious inventors, the finding regarding liberalism may be seen as a benefit—to the extent that observers desire more RPS invention—of ideological extremism in government, which is typically seen through a negative lens.

I also evaluate the potential that legislative electoral vulnerability could influence legislative RPS inventing and borrowing, and I test for both of these possibilities. While I find no meaningful link between legislative electoral vulnerability and legislative RPS invention, I do find a link with RPS borrowing (greater vulnerability leads to more RPS borrowing), which I argue emanates from vulnerable lawmakers wanting to tell potentially skeptical constituents that they are trying to replicate results seen elsewhere. Normatively, some may believe that legislative electoral vulnerability's connection with RPS borrowing but not RPS invention is desirable, as it suggests that lawmakers are not subjecting voters to the risk of adopting novel policy for the sake of lawmakers' own electoral vicissitudes. However, if one believes that lawmakers' electoral concerns *should* motivate them to tackle renewable energy challenges by embracing novel and untested policy, then the finding here may be potentially problematic.

Chapter 6. While the fifth chapter contains a theoretical and empirical exposition about legislative RPS invention, the sixth chapter does the same regarding public utilities commission–led RPS invention. Public utilities commissions are bound by mission statements upholding a central objective of fairness in regulatory behavior and conceivably attempt to maintain an appearance of being neutral arbiters in decision-making. This desire to conform to the appearance of being a neutral arbiter arguably influences·when public utilities commissions choose to invent RPS policy. RPSs potentially raise costs for entrenched or long-standing electric utility companies by pushing these companies to change their electricity sourcing or procurement.[12] Novel RPS policy arguably carries greater uncertainty for these firms than borrowing, where the experiences of companies in other states can inform firm observers. As surveys of firms have shown that they generally abhor uncertainty (Lagerberg 2015; Baker and Raskolnikov 2017), it is not a leap to surmise that entrenched electric utility companies dislike RPS invention. Public utilities commissions ostensibly know about the feelings of entrenched electric utility companies and strategically invent when these companies are weak to minimize chances of company-led pushback. This condition is more likely to obtain when states have undergone electricity sector deregulation, as entrenched electric utility companies have lost monopolistic or near-monopolistic power and are plausibly more likely to accommodate regulatory wishes to preserve the position (essentially holding on to control over distribution) that they still retain.

I use a pooled event history dataset encompassing public utilities commission-led instances of RPS invention to test the deregulation argument, and I find evidence in support of the deregulation argument. I also evaluate the possibility that deregulation could influence public utilities commission–led borrowing and do not find support for this, which comports with the idea that entrenched electric utility companies are less hostile to borrowing than they are to invention. The deregulation finding not only helps us identify when public utilities commissions are likely to adopt novel RPS policy, it shows how regulators might take potential pushback from regulated entities into consideration when adopting novel policy, and highlights a potential benefit that might accrue from electricity sector deregulation.

---

12. In chapter 6, I give readers a thorough explanation of what I mean by *entrenched* electric utility companies.

Chapter 7. This chapter provides complementary case studies for the phenomena discussed in chapters 5 and 6. I first discuss the RPS policy feature adoption experiences of the state legislatures of Illinois and Indiana. Illinois and Indiana are Midwestern neighbors that have similar economic profiles, energy profiles, and renewable energy development potential. However, the experiences of the two state legislatures in crafting RPS programs have been different: while lawmakers in Illinois made the state a leader in renewable energy policy-making and have shown a willingness to shape their state's RPS program by inventing novel policy features, Indiana lawmakers adopted their RPS program only after such programs had diffused widely across the United States and also chose to adopt policy features that were almost entirely unoriginal and not novel. I walk through the experiences of both state legislatures and show how the relatively liberal ideological orientation of the Illinois legislature vis-à-vis Indiana's played a role in the more inventive RPS path of the Illinois legislature.

To buttress findings from chapter 6, I present a case comparison of the RPS policy feature adoption experiences of two state public utilities commissions, those of New York and Arizona. New York and Arizona are noteworthy in that the public utilities commissions of both states were pioneers in devising the RPS programs in each state and also inventing novel RPS policy solutions. However, whereas New York regulators have continued to position their state as a leader in crafting renewable energy policy, Arizona regulators have been under siege and face pressure to halt development on the state's RPS and even roll it back. A big reason Arizona's regulators have faced greater challenges than New York's is that Arizona has a regulated electricity sector, which gives entrenched electric utility companies a firmer position from which to challenge new regulatory policy proposals. Together, the case studies provide an illustrative and accessible visualization of core themes of the book.

Chapter 8. While the previous seven chapters have explored state novel policy adoption from the vantage point of RPS, in this chapter, I veer from the terrain of RPS policy-making and examine state-level novel adoption from the area of anti-abortion policy-making. Although RPS programs have been adopted by an ideologically heterogeneous set of states, using regulation to advance renewable energy development is generally regarded as a liberal ideological prerogative (Potrafke 2010). Given that one of the book's central findings regarding legislative RPS invention is that ideological extremism leads legislatures to overlook the absence of a track record and support the adoption of a policy proposal comporting with their worldview (shown in chapter 5 with respect to legislative liberalism and RPS invention), observers may wonder if the same dynamic occurs with respect to increased legislative conservatism regarding policy adoption comporting with a conservative worldview. Anti-abortion policy is not within the lexicon of renewable energy policy, but it is solidly conservative in character and has been overwhelmingly adopted through state legislative action (Kreitzer and Boehmke 2016). Moreover, even though the famous *Roe v. Wade* Supreme Court case represented federal-level intervention in the abortion policy area, the panoply of state-level attempts to limit abortion access is emblematic of state efforts to craft their own policy solutions (in this case, of a conservative stripe) in the aftermath of imprecise federal resolution (Kreitzer and Boehmke 2016). State legislative attempts to forge anti-abortion policy thus serve as a useful conservative extension of the analysis of legislative RPS invention, and this extension provides a glimpse of how the framework utilized in this book could be applied to other policy areas in the future.

To facilitate this extension, I take anti-abortion policy feature adoption data, as recorded by the authors of a paper on this issue (Kreitzer and Boehmke 2016), and I transform this data to capture instances of anti-abortion invention and borrowing using the same procedure that I utilized to capture RPS-related instances of invention and borrowing. I then see how the same variables influencing legislative RPS invention (and borrowing) in the fifth chapter measure up when the area of analysis is changed to the issue of anti-abortion. I ultimately find congruence on the conservative side with respect to ideological extremism, as increased conservatism of a state legislature makes that legislature more likely to adopt novel anti-abortion policy. Also similar to the fifth chapter, ideological extremism has a more prominent statistical association with legislative invention compared to legislative borrowing, suggesting that more ideologically diverse legislatures tend to embrace borrowing. The finding linking ideological extremism to legislative invention suggests that insofar as a policy area takes on a liberal or conservative bent, ideology will play a large role in dictating whether a state legislature enacts novel policy comporting with that policy area.

A second noteworthy finding from this chapter regards the inversion of the electoral vulnerability variable in comparison to the fifth chapter.

While electoral vulnerability influenced legislative borrowing but not inventing in the RPS area, this same variable influences legislative inventing but not borrowing when we turn to analyzing anti-abortion adoption. One potential reason for why this could be the case has to do with the possibility that abortion may be considered to be more of a moral issue area than renewables. Moral issues tend to be viewed through a prism of right versus wrong (Mooney 1999), which can diminish the importance of evidence as a tool to communicate with constituents about a policy. At the same time, viewing an issue area as a matter of good versus evil may create an expectation that policymakers are showing a commitment to advancing a worthwhile crusade, and adopting novel policy could be a way for vulnerable policymakers to demonstrate that they care about taking part in the crusade. Systematic study across a host of morally and less-morally perceived issue areas is needed to provide affirmation for the idea that I put forth here—and in the conclusion, I discuss how this systematic study can be carried out—but the result here preliminarily suggests that those wishing to create a stronger electoral connection for RPS invention would do well to frame the renewable issue as one of right versus wrong or good versus evil.

Chapter 9. In the concluding chapter of the book, I not only recap key findings and implications regarding legislative and regulatory RPS invention but also outline how the framework devised here can be applied to examine the inventive capacity of the states in a number of different ways. Spillovers include (i) extending the analysis to incorporate more policy areas; (ii) extending the analysis to include changes in federal-level intervention; (iii) extending the analysis to include the study of ideologically "moderate" policy areas; (iv) extending the analysis to incorporate regulatory adoption in "conservative" policy areas; and (v) extending the analysis to systematically compare policy areas on the basis of whether they are perceived to be moral in nature.

Other extensions discussed in the conclusion involve moving beyond an adoption-based conceptualization of invention and entertaining the possibility that my distinction of invention and borrowing could apply to other kinds of governmental policy-making. State public utilities commissions, for example, have played a major role in enforcing electric utility companies' compliance with RPS program stipulations. Based on the analysis that I put forth here, it is possible that (vi) the type of enforcement regime pursued by a state's public utilities commission (in terms of whether it is a novel enforcement strategy or one that has been pursued by other state public utilities commissions) could be influenced by the status of a state's electricity sector (whether it's regulated or deregulated), and this potential difference, if true, would have bearing on the health of RPS programs as tools to spur renewable energy development. Another extension (vii) along the same lines could involve analyzing novelty in policy abandonment or termination (Volden 2015). A different spillover project (viii) related to better capturing the preferences of regulatory agencies involves devising a convincing way to measure regulatory agency preferences. And finally, (ix) one could look at factors predicting individual legislator support for novelty in policy-making by examining the amount of novel content in legislation sponsored by specific legislators. This set of ideas encompasses an entire research agenda that could inform our understanding of American federalism and state politics and policy-making for years to come.

Final Thoughts

In the book, I ultimately address a big issue—the hope that the individual states will serve as a reservoir or repository of policy solutions that compensate for federal-level dysfunction, and the related expectation that the states will pursue novel policy solutions that can then potentially be utilized by other states—and not only devise a method to identify invention in state policy adoption but also address when such invention is more likely to occur. The policy area that I predominantly use to anchor my analysis, state renewable portfolio policy, touches on an issue of enormous normative importance (encouraging the development of renewable energy utilization in the electricity sector of the United States) where the states filled a void arguably left by federal inaction, allowing us to see how the states are fulfilling Brandeis's promise of being courageous policy leaders. And my exploration of invention across two different institutions conjures up the possibility that different stimuli could influence inventing across different institutions. The book ultimately provides a snapshot that could be used to better understand the states' position as engines of invention, and I now turn to more fully developing that snapshot.

CHAPTER 2

Renewable Portfolio Standards in the U.S. States

Given that the bulk of the book deals with renewable portfolio standards as an area of interest, in this chapter I situate the standards within the wider context of U.S. environmental policy. Renewable portfolio standards (RPSs) generally mandate that electric utility companies procure some amount of the electricity they provide to consumers from renewable sources, and these standards have emerged as one of the preeminent ways in which the U.S. invests in renewable energy development (Rabe 2004, 2007; Äklin and Urpelainen 2018; Parinandi 2020; Parinandi, Langehennig, and Trautmann 2020; Stokes 2020). While all RPSs share a commonality of pushing electric utility companies to procure renewable energy and even though the vast majority of state RPSs require participation from electric utility companies, voluntary programs also lie within the Rubicon of state RPS policy-making; in some cases (e.g., Illinois), they were precursors to the formation of required programs (North Carolina Clean Energy Technology Center 2016). Here, it is useful to briefly address why RPSs have become a central tool in American renewable energy policy and also address why the states have been the locus of this activity.

RPSs were conceived to increase renewable energy development through intervention on the supply side of electricity (Allison and Parinandi 2020). RPSs have also been connected to climate-change-related mitigation efforts, and to the extent that these policies have increased the proportion of low carbon emissions fuel sources that are utilized to generate electricity, RPSs *have* attempted to reduce the carbon footprint of the electricity sector. However, it is important to recognize that what counts as renewable is subject to definition by policymakers and that states have crafted their RPSs in different ways, suggesting that no two states' RPS approaches would share the same level of effectiveness in either mitigating climate change or bolstering renewable energy development based on the traditional understanding of "renewable" energy as encompassing non-fossil-fuel-based sources (Stokes 2020).

One reason for why RPSs became a preferred policy device in the United States is that they typically do not impose direct costs on end-use consumers—imagine a person at home turning on their light switch—nor do they impose direct costs on a wide variety of industries. A carbon tax levied on individuals, such as that existing in the Canadian province of British Columbia, has been prescribed as one of the best methods to reduce carbon emissions (Marron and Morris 2016; Province of British Columbia 2020); this kind of tax, however, places a direct cost on individuals and has had difficulty gaining traction within the United States, as many Americans believe they should not have to pay directly to confront climate change (Leiserowitz et al. 2018; Rainey 2019). In a related vein, a largescale cap-and-trade system such as the European Union's Emissions Trading System could reduce carbon emissions by linking permits to emitting carbon, requiring companies to buy permits if they want to emit carbon, and reducing the number of permits in circulation over time to lower total carbon emissions (Bayer and Äklin 2020). However, a system like the EU's Emissions Trading System imposes direct costs across a host of different industries, which have largely been able to convince policymakers and much of the public that such a system will impact businesses adversely and raise costs for the public (National Federation of Independent Business 2017; Sickinger 2019; Allison and Parinandi 2020).

RPSs, in contrast, are levied on electric utility companies. In turn, electric utility companies have a largely adversarial relationship with the public, which chiefly interacts with these companies while paying bills or dealing with electricity outages, and which has low levels of trust concerning how fairly it is treated by these companies (Consumer Reports 2018).[1] The fact that RPSs are imposed on parties—electric utility companies—

---

1. This survey, conducted on a nationally representative sample of electricity consumers, revealed that just one-third of respondents expected "fair rates and service" from their electric utility company (Consumer Reports 2018).

with which the public does not have especially cordial relations, combined with the fact that costs borne by the public due to RPSs are largely indirect (meaning that they are folded into electricity bills instead of being stand-alone items), might account for why RPSs have taken hold across the bulk of the United States while policies like carbon taxes have not.

Even though RPSs have found acceptance in much of the United States, it is worth noting that RPS policy adoption has been a state rather than federal phenomenon. To be sure, there has been a federal-level attempt to enact a policy similar to an RPS: the Obama administration's Clean Power Plan functioned like an RPS in that states were expected to achieve clean energy targets through regulating electricity generation and procurement.[2] However, RPS-like policies have failed to gather steam at the federal level, and the states have taken the leading role in advancing these policies (Parinandi 2020). Federal inaction has occurred not only because the U.S. Senate amplifies the interests of rural states with fossil-fuel-related industries (e.g., Alabama or Alaska), which may generally be skeptical of environmental regulation at the expense of urban states with less dependence on fossil fuel-related production (e.g., California or Rhode Island), which may be more receptive to environmental regulation (Warf 2008). It has also occurred because the individual states (and many of the members of Congress who represent these states) arguably desired flexibility to craft their energy and environmental policies in ways that they themselves saw fit (Peterson 1995; and Karch 2007).

While the lack of meaningful federal involvement has been lamented for contributing to a renewable energy regulatory landscape that is best described as a patchwork (Allison and Parinandi 2020; Mildenberger and Stokes 2020), the state-led response regarding renewable energy policy is fortuitous for learning about when states invent original policy as opposed to borrowing existing policy. Moreover, the institutional variation in how states have invented and borrowed RPS policy—with legislatures and public utilities commissions playing sizeable parts in inventing and borrow-

---

2. Although RPSs have arguably increased American renewable energy use and development compared to the status quo prior to the creation of RPSs (Rabe 2004, 2007; Allison and Parinandi 2020), it is important to not automatically draw a one-to-one correspondence between RPS policy-making and carbon emissions reduction, since some states (e.g., Ohio, Pennsylvania, and West Virginia) defined "renewable" energy to include fossil fuel-based sources. However, even given this acknowledgment, the majority of state RPS programs have defined "renewable" energy to consist of conventional "renewable" sources of energy.

ing in this area—allows us to see how different institutional actors might approach the process of inventing and borrowing. In this brief chapter, I provide a quick chronology of RPS adoption during the time span of this study (1983–2011). I then discuss how different institutional actors played a role in adopting RPS policies across the states. Both the chronology and the institutional discussion offer a useful foundation for explorations encountered later in the book.

A Chronology of State RPS Adoption

The state RPS adoption story is one that comports with other areas of policy experimentation (e.g., lottery adoption as in Berry and Berry 1990, or antismoking adoption as in Shipan and Volden 2008) where a few jurisdictions serve as initial adopters while a greater number of jurisdictions are later adopters who aid in the diffusion of the policy (Rogers 1962; Walker 1969; Gray 1973). What this study offers beyond those accounts is both a systematic distinction between invention and borrowing at the subpolicy or policy feature level that recognizes the fact that later adopters could still invent at the subpolicy level (thereby permitting us to observe invention and borrowing regardless of when a state adopted an RPS policy writ large) and the existence of institutional variation vis-à-vis legislatures and public utilities commissions that lets us study the factors influencing invention and borrowing in each of these two institutional actors.[3]

The first cluster of states that adopted policies that would later functionally become known as RPSs was located in the Upper Midwest. Under the auspices of building up its renewable energy sector, Iowa adopted a prototypical RPS program with its 1983 Alternative Energy Law requiring that some amount of electricity be procured from specific energy sources (Sarkisian 2016). Iowa's effort was followed by Minnesota, which in 1994 required its largest investor-owned utility to set aside a certain amount of mega-wattage capacity from biomass-related and wind-based sources (Minnesota Legislature 1994).

Following this point, state policy experimentation concerning RPS took root in two new regional clusters. One cluster, centered on the

---

3. In the next chapter, I provide a much more exhaustive explanation of the value added through using my analytical framework.

American Southwest, involved states like Arizona (1996), Nevada (1997), Texas (1999), and, later, New Mexico (2002) adopting RPSs in trying to harness the region's considerable solar and wind-based energy potential (Arizona Corporation Commission 1996; Rabe 1999; North Carolina Clean Energy Technology Center 2016). The second cluster, focused on the Northeast, involved states like Massachusetts (1997), Maine (1997), and Connecticut (1998) enacting RPSs centered on (but not exclusive to) hydroelectric and ocean-based energy sources (North Carolina Clean Energy Technology Center 2016). While new clusters were emerging, the Upper Midwest remained a locus of experimentation with Wisconsin adopting its own program in the late 1990s (North Carolina Clean Energy Technology Center 2016).

By the mid-to-late 2000s, RPSs began gaining traction among a wider group of states and were adopted more broadly across the United States. A large swath of states stretching from the mid-Atlantic to the nation's interior, including Pennsylvania (2004), Michigan (2008), Ohio (2008), and West Virginia (2009), adopted their own RPS programs (North Carolina Clean Energy Technology Center 2016). The four states above are noteworthy because they did not merely craft their programs around bolstering conventional (e.g., "clean" with respect to carbon emissions) renewable sources but also included decidedly fossil-fuel-based sources (e.g., "coal mine methane" with respect to Pennsylvania's RPS) within their RPS programs (e.g., Pennsylvania Legislature 2004). Another later adopter, North Carolina (2007), made concessions to its own locally dominant industries by mandating that, in its RPS program, some electricity be procured using swine and poultry waste (North Carolina Legislature 2007). In fact, there are dozens and dozens of different kinds of sources and technologies (such as microturbines as well as combined heat and power) that states could incorporate into their RPS programs. Other later adopters, such as Indiana (2011), adopted RPS programs but made them voluntary rather than mandatory in orientation (Indiana General Assembly 2011). State RPSs can also differ in terms of how quickly they aspire to reach their target levels.[4]

The diversity in state-related RPS program design not only helps with one of the objectives of this project—identifying and studying cases of

---

4. Although I analyze target levels (the amount of renewable energy that a state RPS aspires to procure), I do not analyze timelines in this book.

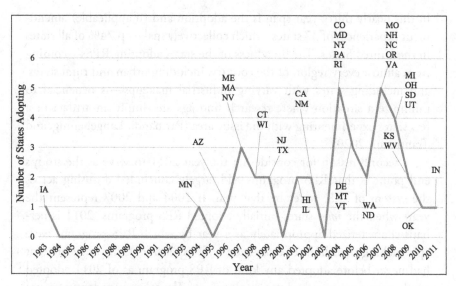

Fig. 2. When States Initially Adopted RPS Programs
Source: Data on state adoption dates primarily comes from the Database on State Incentives for Renewables and Efficiency.

invention as opposed to borrowing—but perhaps also accounts for why RPSs became so widespread (one wonders whether a standardized one-size-fits-all approach would have had such deep acceptance among policy-makers across the states, and the lack of a federal renewable energy standard suggests that standardization would have failed). In figure 2, I display when states adopted their respective RPS programs during the time period (1983–2011) analyzed in this study. It is important to keep in mind that the years in the figure only capture when states initially adopted their RPS programs. States frequently amended their RPS programs via policy feature adoption outside of when they initially adopted their RPS programs, and my framework—discussed further in the next chapter—incorporates both initial program adoption as well as subsequent amendment into the examination of invention as a process distinct from borrowing.

Figure 2 largely corroborates the diffusion outline expressed in the past few pages. While the starting point of Iowa's action in 1983 makes sense given that this was the first instance of a state adopting a prototypical RPS program, I would like to elaborate about why the year 2011 makes a worthwhile end point. First, choosing the year 2011 provides observers with nearly three decades' worth of data on RPS policy-making. Included in this nearly thirty-year span is the adoption and (if applicable) amendment experiences of 37 states, which collectively make up 74% of all states in the United States. The broadness of the states adopting RPSs—coming from almost every region of the country, including urban and rural states, and including states with varying industrial makeups—is beneficial to minimize a situation where research findings are simply an artifact of a few states experimenting with the issue area (Parinandi, Langehennig, and Trautmann 2020).[5]

A second reason for considering the year 2011 to serve as the study's end point is that RPS programs had largely concluded diffusing across the system of U.S. states by that year. If 2004 and 2007 represent the years when the *most* states initially adopted RPS programs, 2011 is perhaps characterized appropriately as a year by which RPS programs were approaching their limit of cross-state U.S. expansion. Only one state that had never before adopted any kind of RPS program as of 2011 adopted one between that year and the present time.[6] The other nonadopting states as of 2011—Alabama, Alaska, Arkansas, Florida, Georgia, Idaho, Kentucky, Louisiana, Mississippi, Nebraska, Tennessee, and Wyoming—had still never adopted an RPS program as of 2021.

Moreover, the years following 2011 actually witnessed more of a rollback and abandonment of RPS programs across the states as opposed to an expansion of these programs (Stokes 2020). In 2014, for example, Ohio instituted a freeze on its RPS program (Nangeroni 2014). The next year, neighboring West Virginia went even further and repealed its fossil fuel and particularly coal-centric RPS program (Eick 2015). Combined with the lack of a substantial number of new states initially adopting RPS programs, the dismantling of existing programs offers further evidence for the idea that the cross-state diffusion cycle for RPS policy had largely abated by 2011.

Although it is possible that dynamics similar to those driving invention and borrowing in the adoption of policy could also play a role in accounting for hypothetical invention and borrowing in the abolition or termination of policy, the field of political science has typically isolated the study of adoption (which is ensconced firmly within literature on how

---

5. This may have been the case if we focused on a program (such as carbon tax policy or autonomous vehicle regulation) that has been adopted in only a handful of states.

6. South Carolina adopted a voluntary RPS standard in 2014 (North Carolina Clean Energy Technology Center 2020).

adopted policies spread or diffuse as typified by Walker 1969; Gray 1973; Berry and Berry 1990; Shipan and Volden 2006; and Boushey 2010) from the much less well-established study of policy abolition or termination (one example of this nascent literature can be found in Volden 2015). This monograph lies within the larger tradition of studying adoption and seeks to investigate how inventing occurs across different institutional actors in the course of adoption using a policy area that has diffused across a broad number of states. The revelations in this monograph are meant primarily to inform future work on adoption and could potentially inform our knowledge about how invention occurs in non-RPS related policy-making that may be diffusing across the U.S. states. In advice intended to guide future scholarship in the conclusion of the book, I discuss how the central framework utilized in this study could also be applied to policy abolition and also discuss how scholars can begin the arduous yet important task of extending the framework across a diverse range of policy areas. In the meanwhile, I encourage readers interested in learning more about the recent freezing and repeal of RPS policy to consult the pathbreaking work of Stokes (2020).[7]

Figure 3 displays the familiar "S-curve" that is ubiquitous in studies of policy diffusion (Rogers 1962; and Boushey 2010). According to this curve, as time elapses, a greater number of states are likely to adopt a given program, such as RPS. While many previous studies of diffusion (for example, Rogers 1962) focus on how a program may drift through the population of states based on the S-curve, I am less concerned with the S-curve here and instead seek to evaluate why a state would invent within a program (at the subpolicy level) even if that state is adopting a program that has already been adopted in other states. Even a late program adopting laggard (such as West Virginia in the RPS space) can invent, and I want to explain that invention.[8]

---

7. One difficulty with applying the framework advanced in this book to the issue of policy abolition or termination is that such activity might be rare. For example, in the RPS policy space, full repeal of a state's entire renewable energy policy infrastructure has occurred in only one state (West Virginia). I offer advice on potential ways to overcome this data limitation issue in the book's conclusion.

8. The framework I advance is flexible enough to accommodate programs that spread slowly across the U.S. states (such as RPS) along with programs that spread rapidly (such as Megan's Law). I do not evaluate whether the dynamics uncovered with respect to RPS also apply to a rapidly spreading program like Megan's Law and believe that this is a worthy subject of future research.

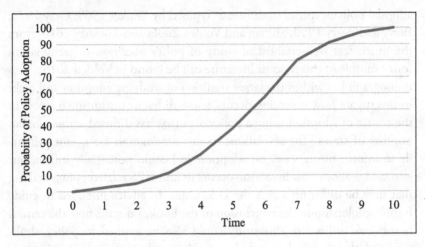

Fig. 3. Cumulative Adoption Curve

In spite of the fact that RPSs have largely stopped diffusing to new states and that some states have made attempts to dismantle their RPS infrastructure, RPSs are arguably the most widespread and durable policies falling under the aegis of clean energy to have been adopted in the United States (Allison and Parinandi 2020). Furthermore, even though the federal government was unable to implement the Clean Power Plan that it devised in the mid-2010s (recall that the federal government had a laissez-faire attitude toward the issue of fostering renewable energy development in the nation's electricity network until the attempted promulgation of the Clean Power Plan),[9] the federal plan overwhelmingly borrowed ideas from state RPS programs (United States Environmental Protection Agency 2015). Insofar as the federal government might revisit implementation of the Clean Power Plan in the years ahead, we can rest assured that state-led RPS experimentation will form much of the bedrock of any future federal clean energy electricity mandate. Evaluating the novel policy creation that took place when RPSs became the preferred renewable energy development instrument across the U.S. states thus might help us make sense of the origination of policies that could comprise a future federal electricity

9. For more information about federal inaction in the RPS space, consult Rabe (2004), Carley and Miller (2012), and Allison and Parinandi (2020).

agenda.[10] In the next section of this chapter, I move on to discussing how that different institutional actors played a role in crafting state RPS policy.

Different Institutional Actors and the Adoption of RPS Policy

RPS programs operate via the electricity sector, and one noteworthy aspect about this sector is that different institutional actors have historically had the ability to adopt policy governing this sector. By virtue of being designated as the chief lawmaking branch and having a concomitant responsibility to use the lawmaking process to cater to the interests of their constituents (Mayhew 1974; Fenno 1978; Binder 1999; Kousser 2005; Volden and Wiseman 2014), legislatures have naturally taken a leading role in crafting policy about an issue as important as renewable energy. And yet legislatures are not the only institutional actors that can claim a mandate to directly enact policy regulating a given state's electricity sector and specifying how firms operating within that sector should behave. Public utilities regulatory commissions were predominantly set up across the U.S. states in the early twentieth century (Troesken 2006). These commissions were largely set up with the blessing of electric utility companies, which feared that they were being fleeced by municipal governments and thought that state-level regulation would be more even-handed (Troesken 2006).[11]

In turn, state public utilities commissions were created explicitly to attempt to adjudicate equitably between the interests of electric utility

---

10. In chapter 3, I utilize a time-based definition of invention and classify an instance of state RPS policy feature adoption (so long as it comports with the time-based definition) as invention even if such adoption is not within the mold of what we might conventionally expect renewable policy to look like (so, for example, the Pennsylvania legislature's decision to make that state the first to allow coal mine methane to be considered a renewable source would be classified as invention). My rationale here is based on the idea that the classification of invention should reflect the on-the-ground reality where states have been extremely flexible and diverse in crafting their own RPS programs.

11. I uncover the history and impetus of state public utilities commissions in greater detail in chapter 6. The short story is that the electricity sector was mostly initially unregulated, leading to the price gouging of consumers by electric utility firms. A response to this price gouging in some states was to give municipal governments the ability to regulate electric utility firms directly (Gormley 1983; Troesken 2006). However, this led to antifirm price pandering on the behalf of consumers by municipal politicians (Gormley 1983; and Troesken 2006). State public utilities commissions were conceived to ostensibly be impartial arbiters of electric utility firm and consumer demands, and these commissions now exist across all 50 states.

companies and the rate-paying consumers constituting the general public, and the mission statements of the public utilities commissions commonly invoke this raison d'être. Colorado's public utilities commission, for example, states that a primary goal of its electricity section is to ensure "safe, reliable, and quality services to electric utility customers on just and reasonable terms" and maintain "the public interest by balancing the needs of customers and utility service providers on just and reasonable terms" (Colorado Department of Regulatory Agencies 2020). Michigan's public utilities commission includes similar language about "ensuring safe, reliable, and accessible . . . services at reasonable rates" (Michigan Public Service Commission 2020), and Georgia's public utilities commission emphasizes that the regulatory body "must balance Georgia citizens' need for reliable services and reasonable rates with the need for utilities to earn a reasonable return on investment" (State of Georgia Public Service Commission 2020). The analogous phraseology across different state public utilities commissions speaks to the ubiquitous role that these commissions play in regulating their respective electricity sectors.

Although the core missions of state public utilities commissions may seem mundane, commissions have invoked their missions to adopt a bevy of policies including conservation and public-health-related regulations (Filipink 2009). The actions of regulatory commissions in going beyond their explicit original responsibilities (in the case of state public utilities commissions, think rate setting) and adopting broader regulations in the name of upholding their regulatory missions or mandates have been upheld by the United States Supreme Court (Filipink 2009; *National Association for the Advancement of Colored People v. Federal Power Commission* 1976). Moreover, state public utilities commissions have amassed a great deal of institutional expertise and deference, and they have enjoyed and do enjoy substantial autonomy as a result (Teske 2003).

Consequently, based on being able to mediate the participation of electric utility firms in a state's electricity sector, state public utilities commissions have possessed the jurisdictional authority to adopt RPSs. The RPS policy space, then, merits attention insofar as multiple institutional actors had the opportunity to adopt RPSs; the RPS adoption experiences of the U.S. states confirm institutional heterogeneity in RPS involvement, as some states' RPS programs were crafted wholly by legislatures, other states' programs were crafted wholly by public utilities commissions, and still other states' programs were crafted by a mix of legislative and public utilities commission activity.[12] In figure 4, I display the breakdown of RPS policy feature adoptions by state based on the type of institutional actor doing the adopting.

Figure 4[13] reveals the distribution of the different institutional adopters of RPS policy features across the U.S. states. One immediate takeaway is the relative ubiquity of legislative adoption, with most states adopting most of their policy features legislatively. This probably makes sense given that the legislative branch is considered the chief policy crafting branch and given that energy-related issues represent a potentially important area of legislative policy-making. The preponderance of legislative adoption comports with the traditional literature on state policy adoption (e.g., Berry and Berry 1990; Boushey 2010; Boehmke and Skinner 2012; Parinandi, Langehennig, and Trautmann 2020) that characterizes adoption as a primarily legislative endeavor. What this book adds to that literature is a systematic way to identify novel adoption (invention), distinguish it from already-tested adoption (borrowing), evaluate what makes legislatures more likely to invent policy, and discern whether the factors influencing invention are similar to those influencing borrowing.[14] To do this effectively, I identify the components of an RPS program that could be adopted (I call these policy features), and I then determine whether these instances of policy feature adoption are either invention or borrowing. Concrete examples of policy feature adoption include sources that a state considers to be renewable (such as solar thermal energy) as well as the final target rate of an RPS (say, requiring 30% of a utility's procured electricity to be from renewable sources).

Another takeaway from figure 4 relates to the relevance of public utili-

---

12. A third institutional actor was involved in RPS policy adoption in some states, as voters directly adopted RPS policies through the ballot initiative process. I discuss the ballot initiative pathway later in this chapter but do not focus on this pathway in the book (unlike the legislative and regulatory pathways, which receive far greater attention) since it is the least common and almost entirely absent with respect to invention (e.g., in the RPS space, invention almost never occurred via the ballot initiative process).

13. Percentages are rounded to the nearest whole numbers to enhance readability in the figure.

14. In the next chapter, I go over how invention and borrowing are identified in adoption data and also discuss how the legislative and regulatory datasets that form the bases for empirical analysis in chapters 5 (legislative RPS) and 6 (regulatory RPS) are constructed. The same procedure discussed in chapter 3 is then utilized in chapter 8 to transform an existing legislative dataset on abortion restrictions (Kreitzer and Boehmke 2016).

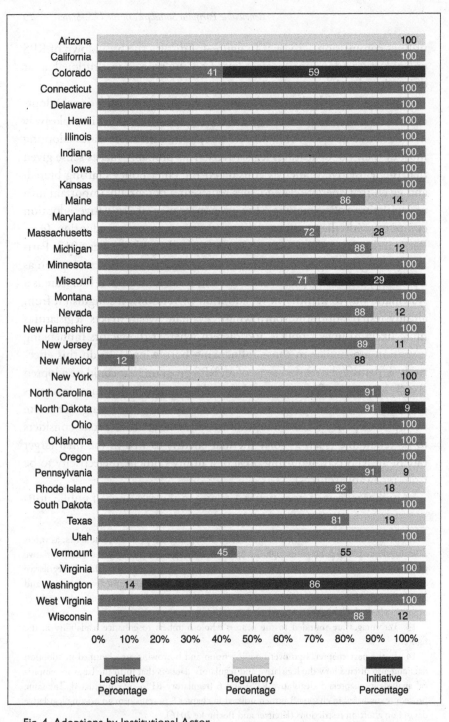

Fig. 4. Adoptions by Institutional Actor
Source: Data on state adoption primarily comes from the Database on State Incentives for Renewables and Efficiency.

ties commission, or regulatory agency-led, adoption. Although legislative action has been the preeminent method to achieve adoption, public utilities commission-led adoption has been nontrivial. Fifteen states adopted at least one RPS policy feature via public utilities commission rulemaking, with two states (New Mexico and Vermont) adopting the majority of their RPS policy features through such rulemaking and two others (Arizona and New York) adopting *all* of their RPS policy features through such rulemaking. This collection of states, like all other states, had public utilities commissions that possessed the jurisdictional authority to adopt RPS policy features under the guise of managing the relationship between electric utility companies and the consumers of electricity. Finding out what made public utilities commissions in this collection of states more likely to use their jurisdictional authority to adopt RPS policy features compared to public utilities commissions outside this collection of states is valuable insofar as we can identify when commissions would be more likely to expand their regulatory mandates and choose to invent or borrow policy.

The point that *both* state legislatures *and* public utilities commissions had the opportunity to adopt RPS policies is worth reiterating. Of course, some state public utilities commissions are more attuned to influence from their respective state legislatures than are other public utilities commissions. In my close reading of state legislative and regulatory RPS documents, however, I do not find systematic evidence of state legislatures detailing how state public utilities commissions should approach the adoption of RPS policy nor do I find evidence about how much RPS policy crafting state legislatures ask public utilities to take up.[15] What I observe is that RPS represents an area where multiple institutions had and took advantage of the opportunity to adopt and invent policy, allowing us to better study invention. Nonetheless, in chapter 6 of the book, which contains the quantitative empirical analysis of public-utilities-commission-led RPS policy feature adoption, I account for how much a state's legislature could influence regulatory agency workings by including variables capturing whether a state's legislature has term limits (under the assumption that

15. This is in stark contrast to the administration of firm or company *compliance* with RPS policy. State public utilities commissions appear to almost universally be expected to audit and ensure that electric utility companies are complying with RPS regulations. This book is about the role of institutions in adopting policy, but a potential follow-up study could examine how different institutional parameters influence firm auditing and compliance enforcement. I discuss this follow-up in greater detail in the conclusion.

term limits weaken the ability of legislatures to learn about regulatory matters) and the resource endowment or professionalism of a state's legislature (legislatures with higher endowments may be better able to monitor regulatory developments). In the same chapter, I also include a variable capturing whether or not public utilities commissioners are appointed (and thus subject to legislative confirmation and monitoring).

Before moving on, I would like to address the phenomenon of ballot-initiative-led RPS policy feature adoption. Of the three pathways, the ballot-initiative-driven one was by far the least common, appearing in only 4 states (there are 37 states that adopted RPS programs during the time span of this analysis) and being the majority of policy feature adoptions in only 2 states (Colorado and Washington). If we drill down further and look at how often the ballot initiative pathway introduced *novel* policy features into circulation across the U.S. states, we will see that the record of ballot initiatives producing invention in the RPS area is exceptionally poor, with only three instances of invention occurring through the ballot initiative process. Such a low number not only pales in comparison to the legislative and public utility commission/regulatory pathways—which have 169 and 36 instances of RPS policy feature invention, respectively— but makes quantitative analysis of ballot-initiative-led invention exceedingly difficult.

While one could speculate why ballot-initiative-led RPS policy feature invention was so rare and also speculate how this pathway of invention *may* be more common in other areas (recreational marijuana legalization may be one such area worth exploring), I focus in this book on unpacking the determinants of invention in the overwhelmingly most common institutional pathways of invention in the RPS space and save discussion of how ballot-initiative-led invention could be investigated for the book's conclusion.[16] In the book's appendix, I include a variable corresponding to whether a state allows for laws to be adopted via direct ballot initiative in my analyses; adding this variable does not change empirical results discussed in chapters 5, 6, and 8.

Ultimately, the RPS policy space represents perhaps the central way in which the United States has spurred renewable energy development (Rabe

16. Even though I do not look at the determinants of ballot-initiative-led RPS policy feature adoption, it is important to mention that I remove a state's opportunity to adopt a given policy feature if that state already adopted the policy feature through ballot initiative action. I describe this process more fully in the next chapter.

2004, 2007; Äklin and Urpelainen 2018; Allison and Parinandi 2020; Parinandi 2020; Parinandi, Langehennig, and Trautmann 2020; Stokes 2020), and it may continue to be a leading policy mechanism to propagate renewable energy development into the future. Deciphering how novel policy features enter the ecosystem of RPS policy-making—and crucially, deciphering how two prominent institutional actors partake in the entry of novel policy features into that ecosystem—has important implications for how we might see state responses in the renewable energy space progress moving forward. In the next chapter, I walk through how "invention" is identified and operationalized, and I provide a blueprint for the empirical chapters that follow later in the book.

CHAPTER 3

Identifying Invention in State Subpolicy

Subnational governments adopt lots of policies. And in federal nations, the concept of subnational units as semi-sovereign and quasi-independent entities with their own unique policy-making needs implies that subnational governments are a major site of policy creation and experimentation (Strumpf 2002; Karch 2007; Bednar 2008; Boushey 2010). The American states are no exception to this pattern and adopt their own policies quite frequently. A quick glance at law enactment data provided by the *Book of the States* shows that the 50 states collectively adopted 409,941 laws in the twenty-year interval spanning 1990–2010 (Council of State Governments, multiple years). Furthermore, policy adoption in the American states is not just a legislative enterprise. As state-level executive agencies have grown to administer an increasing array of programs, state bureaucrats or regulators have emerged as significant policy adopters in their own right. The authors of a recent publication, for example, identify that bureaucratic agencies across the 50 states adopted 292,568 rules in the same 1990–2010 period (Boushey and McGrath 2017).

What is the point behind adopting all these policies? At a very general level and without getting into the classic debate about whether governments *should* adopt so many policies, the simple answer is that state governments adopt policies to satisfy and implement the demands of their constituents. This is true for both legislatures and bureaucratic agencies. Legislatures adopt policies that they think will best cater to the wishes of the median voter in a legislative election.[1] And bureaucratic agencies

---

1. In my opinion, this assumption is not problematized by the finding linking legislative

adopt policies that they think will best allow them to fulfill their executive responsibilities while minimizing gubernatorial and legislative pushback or in the occasional case where agency members are elected, cater to the wishes of the median voter in an agency election.[2]

Policy adoption rates by the states show little sign of slowing down and may actually increase given gridlock and polarization in the federal government (McCann, Shipan, and Volden 2015). In deciding to adopt policy, state governments must grapple with the issue of adopting one of two types of policy: *borrowing* existing policy solutions from other states or *inventing* their own particular policy solutions. Invention implies "customization" and gives the adopting state government the benefit of selecting a policy that is uniquely tailored to address that state's problems (Karch 2007).[3] Borrowing, on the other hand, implies copying and gives the adopting state government the benefit of selecting a policy that has already been adopted and tried in other states. While invention is potentially risky for the adopting state government in the sense that the adopted policy has never been tried and may produce unintended negative consequences, borrowing is potentially risky for the adopting state government in the sense that the adopted policy may not be a good fit for the borrowing state and could be a "square peg in a round hole." For the adopting state government, the strengths and drawbacks of invention and borrowing are essentially mirror images of each other.

There are plenty of examples where state governments customize by choosing to invent and adopt untried policies. One recent famous example involves Kansas governor Sam Brownback's successful and unprecedented

---

ideological extremism to invention. This is because median voters elect the legislatures that serve them, including legislatures that are extreme ideologically.

2. I am thinking mainly of state public utilities commissioners, since these commissioners are elected in some states.

3. In terms of how invention might be considered to be unique tailoring, it is helpful to remember that invention represents a state adopting novel policy that has not been tested in other states. In thinking about why a state would invent (rather than say, borrow and adopt something that has been adopted in other states), it is useful to recognize that an inventing state is implicitly making an admission that existing policies that have been adopted across the states are by themselves insufficient in addressing the inventing state's desires; if such existing policies were sufficient, then the inventing state ostensibly would not feel the need to invent. Seen in this vein, invention does capture the idea that a state is trying to fit policy to meet its circumstances. Moreover, this conceptualization of invention comports with Brandeis's characterization, which describes a "courageous" state adopting novel policy to meet its own circumstances.

2012 effort to lower the tax rate on "pass-through business income to zero" (Gale 2017). Brownback and the Kansas legislature ostensibly believed that dramatically reducing the pass-through business income tax rate would increase corporate investment in Kansas and ultimately lead to growth in the state's economy. This action, however, had not been tried before and there was a possibility that a drastic reduction in taxation would instead contribute to economic distress rather than growth. Under the novel tax system, Kansas's economy did not grow as fast as the economies of neighboring states and even experienced a slowdown compared to its own (pre-tax-reform) level of growth. Moreover, Kansas's policy invention encouraged residents to reclassify their income as being from business instead of labor to benefit from the zero percent rate (Gale 2017). The resulting stagnation in economic growth combined with a drop in public budgets led the Republican-controlled Kansas legislature to override the veto of a Republican governor and end Kansas's policy invention with respect to business income taxation.

The Kansas tax experiment is an example of invention that carries a great deal of notoriety, but there are more mundane examples of state policy invention. For example, Michigan has long had the highest truck gross weight limit of any state and allows trucks with gross weights of up to 164,000 pounds to traverse its roads (Oosting 2014).[4] Michigan could have chosen a more common weight limit but opted for a unique (and uniquely high) one. Michigan's policy invention may have brought unique benefits to the state: for example, it is possible that domestic auto production has not declined in the state as much as it would have absent the invention since automakers can reduce the number of trips between production facilities due to a higher weight allowance and lower their own costs. It is also possible that the same logic (firms lowering transaction costs by taking advantage of high weight restrictions) might link the higher weight to the consolidation of Michigan's position as a key conduit in American-Canadian international trade. However, Michigan's policy invention has also brought about a disadvantage—which may have been avoided had the state adopted the federal weight standard—in the form of a transportation infrastructure that is deteriorating in part due to the stress placed on roads by heavy trucks.[5]

---

4. The vast majority of states set their gross weight limits at the federal level of 80,000 pounds. Michigan's level is therefore more than double the federal level.

5. See Tom Greenwood, "Metro Detroit Roads Ranked Fourth Worst in U.S.," *Detroit News*, July 23, 2015.

Just as there are many examples of state governments inventing during policy adoption, there are also ample examples of state governments borrowing during policy adoption. For example, states have been shown to copy other states in adopting lotteries in order to prevent their residents from traveling to other nearby states to purchase lottery tickets (Berry and Berry 1990; Baybeck, Berry, and Siegel 2011; Shipan and Volden 2012). States not only borrow for competitive reasons but also for cooperative ones. America's ongoing opioid epidemic has affected every state and created a need for coordinated and streamlined policy-making in order to shut down pill mills and disrupt drug distribution networks. The need for interstate coordination in this example has provided the states with a golden opportunity to borrow best practices from one another in an attempt not only to utilize the most effective anti-opioid policy tools but also to work together to mitigate a severe and widespread public policy challenge.[6]

As the Kansas tax and opioid epidemic examples show, invention and borrowing are discernible from one another in the public imagination and in the minds of policy practitioners. However, apart from uncovering the insight that invention and borrowing represent different kinds of policy adoption, the fields of political science and public policy have not found a way to systematically distinguish invention from borrowing in actual policy adoption data. One reason why we have not found a way to differentiate invention from borrowing is that the literature on policy diffusion utilizes a conceptualization (what diffusion scholars call "innovation") of policy adoption that does not substantially separate policy adoptions that resemble invention from those that resemble borrowing. Another reason why we have been unable to differentiate invention from borrowing is that most policy diffusion scholars have analyzed policy adoption at a level—that of adopting the *entire* law or regulation—that is too broad to determine the components of that law or regulation that are novel or original in character as opposed to being borrowed from other states' laws or regulations. Simply put, we have to focus on the subpolicies that make up a state's adopted policy in order to identify the elements of that policy that represent invention and the elements that represent borrowing.

Our inability to identify and distinguish invention from borrowing

---

6. Sometimes, states will work with each other and (occasionally) with the federal government to identify streamlined best practices. For example, the National Alliance for Model State Drug Laws, http://www.namsdl.org/index.cfm

means that we cannot uncover systematic causes of invention and borrowing and cannot discern what, in Brandeis's words, makes "a single courageous state . . . serve as a laboratory" and "try novel social and economic experiments without risk to the rest of the country" as opposed to trying existing and already-tested policy (*New State Ice Company v. Liebmann* 1932). In this chapter, I devise and describe a systematic way to distinguish invention from borrowing in policy adoption data. My method of isolating invention from borrowing can be applied to any issue area, but I use the method with the issue area of renewables portfolio regulation. I discuss how I scan state renewables portfolio laws and regulations to identify and then categorize policy adoptions as instances of invention and borrowing; and by doing so, I set the stage for the bulk of the rest of the book in which I evaluate the causes of invention and borrowing in renewables portfolio policy adoption among state legislatures and regulatory agencies.

Delving into Policy Adoptions to Help Distinguish Invention from Borrowing

I begin separating invention from borrowing in policy adoption by defining terminology that is crucial to this chapter and the overall book, starting with the concept of a *policy feature*. A policy feature is the most basic component of a policy adoption and describes in granular detail how a government plans to achieve a programmatic goal that in part motivated the policy adoption. Suppose that a state government wants to ensure the cleanliness of its waterways and adopts a policy to monitor activity from businesses and punish those businesses that are considered to be polluting the waterways. A policy feature allows the state government to operationalize its programmatic goal (cleaning the waterways) by describing *how*, in *specific* terms, the state government plans to achieve its goal. Actual policy features in this hypothetical example could include how the state government defines the cleanliness of its waterways, what businesses will be inspected, how often businesses will be inspected, and how businesses will be punished for polluting the waterways. Policy features give specificity to the state government's programmatic goal and provide the analyst with concrete ways in which the government will try to achieve its programmatic goal.

A *policy regime* is simply the set of all policy features adopted by the state government to meet the programmatic goal motivating the state's adoption of a policy. In the working example of waterway cleanliness, a policy regime is the set of all policy features that a state government has adopted within its policy aimed at ensuring clean waterways. Continuing from the working example, this means that the state's policy regime for ensuring clean waterways is the combination of all of the policy features— how a state government defines the cleanliness of its waterways; what businesses will be inspected; how often businesses will be inspected; and how businesses will be punished for polluting the waterways—that the state selected in its macro-level policy adoption (or policy regime) geared toward cleaning its waterways. A state government adopts a policy regime when it initially adopts any set of policy features that taken together encompass how the state will accomplish the goal motivating its policy adoption (or in the parlance of diffusion studies, a state government adopts a policy regime when it adopts a policy). However, the state government can change its policy regime over time by adopting new policy features or dropping existing policy features from the combination of policy features it has chosen to operationalize its policy. Two states have identical policy regimes if they have each adopted the exact same set of policy features:[7] if not, then the states have different policy regimes.

A *policy domain* is the broadest term and is simply the entire set of policy features that have been adopted across all governments that share the same programmatic goal. In order to analyze policy-making across units that are comparable to one another and to interrogate the mechanics of Brandeis's famous opinion (which pertains to the American states), I define "all governments" throughout this book to mean the 50 state governments of the United States. A scholar analyzing cross-national policy-making, however, could define all governments in terms of some set of national governments in the world.

In our running example, the clean waterways policy domain consists of the set of all policy features that have been adopted across the 50 states to achieve the programmatic goal of clean waterways. It is hopefully clear from this discussion that the order of concepts from most-to-least granular is policy feature followed by policy regime followed by policy domain. Since

---

7. In our example, this would mean that two states adopted clean waterways laws where cleanliness is defined in the same way; the types of businesses that will be inspected are the same; the frequency with which businesses will be inspected is the same; and penalties for violation are the same.

a policy domain consists of all policy features pertaining to some programmatic goal that have been adopted across the states, a policy domain also includes all policy regimes—which by construction capture each state's individual collection of policy features—that have been adopted across the states. By identifying the set of policy features that have been adopted across the states for a given policy domain and by determining when (and in what order) states adopted their respective policy features and making policy feature adoption the key unit of analysis, we can separate invention from borrowing and test theories about how the causes of invention and borrowing may differ from one another.

It should also hopefully be clear from this discussion about terminology that much noteworthy work on policy diffusion (e.g., Berry and Berry 1990; Shipan and Volden 2006; Shipan and Volden 2008) treats policy adoptions across units as equivalent in terms of content and ignores the richness and granularity that comes from including and utilizing information on policy features to analyze adoption. While this assumption of policy adoption content equivalence is understandable given that these scholars were explaining how a general policy (such as the creation of a public lottery or the adoption of a smoking ban) spreads across a system of actors, what the assumption leaves out is an explanation of how a general policy undergoes "customization" or "reinvention" as it spreads across that system of actors (Glick and Hays 1991; Karch 2007).

Other canonical work on policy "innovations" (e.g., Walker 1969; Boehmke and Skinner 2012) uncovers factors that make states leaders in terms of adopting policies that they previously lacked but still does not differentiate invention from borrowing within a single policy domain at the level of a policy feature, meaning that we still cannot unpack Brandeis's statement about what drives invention (or original or novel adoption) as opposed to borrowing. Following the lead of Rogers (1962), who recognized that the nature of a technological adoption may change as later adopters manipulate that adoption to suit their own particular needs, Glick and Hays (1991) acknowledge that policy adoption should be studied at the level of "provisions" (what they call policy features) rather than meta-policies but neither derive a systematic way to separate invention from borrowing nor do they uncover how political variables can have different influences on invention as opposed to borrowing (Glick and Hayes 1991, 839). Karch (2007) similarly identifies how local jurisdictions customize policy adoption (with the assumption that local customization implies sometimes creating novel, original, or untested policies) but gives future scholars the job of figuring out why "the same policy innovation takes on a variety of different forms in the states in which it is adopted" and also gives future scholars the job of figuring out how to consistently detect customization for quantitative analysis (191).

I now use my terminology of policy features, policy regimes, and policy domains to show how invention can systematically be distinguished from borrowing, and the method that I display here will be used for a theoretical investigation of invention and borrowing that takes place in chapters 4, 5, 6, 7, and 8. The policy domain that I use to display my method and explore causes of invention and borrowing is that of the renewable portfolio standard (RPS), and it is worth recapping why this is such a good policy domain to study. First, from an environmental perspective, state-level RPSs are the preeminent carbon mitigation tool used in the United States, meaning that if we can understand what caused the states to invent and borrow with respect to RPS, we may be able to also understand what caused the states to invent and borrow with respect to other green energy policy domains (Rabe 2004, 2007; Carley, Nicholson-Crotty, and Miller 2017; Stokes and Warshaw 2017). And second, from a purely political science and public policy-driven perspective, the RPS policy domain is ideal to analyze for two reasons. First, the federal government has essentially left RPS policy-making entirely in the hands of the states. And while this may seem like a problem at first glance, the lack of federal intervention in RPS policy-making is highly desirable for our purposes since it allows us to assess authentic state-driven explanations of invention and borrowing; through the classic use of sticks and carrots, after all, the federal government may distort state incentives to develop original policy (Peterson 1995). This suggests that analyzing state-level invention and borrowing in a policy domain where the federal government intervenes substantially (such as welfare provision or transportation policy) can create false impressions of what influences state-level invention and borrowing absent federal intervention.[8] The second desirable reason for studying the RPS policy

8. One may wonder whether the federal government leaves policy-making in the hands of the states in other areas. I can think of several. One example from the past involves state-level experimentation with air pollution restrictions in the 1950s and 1960s prior to the adoption of the Clean Air Act and the creation of the Environmental Protection Agency. An example from the present involves state-level policy experimentation with recreational marijuana legalization, as the federal government has chosen not to enforce its own law on recreational marijuana

domain is that different kinds of institutions across the states (namely, legislatures and public utilities commissions) have taken the lead in crafting and adopting RPSs, and we can use the policy adoption experiences of each kind of institution to understand how the drivers of invention and borrowing might differ between legislatures and regulatory agencies.

In the remainder of the chapter, I first describe the RPS policy domain in great detail. I then show how I use adoption data on policy features within the RPS policy domain to distinguish invention from borrowing. Part of this process involves discussing the coding procedure that I utilize throughout this book. I conclude by explaining how I use my data throughout the rest of the book.

The Characteristics of the RPS Policy Domain

Renewable portfolio standards are a set of *policy features* that state governments use to encourage (and in most cases, mandate) electric utility companies to procure and distribute electricity from renewable sources of energy (Rabe 2007). Electric utility companies typically deliver electricity from producers to end-use consumers,[9] and state RPS *policy regimes* (or the set of policy features that each respective state adopts to operationalize its own RPS program) promote renewable energy use by placing the onus on electric utility companies to supply their consumers with electricity derived from renewable raw materials. RPS policy regimes have emerged as the preferred tool that state policymakers use in trying to spur renewable energy consumption: an RPS policy regime is more viable politically than alternatives that impose direct and observable costs on end-use energy consumers (a carbon tax is an example of an alternative that

---

within states that have legalized it, thereby giving those states freedom to create their own policy. Another example involves state-level experimentation in lockdown policy-making at the outset of the COVID-19 pandemic, as the federal government left it to the states to determine how to establish their own shutdown policies. Finally, given contemporary concerns about federal-level dysfunction (Binder 2015), it is possible that other areas may enter the realm of state-level policy freedom in the future.

9. *Some* electric utility companies produce *and* deliver electricity to end-use consumers. However, all electric utility companies deliver electricity to end-use consumers. An end-use consumer (or retail consumer) is defined as any electricity consumer who sits at the very end of an electricity supply chain and consumes electricity. The vast majority of electricity consumers are end-use consumers (Besley and Coate 2003).

imposes direct and observable costs on end-use energy consumers), and an RPS policy regime typically imposes direct costs on actors—electric utility companies—with whom the vast majority of end-use energy consumers have an oppositional relationship (Besley and Coate 2003; Holland, Hughes, and Knittel 2009).[10]

RPS policy regimes are also viable politically because they are not purely associated (in the eyes of the public and some policymakers) with climate change (Rabe 2004, 2007). Policy alternatives that promote renewable energy use, like fossil fuel taxes or cap and trade systems, have directly been labeled as anti-fossil-fuel policies and face opposition from climate change skeptics; RPS policy regimes, on the other hand, have been lauded as an effective way to reduce dependence on foreign petroleum while creating jobs and have even won support from policymakers in several politically conservative states where the domestic fossil fuel industry represents an important constituency (Rabe 2004, 2007).[11]

As mentioned earlier, the federal government has not provided incentives or advice to the states on whether the states should adopt RPS policy regimes or how the states should craft their RPS policy regimes. The states have crafted their own RPS policy regimes in diverse ways, and policymakers across many states have invented by adopting RPS policy features that have not previously been adopted in any other state. Policymakers across the states have also borrowed by adopting RPS policy features that have already been adopted in other states. And although the lack of federal intervention means that I am unable to evaluate how the centralization of policy-making in the hands of the federal government (e.g., Chhibber and Kollman 2004) influences state-level invention and borrowing, I establish an understanding of state-level invention and borrowing given a baseline

10. This is not to say that the majority of end-use energy consumers *hate* their electric utility providers. But it is reasonable to assume that end-use energy consumers may have favorable opinions about RPS since it places direct costs on electric utility companies, a group that end-use energy consumers mainly interact with when they have power outages or pay their electricity bills.

11. Texas is the best example of a politically conservative state with an important domestic fossil fuel industry that has a robust RPS program. Oklahoma also has an established RPS program. I should note that electric utility companies and the coal industry have fought back against RPS programs in recent years and achieved success in temporarily freezing the RPS program in one state (Ohio between 2014 and 2017) and repealing it in another (West Virginia in 2015). However, recent developments do not change the fact that RPS programs have had more support from politically conservative policymakers than any other green energy policy.

of no direct federal intervention that can be extended by future scholars using different policy domains to incorporate variation with respect to the level of federal intervention on state policy-making.

An RPS policy regime consists of a set of policy features that dictate how an electric utility company should provide renewable-energy-derived electricity to consumers. Each state RPS policy regime typically includes four types or groups of policy features that specify how an electric utility company should provide renewable energy-derived electricity to consumers: (1) policy features belonging to the first group specify the exact energy sources or technological processes that are considered to be "renewable" (such as electricity derived from "hydroelectric" or "wind" sources) for the purposes of meeting the requirements of a state's RPS program; and (2) policy features belonging to the second group deal with the final target rate (which can either be mandatory or voluntary) that a state imposes on electric utility companies to be in compliance with its RPS program: for example, many states specify that electric utility companies procure some amount of electricity sold to end-use consumers from renewable sources, and each unique procurement target amount combined with whether that target is mandatory or voluntary represents its own policy feature. (3) Policy features belonging to the third group deal with whether a state requires that part of its RPS be met using a specific energy source or technological process: New Hampshire, for example, requires that electric utility companies operating in that state must meet part of their RPS obligations by procuring electricity from biomass sources.[12] And (4) policy features belonging to the fourth group deal with whether a state allows electric utility companies to trade credits to meet RPS requirements. I list all of the policy features utilized in this book in the appendix. Furthermore, the policy features were identified by renewable energy policy experts who assembled the Database of State Incentives for Renewables and Efficiency, or DSIRE. DSIRE is an initiative of the North Carolina Clean Energy Technology Center at North Carolina State University. Experts at DSIRE have compiled and maintain overview pages of each state's RPS program, and these overview pages list which policy features have been included in each state's RPS program.

---

12. Policy features requiring electric utility companies to meet part of their RPS obligations from specific energy sources or technological processes are called "carve-outs" or "technology minimums" in the renewable energy policy community.

It is hopefully clear from the above discussion that a state operational-izes its RPS policy regime (or program) based on the specific policy features it selects, and that a state's chosen *combination* of RPS policy features can also represent an important selection that the state makes when crafting its own RPS policy. Michigan's RPS policy regime, for example, consists of several policy features that taken together give that state's RPS program a particular character. First, Michigan adopted policy features correspond-ing to which energy sources and technological processes are considered to be renewable: some, like "tidal energy" and "wind," are firmly in the wheelhouse of what is regarded as conventional renewable energy while others, such as "coal combined with carbon sequestration," are assuredly not. Michigan also adopted a mandatory final target rate specifying that 10% of the electricity sold by electric utilities to end-use consumers should be derived from renewable sources. While Michigan chose not to include a carve-out or technology minimum in its RPS, it did choose to allow electric utility companies to meet RPS obligations through the trading of credits. Michigan's choice to mix individual policy features together to cre-ate a comprehensive RPS policy regime is far from atypical, as every state with an RPS policy regime has done the same. However, the way in which Michigan crafted its RPS regime through its adoption of specific policy features as well as the combination of those policy features can give insight into when Michigan "customized" or invented with respect to RPS versus borrowing from other states (Karch 2007). And next, I detail why looking at the policy feature (and a state's combination of policy features) is useful for distinguishing invention from borrowing.

Using Policy Features to Distinguish Invention from Borrowing

Looking at state policy-making at the level of policy feature adoption gives the analyst a more accurate picture of the true uniqueness of a state's RPS policy regime compared to looking at state policy-making at the more macro level of RPS policy regime or program adoption. Imagine that I compare the RPS policy regimes of Michigan and Ohio but ignore adop-tion at the granular level of policy features and only look at whether Mich-igan and Ohio adopted RPS policy regimes.[13] The RPS policy regimes of

---

13. When I refer here to how extant literature analyzes adoption at the level of the policy

the two states would appear identical even though they differ substantially in terms of what sources and processes are considered to be "renewable" and whether electric utility companies must meet carve-outs or technology minimums. Focusing instead on policy feature rather than policy regime adoption would allow us to better discern the diversity of RPS policy-making within and across states.

Since focusing on policy feature adoption reveals the diversity and uniqueness of state policy-making more than focusing on policy regime adoption, it follows that tracing the novel or borrowed quality of policy features within a state's RPS policy regime allows us to better discern the novel or borrowed quality of a state's RPS policy regime compared to tracing novelty and borrowing at the level of the state's RPS policy regime. Analyzing policy invention at the level of policy features represents a divergence from much existing literature (e.g., Walker 1969; Gray 1973; Berry and Berry 1990; Boushey 2010), which has largely looked at the adoption of entire policy regimes rather than policy features. Berry and Berry (1990) study the adoption and diffusion of lottery programs across the U.S. states but ignore the adoption of various policy features that could distinguish one state's lottery regime from the lottery regime of another state. The study of lotteries has been central to work on policy adoption and diffusion, and treating lotteries as if they are equivalent makes sense in that lotteries are similar (they all represent government sanctioned gambling) and that data is easier to obtain (since one does not have to capture all of the ways in which lotteries are different from each other). Treating lotteries as equivalent, however, comes at a cost of not taking into account the heterogeneous design choices that went into the universe of state lottery adoption, as Pierce and Miller (1999) show in their study of general fund and educational fund lotteries, and suggests that attention be paid to diversity in understanding policy-making.

More generally, while the extant literature's focus on adoption at the level of an aggregate policy regime rather than an individual policy fea-

---

regime rather than the policy feature, I am describing how scholars analyze "whether the state in question has adopted the given policy" without giving attention to the content of the policy adoption. This is different from looking at policy regime adoption as I do in this book. As I mention later in this chapter, I analyze a state's policy regime adoption by identifying the full combination of policy features (and coding whether this *combination* is an example of invention or borrowing) that make up that state's RPS program instead of only identifying whether a state adopted an RPS program or not.

ture is understandable, the choice to analyze aggregate policy regimes has affected how we in political science study policy innovation. Looking at the adoption of an aggregate policy regime rather than individual policy features leads to misleading inferences about the novel or inventive versus borrowed quality of a state's RPS policy regime. If I looked only at the initial adoption of state RPS policy regimes rather than the adoption of individual policy features, I might mistakenly conclude that later adopting states borrowed the policy specifics of earlier states even in cases when the later states were actually big inventors and adopted several policy features that had not been previously adopted by other states.

The mistaken conclusion mentioned above can occur with respect to the RPS policy domain. If I looked at the initial adoption of RPS policy regimes but did not consider the policy-feature-specific content of those regimes, I may conclude that West Virginia, the third to last state to adopt an RPS policy regime in the time span of this book, is a laggard that has entirely borrowed the policy-making choices of states that established their RPS policy regimes earlier. However, looking at the adoption of policy features reveals West Virginia to be a big inventor that has adopted several policy features, mainly related to the incorporation of coal and fossil fuel sources and technologies within the RPS landscape, which were previously not adopted by any state.[14]

Focusing on the initial adoption of state RPS policy regimes rather than the adoption of individual RPS policy features also prevents us from identifying when states invent by amending or modifying their own already established RPS policy features. Many states continue to add policy features to their RPS policy regimes after these policy regimes have been established, and the added policy features can be prominent examples of invention and borrowing. Nevada, for instance, initially established its RPS policy regime in 1997 and adopted eight policy features corresponding to six instances of invention and two instances of borrowing. However, Nevada chose to amend its RPS policy regime in 2001, 2002, 2003, 2005,

---

14. Among West Virginia's inventions were the inclusion of "coal bed methane" and "natural gas" as eligible RPS sources, as the state was the first to incorporate these sources within its RPS. Although West Virginia's actions here do not conform to stereotypical conceptualizations of renewable energy policy-making, they still count as novel additions to the corpus of RPS policy and could serve as the inspiration for other states' borrowing. Therefore, West Virginia's inventions still fit Brandeis's mold of a state explicitly formulating novel policy and creating templates to follow and should therefore be included in the analysis.

2007, and 2009, and the state adopted 18 policy features across all of those amendments. The 18 "noninitial" (meaning that they were not adopted in 1997 during Nevada's adoption of its RPS program or policy regime) policy feature adoptions break down into 10 instances of invention and eight instances of borrowing. If I had looked only at the initial adoption of Nevada's RPS policy regime, I would have thrown away important policy adoption activity that occurred in Nevada subsequent to the initial adoption of that state's RPS policy regime.

Scholars of policy reinvention (e.g., Clark 1985; Glick and Hays 1991; Hays 1996; Karch 2007) would recognize the problem I describe above, as their use of the word *reinvention* conveys the idea that a given state's policy regime potentially can change (in a sense, the policy regime or program gets reinvented) from its initial form. Reinvention, according to this literature, occurs from initial adoption all the way through modification or amendment. Policy reinvention scholars would also recognize my focus on the policy feature, as this is the level of analysis where changes to a program are discernible. One goal with my framework is to not only devise a way to systematically capture novel adoption in policy-making but to also capture it regardless of when it occurs over the existence of a given state's program: my framework therefore in a sense pays homage to reinvention scholarship by identifying how invention can be captured and analyzed across the life cycle of a program. In short, analyzing inventing and borrowing at the level of policy features at both the time of an RPS policy regime's initial creation and the time of an RPS policy regime's modification allows us to better visualize the diversity of RPS policy-making within and across the states and gives us a much better picture of the totality of inventing and borrowing within and across the states. The benefit of much greater detail about state policy-making activity justifies the use of the policy feature as the unit of analysis in this book.

Coding Policy Features as Invention or Borrowing

A key hallmark of this book is that I define invention and borrowing at the level of policy features and also discuss how to identify invention and borrowing in the adopted policy features associated with state RPS policy regimes. Although I utilize my coding process with respect to the policy domain of RPS, I emphasize that this process is extendable to policy domains besides RPS. The one caveat, however, is that the analyst must have knowledge about what policy features are actually associated with a policy domain.[15] As I have mentioned, I use policy features that have been identified by analysts at DSIRE. Utilizing the DSIRE database is valuable insofar as it gives me confidence that I am taking the correct policy features into consideration in my analysis. I am aware, however, that the DSIRE database is not perfect in listing policy features associated with each state's RPS program. Therefore, I supplement information gathered from the DSIRE database with state RPS program fact sheets provided by the Union of Concerned Scientists. Two different states may use different terminology to refer to the same policy feature in their respective RPS policy regimes, and I consequently devise and utilize a method of identifying and merging synonymous policy feature names (e.g., different names that actually describe the same policy feature) to avoid the situation where counts of invention and borrowing are incorrect because synonymous policy features are mistakenly treated as different and distinct policy features. I utilize the synonyms identification and merging process prior to quantitative analysis and describe this process later in this chapter.

My coding strategy centers on two key assumptions. First, I assume that invention and borrowing are distinct and separable types of policy adoption available to policymakers. The distinction between invention and borrowing, I argue, is one of relative timing and boils down to whether a specific policy feature that is being adopted by state i has already been adopted by at least one other state j. If state i adopts a specific policy feature that has never been adopted by another state, then I claim that state i's policymakers are inventing; on the other hand, if state i adopts a specific policy feature that has already been adopted by another state, then I claim that state i's policymakers are borrowing. Invention and borrowing differ because borrowing provides adopting policymakers with a visible track record while invention does not. Borrowing policymakers in state i in some sense know what to expect from adopting a policy feature that has already been adopted in state j because the policymakers in state i can observe what happened when state j adopted the same policy feature.[16] Inventing

---

15. This is to avoid the situation where a naïve analyst incorrectly identifies (or fails to identify) policy features associated with a policy domain and thereby mistakenly inflates (or deflates) the number of instances of policy feature adoption that occur in the data.

16. In this book, I utilize a technocratic conceptualization of borrowing (i.e., when a state borrows, it can visualize the impacts of another state's policy-making) because this technocratic

policymakers in state i know comparatively less about what to expect when adopting a novel policy feature because they do not have access to some other state's track record with that same policy feature. Following Volden, Ting, and Carpenter (2008) and Cai and Treisman (2009), I assume that the existence of a track record generally makes borrowing less risky than inventing, and I use the idea that borrowing offers adopting policymakers a visible track record while inventing does not to give invention and borrowing different empirical forms.[17] Importantly, a track record can be visible even accounting for the granularity of analyzing policy at the level of a policy feature: for instance, policymakers considering whether to borrow would be able to see the impacts of another state designating "wind" as a renewable resource and then could decide whether to follow suit.

Two questions arise: Is invention so easily distinguishable from borrowing? Isn't the distinction between invention and borrowing more nuanced than I suggest here? I acknowledge these concerns. First, not only do I code each state's individual policy feature as an example of invention or borrowing but also code each state's combination of policy features (or each state's policy regime) as an example of invention or borrowing. I am able to identify the specific set of policy features that make up each state's RPS policy regime because I already identified the individual policy features that have been adopted by each state. Looking at each state's policy regime is a reflection of the complexity and nuance of state policy choices. A given state i (Indiana, for example) could adopt a policy regime that consists entirely of individual policy features that have already been adopted in other states, but if Indiana is adopting individual policy features that have never before been combined together, then we would want to acknowledge Indiana's invention of combining individual policy features in a novel and untested manner.[18]

conceptualization is derived from Brandeis (the *New State Ice Company* case has been cited over 8,000 times in Google Scholar's "Case Law" feature as of November 2021). However, it is entirely possible that borrowing could have a political conceptualization (for example, politicians in state Y see that politicians in state X benefitted from adopting a policy and then try to mimic those politicians in state X), and I discuss this possibility in the book's conclusion.

17. Although there may be certain instances where borrowing is riskier than invention, I follow the lead of Volden, Ting, and Carpenter (2008) and Cai and Treisman (2009) in assuming that borrowing is generally less risky than invention.

18. There are two additional points worth mentioning. To address a concern that I lump together stark and minor differences across policies in my analysis, I drop rates from the analysis in robustness checks mentioned in chapters 5 and 6. Dropping rates also helps address the

And, second, a natural criticism of my coding enterprise may be to suggest that I use quantitative methods to distinguish invention from borrowing. While I acknowledge that qualitative analysis can help us better elucidate the concepts of invention and borrowing, I point readers toward Andrew Karch's masterful discussion of "customization" in *Democratic Laboratories* (2007). Karch employs the case study method to determine how various states customized (or made unique) their own health and welfare programs, but then implores political science scholars to identify a quantitative way to distinguish invention from borrowing so that we can investigate general determinants of invention and borrowing based on studying large sample sizes. It is partly with the goal of working toward Karch's imperative that I devise and employ the technique used in this book.

My second main assumption deals with how I empirically distinguish invention from borrowing: namely, I code the adoption of a specific policy feature as an example of invention if state i either (a) adopts that policy feature *before* any other state has adopted the policy feature or (b) adopts that policy feature by the next calendar year after another state j became the very first state to adopt the policy feature. I build the "by the next calendar year" grace period into the definition of invention to account for the situation where state i essentially adopts a policy feature at roughly the same time as state j (states i and j adopt a feature at different times but are close enough in their adoption that we cannot say definitively that one is the inventor while the other is not). The "by the next calendar year" grace period builds a cushion for invention that effectively pushes borrowing on a given policy feature adoption out until two years after the calendar year in which the first state adopted the same policy feature. For example, if Ohio is the first state to adopt a particular policy feature in 2008, any other state's adoption of that same policy feature that occurs from 2010 onward would be borrowing. Having this amount of time to distinguish invention from borrowing (e.g., a policy feature adoption counts as borrowing once two years have passed since the calendar year in which that feature was first adopted by any of the U.S. states) is arguably more generous than work by Beck, Gleditsch, and Beardsley (2006), Swank (2006), and Volden, Ting, and Carpenter (2008), who argue that one year is suf-

concern that the timetables of RPS programs (rates are linked to timetables) could complicate the analysis.

ficient for one state to observe another state's policy-making. While the distinction is not perfect (some states could ostensibly be myopic borrowers), it conforms to the fairly straightforward assumption that later adopters could be informed by first movers if they chose to do so. I therefore code the adoption of a specific policy feature as an example of borrowing if state i adopts a policy feature at any time once two years have passed since the calendar year in which state j was the very first state among any state to adopt the policy feature (so, if state j is the first state to adopt a policy feature in the year 2007, state i's adoption of that same feature counts as borrowing if it occurs in the year 2009 or later).[19]

Concrete examples of invention and borrowing are illustrative, and I present some here. First, including electricity derived from "wind" as a renewable source or technological process within a state's RPS policy regime is a common RPS policy feature that has been adopted across many states. In 1983, Iowa was the first state to adopt electricity derived from wind as an eligible source or technological process within its RPS policy regime with the passage of the Alternative Energy Law (1983). By virtue of being the first state to act in this manner, Iowa invented by making wind an eligible source. No state followed Iowa's lead for over a decade until the mid-to-late 1990s, when several states included wind as an eligible source within their own RPS policy regimes. Nevada was one of these states and in 1997 established an RPS program with wind included as an eligible source with the passage of Assembly Bill 366 (1997). Since Nevada's action occurred 13 years after Iowa's, Nevada's inclusion of wind energy within its RPS counts as an example of borrowing. Given the "by the next calendar year" grace period, Nevada would have needed to have included wind energy within its RPS by the end of 1984 (the end of the calendar year following Iowa's 1983 adoption) for this action to count as invention.

My second example illustrates why the grace period is necessary. In November 1997, Massachusetts invented by becoming the first state to include energy from waves as an eligible source or technological process within its RPS program with the passage of Chapter 164 of the Acts of 1997. Neighboring Connecticut followed suit in April 1998 with the passage of House Bill 5005 and also included wave energy as an eligible source within its own RPS program. Although about five months separated the

---

19. I utilize the same rule in distinguishing each state's combination of individual policy features as an example of invention or borrowing.

actions of Massachusetts and Connecticut, it is difficult to say conclusively that Connecticut borrowed from Massachusetts. Connecticut policymakers may have been unable to establish an RPS and include wave energy within it in late 1997 due to having shorter legislative sessions than peers in Massachusetts. Furthermore, the five-month gap in adoption between both states arguably may not have given Connecticut enough time to actually benefit from a visible track record from Massachusetts's adoption. Categorizing Connecticut's adoption as an example of invention is an acknowledgment of the idea that a second state that adopts soon after the original state is inventing in its own right.[20]

My third example concerns the categorization of a state's adoption of a combination of policy features (or in other words, a state's adoption of a policy regime). In 2011, the Indiana legislature established that state's RPS program or policy regime with the passage of Senate Bill 251. Indiana's RPS policy regime consisted *entirely* of individual policy features that have been borrowed from other states. For example, Indiana's inclusion of "nuclear" energy as an eligible RPS source was preceded three years earlier by Ohio's similar action. And Indiana's inclusion of "fuel cells" or "hydrogen" as eligible RPS technological processes followed in the footsteps of 15 other states (Maine, Connecticut, Hawaii, Minnesota, New York, Pennsylvania, Delaware, North Dakota, New Hampshire, Oregon, North Carolina, South Dakota, Utah, Ohio, and West Virginia). However, even though Indiana borrowed with respect to adopting its individual policy features, the state invented by combining individual policy features that had never before been grouped together in the same policy regime. Indiana's action in combining policy features in an unprecedented way is novel and is treated as an example of invention here.

The use of my coding process on adoption data from the RPS policy domain yields 642 instances of policy feature or regime adoption spread out over 37 states during the 1983–2011 time frame. Included in these 642 instances are both instances of the adoption of an individual policy feature (such as the inclusion by Massachusetts of wave energy as an eligible source within its RPS) as well as the choice to combine different individual policy features together in a specific policy regime (such as Indiana's

---

20. Remember that the grace period is "by the next calendar year." Since Massachusetts included wave energy as an eligible source within its RPS in 1997, any state that similarly included wave energy as an eligible source within its RPS in 1998 is categorized as having invented. States that did this from 1999 onward, however, are categorized as having borrowed.

2011 decision to combine several policy features together in a novel way). The richness of this approach is evident considering that if we only focused on the broad issue of whether a state has an RPS program or not, we would have only 37 "yes" observations that would all look identical to each other. By embracing a more granular analytical style, we can see how states' choices about what individual policy features to adopt and about which features should be combined together in an RPS program—decisions that are largely central to the study of policy adoption—represent instances of invention or borrowing. And by making these instances of invention and borrowing dependent variables and using the well-established practice of employing pooled event history modeling (Boehmke 2009; Makse and Volden 2011; Boushey 2016) to evaluate factors influencing invention and borrowing, we can determine how the causes of invention are potentially different from those of borrowing.

In table 1, I display the number of adoptions that occur by state along with a breakdown of how many of those adoptions represent invention or borrowing.[21] The counts by state include adopting individual policy features as well as combining features together within a regime. These choices occur at the same time (when a state is deciding whether to adopt an RPS policy), refer to the same question faced by policymakers ("What shall we include in our policy?"), and are combined together in analyses throughout this book.[22]

A glance at table 1[23] reveals that some states invent more than others. Connecticut invented in 15 of its 22 adoptions (or 68%) and Nevada invented in 16 of its 26 adoptions (or 61%). Other states, such as already-

---

21. One potential concern may be that my operationalization of invention lumps together minor or "marginal" instances of invention from bolder policy-making. Although I hesitate to try to differentiate invention based on how pathbreaking it is, I recognize this concern and in the appendix of the book. I include analyses corresponding to those in chapters 5 and 6 where I alternatively drop inventions consisting of rates as well as combinations.

22. I include instances from the adoption of individual policy features *and* instances from the combination of policy features into a policy regime *together*. This is because both kinds of adoption choices occur at the same time and comprise the "subpolicies" that ultimately become a policy adoption. Analyzing them separately would simply reduce the number of instances of adoption that occur in the data and is not something that I undertake in my study of RPS.

23. If we only looked at the number of instances of invention occurring without including combinations, there are 112 instances of invention. If we are only looking at the number of instances of invention that occur during the calendar year after the year in which a policy feature was first adopted by any of the states, there are 17 instances of invention.

TABLE I. Adoptions by State, Sorted by Invention or Borrowing

State	Number of Adoptions	Inventions	Borrowings
Arizona	22	10	12
California	19	6	13
Colorado	17	4	13
Connecticut	22	15	7
Delaware	20	3	17
Hawaii	23	5	18
Illinois	17	6	11
Indiana	20	1	19
Iowa	7	6	1
Kansas	10	2	8
Maine	21	13	8
Maryland	22	6	16
Massachusetts	18	12	6
Michigan	17	4	13
Minnesota	20	12	8
Missouri	14	3	11
Montana	12	2	10
Nevada	26	16	10
New Hampshire	18	3	15
New Jersey	19	6	13
New Mexico	17	5	12
New York	17	5	12
North Carolina	22	7	15
North Dakota	11	2	9
Ohio	22	6	16
Oklahoma	11	2	9
Oregon	19	4	15
Pennsylvania	22	8	14
Rhode Island	11	3	8
South Dakota	12	2	10
Texas	16	7	9
Utah	19	3	16
Vermont	11	3	8
Virginia	12	3	9
Washington	14	2	12
West Virginia	18	3	15
Wisconsin	24	8	16
Total	642	208	434

mentioned Indiana (which invented in 1 of its 20 adoptions, or 5%) or Montana (which invented in 2 of its 12 adoptions, or 16%), invented much less than other states and tend to borrow during adoption. There is ample variation across states and (in some cases) within states in terms of where invention and borrowing occurred, and this variation aids us in determining why states invent or borrow. However, before delving into theoretical explanations in subsequent chapters, there are two remaining tasks to be completed in this chapter. First, dates of policy adoption—needed to establish whether a given adoption is an example of invention or borrowing, are not listed in the DSIRE database. Consequently, I needed to gather a vast corpus of official documentation across the states that I could use to "time-stamp" each adoption of each state and thereby relate adoptions of the same policy feature across states to one another in order to code instances of invention and borrowing.[24] And second, I needed to take the output from that coding process and create master pooled event history datasets that can be utilized to evaluate the determinants of invention and borrowing. I devote the next two sections to pursuing each of these respective tasks.

Tracing Adoptions in Official Documentation

Although the DSIRE database provides users with the names of the policy features that each state adopts, it does not provide users with dates pertaining to *when* states adopted each of their policy features. However, the DSIRE database provides users with a list of official documents pertaining to each state's RPS policy-making activity. The list of official documentation encompasses all institutional sources in a given state that could change RPS policy. In the vast majority of states, this means lawmaking by a legislature or rulemaking by a public utilities commission, but in rare instances it could also refer to successful ballot referenda. By listing every policy feature that has been adopted by a state and searching through all of a state's official documentation—which has associated dates of adoption—for the earliest mention of a given policy being adopted by a given state,

---

24. There is *never* a case where a state borrows *all* of the policy features (or in other words, the policy regime) of another state. Therefore, all cases of policy regime adoption (remember that I define each policy regime in terms of the combination of policy features that it possesses) represent instances of invention.

we can identify instances of invention and borrowing that can be utilized for statistical analysis.

The first step is to gather the names of all individual RPS policy features listed in DSIRE's state-specific RPS pages.[25] While the full list of features is available in the appendix (in table A1), I have already described several examples of individual policy features. Making wind energy an allowable source or technological process is an example of an individual policy feature. And so too was the adoption of wave energy as an allowable source or technological process by Massachusetts and Connecticut. Another example of an individual policy feature is California's 2011 adoption in Senate Bill X1–2 of a requirement that electric providers procure 33% of electricity sold to retail consumers from renewable sources or technological processes.

The next step is to gather the names of all official RPS policy-making documentation across the states and retrieve these documents. Predominantly using the document names supplied on the DSIRE state-specific RPS summary pages and supplementing these names with other official documentation names contained in the Union of Concerned Scientists' state RPS program description factsheets, I identify a corpus of 280 official policy-making documents that I scan to identify when each state adopted each of its respective policy features. The names and years of the full set of 280 documents are available in the appendix (in table A2). In table 2, however, I list the number of official documents that I scan through for each state with an RPS policy regime. Importantly, not every official document contains an adoption (the DSIRE database just lists the names of the documents and does not identify which features were adopted in them); therefore, I also list the number of documents for each state that actually contain adoptions.

Having identified a master list of policy features that appear in the RPS policy domain as well as a list of official documents in which states made changes to their RPS programs, I can determine when states adopted their respective policy features—by searching through each state's list of official documents to determine when that state first mentions including a policy feature in its RPS program—and then code adoptions across states as instances of invention or borrowing based on the coding rule explained

25. The DSIRE database has state-specific program webpages for state RPS programs. Summary maps for each state open to pages detailing features associated with that state's RPS program.

TABLE 2. Number of Documents Scanned per State

State	Documents Overall (N)	Documents with Adoptions (N)
Arizona	6	4
California	34	4
Colorado	5	3
Connecticut	20	3
Delaware	15	3
Hawaii	7	4
Illinois	13	5
Indiana	1	1
Iowa	20	3
Kansas	2	1
Maine	10	5
Maryland	9	4
Massachusetts	7	4
Michigan	3	2
Minnesota	11	4
Missouri	5	2
Montana	2	2
Nevada	11	8
New Hampshire	3	2
New Jersey	6	4
New Mexico	6	3
New York	15	2
North Carolina	6	3
North Dakota	3	2
Ohio	4	3
Oklahoma	1	1
Oregon	5	2
Pennsylvania	13	2
Rhode Island	3	2
South Dakota	2	
Texas	7	3
Utah	5	3
Vermont	5	3
Virginia	2	1
Washington	4	2
West Virginia	3	1
Wisconsin	6	6
Total	280	108

earlier where a state invents if it adopts a specific policy feature *before* any other state has adopted that policy feature or adopts the policy feature by the next calendar year after another state became the first state to adopt the policy feature (borrowing occurs in all other adoption cases).[26]

Examples are again instructive. Maryland has an ambitious RPS policy regime, and I located nine government documents between 2004—the year in which Maryland established its RPS policy regime or program—and 2011, the final year of analysis in this study, that pertain to policy-making in Maryland's RPS policy regime. Experts at DSIRE have also highlighted several policy features associated with Maryland's RPS policy regime, and here I highlight four: the adoptions of "wind," "tidal," and "wave" energy as eligible renewable sources or technologies within Maryland's RPS policy regime; and the requirement that suppliers providing electricity to retail consumers in the state procure a final target of 20% of electricity provided from renewable sources. Since the DSIRE database does not identify *when* Maryland adopted the four policy features, I search through Maryland's nine government documents in chronological order and look for the oldest document in which Maryland explicitly mentions that each of the policy features is included in its RPS policy regime. Maryland includes "wind," "tidal," and "wave" energy sources within its RPS policy regime with the passage of House Bill 1308 in 2004, and the text of the bill explicitly states that "a renewable source means one or more of the following sources" and includes "wind," "energy from waves," and "energy from . . . tides" among its list of eligible renewable sources. Since Maryland established its RPS regime with the passage of House Bill 1308, I do not need to worry that the state adopted the "wind," "tidal," and "wave" energy source policy features prior to the passage of House Bill 1308 and consequently date Maryland's adoption of these features to be April 10, 2004, the date of the final passage of House Bill 1308 through the Maryland legislature.

---

26. The approval date (used to "date" a policy adoption) of a government document depends on what type of governmental actor does the policy-making. The three actors that adopted RPS policy features were state legislatures, state public utilities commissions, and citizens using the ballot initiative process. For legislatures, the date of approval was the date that the final version of a bill passed both chambers of the legislature. For public utilities commissions, the date of approval was the date that commissioners approved the final version of a rule. And for ballot initiative-driven legislation, the date of approval was the date that voters approved the final version of a ballot proposition.

Incidentally, Maryland's adoption of the three policy features described in the previous paragraph all count as borrowing; this is the case since Maryland adopted "wind" energy as an eligible RPS source roughly 21 years after Iowa first did the same, adopted "tidal" energy as an eligible RPS source roughly seven years after Maine first did the same, and adopted "wave" energy as an eligible RPS source over six years after Massachusetts first did the same. Maryland's adoption of the fourth policy feature— mandating that utilities provide a target rate of 20% of electricity sold to consumers from renewable sources—was not adopted with the passage of House Bill 1308 in 2004. Rather, Maryland initially chose a required final target rate specifying that 7.5% of electricity sold to consumers be derived from renewable energy (House Bill 1308, 2004).[27] Maryland amended its RPS policy regime with the passage of House Bill 375 in 2008, and one area of amendment was an increase in the state's final target rate. Specifically, Maryland adopted a new final target rate specifying that 20% of electricity sold to consumers be derived from renewable sources and included language to this effect, stating that "20%" of electricity will eventually need to be derived "from renewable sources" (House Bill 375, 2008). The Maryland legislature passed the final version of House Bill 375 on April 4, 2008; therefore, Maryland adopted the required 20% final target rate on April 4, 2008. Maryland's adoption of the required 20% target rate based on retail sales was an example of borrowing, since it occurred over five years after California adopted a required 20% final target rate based on retail sales in 2002.

It is hopefully clear from the Maryland examples about why I start with the oldest Maryland document and work in chronological order to the most recent Maryland document when I am determining when Maryland adopted its respective policy features. It is important to start with the oldest document in order to record the correct date during which a state adopted a particular policy feature. Many states (including Maryland) repeat the names of policy features listed in older documents in newer documents in order to maintain consistency and reduce ambiguity in legislation and rulemaking. This means that Maryland repeats that "wind,"

---

27. Language in House Bill 1308 specifies that "the renewable portfolio standard shall be as follows" with the final point specifying that "7.5%" be met using a renewable source. Since no other state had chosen a final target rate of a 7.5% requirement of electricity sold to retail consumers, Maryland's initial final target rate represented an instance of invention.

"energy from waves," and "energy . . . from tides" are included as eligible sources within its RPS policy regime in multiple documents between its earliest document, House Bill 1308 in 2004, and its last document, Senate Bill 717 in 2011. If I started with Senate Bill 717 instead of House Bill 1308, I might incorrectly conclude that Maryland adopted the policy features of "wind," "tidal," and "wave" energy in 2011 instead of 2004. And assigning the wrong date to the adoption of a policy feature is a serious problem since the date of a policy feature's adoption is used to distinguish invention from borrowing.

I repeat the process described in the Maryland examples across every state with an RPS policy regime and identify when each state adopted each policy feature within its RPS policy regime. Then, for each specific policy feature (e.g., the inclusion of "wind" energy as an eligible source within an RPS), I compare adoptions across states using my coding rule to differentiate invention from borrowing.

And what about the process for identifying state policy regimes and coding each of them as instances of invention or borrowing? For each iteration of a state's RPS policy-making, I look at the combination of individual RPS policy features that the state adopts and characterize the choice to adopt that combination of individual features as representing yet another policy adoption decision that the state makes when it adopts the individual features. I do this for all states and often repeatedly for the same state, since a state adopts a different policy regime when it amends its own RPS program and thereby adopts a different combination of individual policy features compared to what it had before.[28] I ultimately am able to identify the distinct combinations of individual policy features that have been adopted within and across the states and can use the exact same coding process described earlier to code these adoptions

---

28. A classic example of this occurs with the Maryland case I discussed earlier. When it adopted its RPS program with the passage of House Bill 1308 in 2004, Maryland adopted a requirement that utilities procure 7.5% of electricity sold to consumers from renewable sources. In 2008, with the passage of House Bill 375, Maryland required instead that utilities procure 20% of electricity sold to consumers from renewable sources. Even if every other individual policy feature (save for the target rates) was unchanged in comparing Maryland's policy-making in 2004 and 2008 (which it was not), Maryland's combination of policy features in 2004 would be different from that in 2008, meaning that Maryland's 2004 and 2008 combinations would represent two distinct adoption choices.

as inventions or borrowings.[29] I can then add these adoptions to the individual policy feature adoptions to evaluate explanations about why invention and borrowing occur.[30]

I stated in the introductory chapter and briefly in this one that the states overwhelmingly adopted RPS programs via legislative action and public utilities commission rulemaking, with a small minority of states adopting RPS programs via ballot initiative. I would like to make explicit here that my coding process is agnostic to the type of governmental actor that adopts a particular policy feature or combination of policy features. A policy feature's adoption (or the adoption of a given combination of policy features) registers as a case of invention or borrowing regardless of the actor doing the adopting: in short, a legislature in one state can borrow from a regulatory commission in another state and vice versa. My coding process yields cases where legislatures and regulatory commissions emerge as major inventors and also yields cases where legislatures, regulatory commissions, and citizens operating through the ballot predominantly borrow. I make my coding process agnostic to the type of actor adopting policy to reflect that any type of actor can potentially take on the risk of inventing and to acknowledge that any type of actor can observe and borrow from the policy choices made by other governments.[31]

---

29. As it turns out, there is *never* an instance where one state borrows by adopting the exact same combination of policy features as another state. Therefore, all instances of adopting a given combination of policy features are instances of invention.

30. There is one important caveat to discuss in terms of how I identify combinations of individual policy features. Specifically, I only identify combinations of individual policy features when a state has at least specified (1) some list of sources and technological processes that are eligible to be used to meet RPS obligations, and (2) a standard or target rate that will hopefully be reached through using the eligible sources and technological processes. I require these policy features to be specified since their specification makes an RPS program operational. This caveat only affects a couple of pioneering states (Iowa and Massachusetts), where the states initially adopted individual RPS policy features dealing with which sources were eligible (in 1983 and 1997, respectively) but then chose target rates—and consequently, policy regimes—later (in 1992 and 2002, respectively). In both of these cases, I date the adoption of the individual policy features dealing with which sources are eligible based on when they were actually adopted (in 1983 and 1997) but date the adoption of respective policy regimes based on when Iowa and Massachusetts adopted target rates that could be applied to their already delineated RPS eligible sources (this occurred in 1992 and 2002).

31. This is a departure from the work of Walker (1969), who only looked at policy-making among legislatures and ignored the role that regulators, for example, can play with respect to policy-making.

Using, Structuring, and Cleaning Adoption Data

The use of the coding process that I describe throughout this chapter results in the identification of cases of invention and borrowing. However, before an analyst can evaluate why invention and borrowing occur, the analyst must structure the cases of invention and borrowing in a way that allows for reasonable inference. Typically, quantitative social scientists have embraced event history modeling as the standard method of analyzing policy adoption across the American states (Berry and Berry 1990; Box-Steffensmeier and Jones 1997; Box-Steffensmeier and Jones 2004). Event history modeling comes from epidemiology, and with event history modeling, an analyst uses statistical regression to evaluate what makes some event of interest more or less likely to occur. While epidemiologists may be concerned with understanding the causes of heart attack occurrence or lung cancer onset, adoption and diffusion scholars are concerned with understanding what makes a state more or less likely to adopt a given policy.[32]

The event of interest for adoption and diffusion scholars, therefore, is policy adoption, and analysts consequently need to select a "period of observation" during which states are "at risk" of adopting a policy (Boushey 2016). Scholars usually select the year in which the first state adopts a policy as the beginning of the period of observation and remove a state from the dataset once it has adopted that policy under the pretext that the adopting state is no longer at risk of experiencing the event of adopting the policy.

Pooled event history modeling takes the principles of event history modeling one step further by creating separate risk sets for different events and pooling these risk sets together. Pooled event history analysis has already been used by adoption and diffusion scholars (e.g., Boushey 2016) to evaluate the factors that make the adoption of policies that fall under a common policy domain more likely.[33] Here, I create a distinct risk set for each policy feature (and each combination of policy features) that appears in the project and pool these risk sets together. Since invention and borrowing are exclusive concepts (meaning that a state cannot simultaneously

---

32. For an example, see the seminal work of Berry and Berry (1990) concerning the adoption of lotteries across the U.S. states.

33. Boushey (2016) evaluates policies falling under the rubric of criminal justice reform.

possess the opportunity to both invent and borrow the same policy feature), I then separate the pooled risk set into two pooled risk sets: one
corresponding to invention and the other corresponding to borrowing.
For each policy feature and each combination of policy features, I start the
invention risk set for all states in 1983, when Iowa became the first state
to adopt a prototypical RPS program.[34] A state loses the opportunity to
invent a given policy feature or combination of policy features once it has
invented that feature or combination (e.g., it is the first state to adopt the
feature or combination or has done so by the next calendar year after the
first state) *or* if two years have elapsed since the year in which that feature
or combination was first adopted by one of the 50 U.S. states.

Provided it has not invented a given policy feature or combination (in
which case it never gains the opportunity to borrow), a state gains the
opportunity to borrow a policy feature or combination once two years
have passed since the calendar year in which the feature or combination
was first adopted by any of the states. A state loses the opportunity to borrow once it has already done so. A state retains the opportunity to borrow
so long as it has not done so.

Examples help once more to clarify. Iowa invented by being the first
state to adopt "wind" energy as an eligible RPS source. Since Iowa did
this when launching the first RPS in 1983, all states have the opportunity beginning in 1983 act in a similar manner. Iowa, of course, exits the
inventing dataset for this policy feature following 1983 but other states
remain in the inventing dataset until 1984, after which they drop out
of this dataset (as it turns out, no other state followed suit by the end of
1984). From 1985 onward, all states except for Iowa have the opportunity
to borrow by adopting "wind" as an eligible RPS source: Connecticut, for
example, borrowed by following suit in 1998 and is removed from being
at risk of adopting "wind" beginning in 1999; similarly, Texas borrowed
by following suit in 1999 and is removed from being at risk of adopt-

---

34. The assumption here is that each state had the opportunity to invent with respect to the
policy features making up the RPS domain when Iowa created the first prototype of an RPS in
1983. This assumption follows advice that was given to me by reviewers in a companion piece to
this book that utilizes the same methodology (Parinandi 2020). If a researcher were analyzing an
area where some invention was impossible until advances in technology occurred (for example,
suppose someone were analyzing the area of car safety regulations but folding self-driving car
policy within the larger aegis of car safety regulations), then that researcher would not begin the
risk set for a given policy feature's invention until the technological breakthrough that made that
policy feature possible had actually transpired.

ing "wind" beginning in 2000. States that never establish an RPS policy regime or program (such as Idaho or Tennessee) remain at risk of borrowing by adopting "wind" as an eligible source through the end of the study in 2011.[35]

Another example pertains to Maryland's 2004 adoption of the requirement that utilities procure 7.5% of the electricity they sell to consumers from renewable sources. No state had adopted this particular feature until Maryland invented it; this design choice could have feasibly been made in 1983 but was not; therefore, all states have the opportunity to invent this particular feature from 1983 onward. Maryland, of course, drops out of the inventing risk set to adopt this feature following 2004. Every other state remains in the inventing risk set through 2005, after which they all lose the opportunity to invent with respect to this feature since the grace period for inventing the feature has expired. From 2006 onward, however, every other state receives the opportunity to borrow with respect to this feature. And since no other state adopts this feature outside of Maryland, every other state retains the opportunity to borrow the feature through the end of the study.

When the risk sets of each policy feature and combination of policy features are created and then separated into pools corresponding to invention and borrowing, we obtain master datasets for invention and borrowing that allow us to evaluate when invention and borrowing occur (there are 642 instances of adoption across all institutional sources translating into 208 instances of invention and 434 instances of borrowing) out of thousands upon thousands of opportunities to respectively invent and borrow.

Before I can explain how I use the master datasets throughout the book, I must first discuss one important processing step that occurred *prior* to the coding of the adoptions and the construction of the pooled event history datasets. This processing step involves dealing with the scenario where different states use different names to describe the same policy feature. For example, Arizona specified that part of its RPS obligations be met

---

35. There are a number of policy features that can only be adopted by states that border a large body of water (e.g., an ocean, the Gulf of Mexico, one of the Great Lakes, or the Great Salt Lake). For example, Kansas cannot include "wave" energy as an eligible RPS source since it does not touch a large body of water. I therefore restrict the inventing and borrowing opportunity sets or "risk sets" for features involving large bodies of water (e.g., ocean thermal energy, tidal energy, and wave energy) to states that border an ocean, the Gulf of Mexico, one of the Great Lakes, or the Great Salt Lake.

using a "distributed generation" carve-out (Arizona Corporation Commission Decision 69127, 2006) while New York specified earlier that part of its RPS obligations be met using a "customer-sited" carve-out (New York Public Service Commission Order for Case 03-E-0188, 2004). A naïve observer may think that a "distributed generation" carve-out is different from a "customer-sited" carve-out and code Arizona's 2006 adoption as an instance of invention, as no state had previously adopted a "distributed generation" carve-out.

However, the phrases "distributed generation" and "customer-sited" refer to the same concept: using local resources and facilities to generate electricity instead of transmitting it over long distances. This means that a "distributed generation" carve-out and a "customer-sited" carve-out refer to the same policy feature. The fact that these two differently named features are the same is important to acknowledge since we would be overcounting cases of invention and undercounting cases of borrowing if we ignored the synonymous nature of New York's and Arizona's decisions.[36]

Prior to coding adoptions as cases of invention or borrowing and prior to constructing the master event history datasets, I therefore devised and utilized a process for identifying when the names of policy features are synonyms of one another.[37] While details of this process are covered in the appendix (in list A3), I consulted a corpus of renewable energy summary fact sheets created by the United States Department of Energy, the National Renewable Energy Laboratory, the United States Environmental Protection Agency, the United States Energy Information Administration, and various industry associations to distinguish features from one another and determine when features are synonyms. My rule for identifying whether features are synonyms is to read descriptions from the fact sheets about features and then ask myself whether the descriptions for multiple features are describing the same process. If the answer to this question is "yes," then the features describing the same process are combined or consolidated into one feature. The incorporation of this combined or consolidated feature into the invention and borrowing datasets follows all of the

---

36. Although DSIRE is an expert-created database, those creating the database did not engage in the exercise of identifying policy feature names that are synonyms of one another.

37. Utilizing this process inevitably reduces the number of individual policy feature adoptions and changes the character of policy regimes (which by definition are combinations of individual policy features) compared to the case when the potential synonymous nature of policy feature names is ignored.

same rules used for features that do not have synonyms. Importantly, for combined or consolidated features, I use the date of the earlier synonym's adoption to distinguish invention from borrowing.

I illustrate my logic in the above paragraph by using the same example of the synonymous features of "distributed generation" and "customer-sited" carve-outs. I consolidate and combine these into one single feature, a "distributed generation/customer-sited" carve-out. Recall that New York adopted the carve-out in 2004 while Arizona adopted it in 2006. New York was the first state to adopt either a "distributed generation" or "customer-sited" carve-out; therefore, while all states gained the opportunity to invent with respect to "distributed generation/customer-sited" from 1983 onward, New York invented this feature in 2004 and then dropped out. No other state invented this feature and after 2005, all other states lose their opportunity to invent the "distributed generation/customer-sited" feature. From 2006 onward, however, every state but New York gains the opportunity to borrow with respect to "distributed generation/customer-sited," and Arizona loses this opportunity following 2006. Importantly, choices corresponding to each state's policy regime do not include policy feature combinations where "distributed generation" or "customer-sited" carve-outs are constituent parts of the combinations but rather mention the "distributed generation/customer-sited" carve-out as the constituent part of each state's combination. Taking synonymous feature names into account allows for a more realistic and credible analysis and therefore represents a vital part of the empirical strategy employed in this book.

How the Master Datasets Are Used Moving Forward

The coding process described here and the master datasets emanating from that process can be used to fill a void in our understanding of policy adoption and federalism and determine when and why invention and borrowing occurs among the American states. One particular opportunity that is opened up through this process is that we can evaluate how state legislatures—the chief institutions charged with crafting policy in the states—handle the task of inventing and borrowing policy; in chapter 5, I document how legislatures approach invention and borrowing in RPS policy-making. In order to pursue this endeavor, I extract adoptions from the master datasets that occurred through legislative action and also extract all nonadoptions from the master datasets to reflect the idea that the opportunity for a legislature in state i to borrow a policy feature is influenced by whether a public utilities commission in state j invented with respect to that policy feature.[38] I additionally extract all nonadoptions to reflect the idea that a legislature in a given state loses the opportunity to adopt a policy feature or combination of policy features if another institution in that state has already adopted the same policy feature or combination of policy features.

In chapter 6, I analyze invention and borrowing from the vantage point of public utilities commissions and evaluate how variation in the structure of state public utilities commissions affects the likelihood of invention and borrowing. Here, I extract adoptions from the master datasets that occurred through regulatory action and also extract all nonadoptions for the same reason as in the legislative case.

In chapter 7, I bore into the details of legislative and regulatory invention and examine comparative case studies related to each kind of invention. I explore the different experiences of Illinois and Indiana with respect to legislative invention as well as the experiences of Arizona and New York with respect to regulatory invention to bring richer and more qualitative insight into my findings.

Finally, in chapter 8, I deploy the same framework to detailed policy feature-level adoption data that others (Kreitzer and Boehmke 2016) have gathered with respect to anti-abortion policy to see how legislative invention unfolds in a conservative policy area. Ultimately, my empirical strategy allows for a granular and in-depth study of invention and borrowing, and I now pursue that enterprise.

---

38. Legislative adoptions account for 526 out of 642 (or almost 82%) of all adoptions. Legislatures also account for roughly 81% (or 169 out of 208) instances of invention and roughly 82% (or 357 out of 434) instances of borrowing.

CHAPTER 4

Situating Legislative and Regulatory RPS Invention in Broader Context

In the preceding chapters of the book, I discussed how the RPS policy area is one where the individual states have crafted their own policy in the absence of federal guidance, how both legislative and regulatory bodies in the individual states ostensibly could claim jurisdictional authority to adopt RPSs, and how invention can be conceptually and empirically identified and separated from borrowing. In chapters 5 and 6, I present theoretical expectations and empirical analyses about the conditions that motivate legislatures and public utilities commissions to invent with respect to RPS policy. What would be useful at this juncture, however, is a discussion about why invention might be a different kind of proposition for legislatures as opposed to regulatory agencies. Recall that in the book's second chapter, I recounted how RPS invention through legislative action has been more common than RPS invention through public utilities commission decision-making. Understanding the reasons why legislative action emerged as the most common pathway for RPS invention can provide context and help shed light on the legislative and regulatory-specific examinations conducted in chapters 5 and 6. Are there insights in political science that help us make sense of the institutional variation in RPS invention seen in the book, and can these insights help contextualize the stories told in chapters 5 and 6?

In this chapter, I situate institutional variation in RPS invention within what we know about legislatures and regulatory agencies, and I offer thoughts that may provide clues as to why legislatures took the lead in

RPS invention. Relatedly, I also discuss how the characteristics of legislative and regulatory bodies can influence the conditions under which these different institutional actors invent. My thoughts here are meant to serve as a bridge between the book's preceding two and following two chapters. First, I discuss why the differing central job responsibilities of legislatures versus regulatory agencies might lead to greater levels of invention among the former. Then, I talk about how different characteristics of legislatures and regulatory agencies themselves might engender different levels of RPS invention. And, lastly, I talk about how the contextualization developed here neatly segues into the book's next chapters.

How Legislative and Regulatory Job Responsibilities Influence RPS Invention

At their core, legislatures and regulatory agencies have different fundamental responsibilities, and these different responsibilities inform where we might expect RPS invention to predominantly occur. In the American political system, the legislative branch is chiefly tasked with making law. This central role is not only referenced in the United States Constitution (United States Constitution, Article I) but also extends to state legislatures, which share the same primary responsibility of proposing, crafting, and adopting legislation as their federal peer (Squire 2007, 2017). In short, legislatures function as policy adoption specialists, and this role, in turn, shapes the behavior of those who serve in legislatures. Legislators are likely to try to get preferred candidate policies adopted into law, are likely to look at policy adoption as one of preeminent ways through which society's challenges can be solved, and are likely to view their own effectiveness through the lens of whether they were able to codify their preferred policy candidates into law (Volden and Wiseman 2014; Bucchianieri, Volden, and Wiseman 2020). Legislators therefore plausibly consider legislating to be an integral if not the integral part of their job.[1]

Legislators' own view about the nature of their job appears to have legitimacy across the broader political system. One aforementioned sign

---

1. This is not to say that legislators do not engage in other responsibilities such as performing constituent service (Fenno 1978) or monitoring the executive branch (McCubbins and Schwartz 1984).

of legitimacy is the United States Constitution and, by extension, state constitutions, which express that legislatures retain the primary authority to adopt law. Another sign of legitimacy is the observation that the judiciary possesses the power of judicial review but generally has not claimed primacy over lawmaking itself. While the judiciary has exercised review since the early nineteenth century (*Marbury v. Madison*, 1803), it arguably has not parlayed the power of review into a demand for control over the job of legislating itself; the absence of such a demand suggests that broader legitimacy exists around the assertion that a prime responsibility of legislators is to make policy.[2] Even the public, for all the reputed and sometimes humorous animosity directed toward the legislative process in surveys, seems to believe that the job of legislators is to make policy.[3] The finding that public disapproval of legislators increases when legislative bodies suffer from gridlock (Flynn and Harbridge 2016) offers additional credence to the idea that the public has some expectation that legislators should try to adopt policy.

While a central part (and many would contend, the central part) of legislative job responsibility is to adopt policy, the situation is arguably different for regulatory agencies. Regulatory agencies exist as executive bodies and are primarily tasked with administering and enforcing policy. Administration refers to running or managing policy while enforcement refers to making sure that the various parties subject to contract stipulations within the policy are following those stipulations. Policy, according to the view that regulatory agencies should be pure executives, is something that is idealized as coming from outside the regulatory organization (canonically originating in the legislative branch) and that is then put into practice by impartial regulatory arbiters. Of course, this view neglects the reality that regulatory agencies do adopt policy. Regulatory agencies might adopt policies to govern their own internal affairs or human resource matters;[4]

---

2. Those alleging that judges "legislate from the bench" might disagree with my statement. However, the judiciary's power to strike down legislation has not resulted in the judiciary usurping the power to propose, craft, and adopt law. Moreover, the power of the judiciary is reactive rather than proactive (Rosenberg 1991). Concern about executive overreach in policy-making is also an acknowledgment of the legitimacy that the legislative branch has with respect to proposing, crafting, and adopting policy because such a concern conceivably would not exist absent the belief that it is the job of the legislative branch to make policy.

3. One humorous example of such a survey comes from 2013, when root canals were found to be more popular than Congress (National Public Radio 2013).

4. In this book, I look at outward-facing policies (which ostensibly directly affect constitu-

they might adopt policies to make their executive responsibilities easier to accomplish;[5] and they might make policies at the behest of the legislative branch.[6] However, the view of regulatory agencies as being primarily executive in character creates an ideal type for how regulatory agencies should behave regarding policy-making and arguably limits their room to maneuver on policy adoption.[7]

Combined with the view that it is primarily the job of the legislative branch to make policy, the ideal-type view of regulatory agencies as pure executives makes justifying policy adoption comparatively more difficult for the regulatory agencies vis-à-vis the legislative branch. While legislatures can simply invoke their authority to make laws on behalf of the public when adopting policy, regulatory agencies have to be ready to argue that their policy adoptions lie within their jurisdictional zones of authority. Even when this issue might seem clear cut—suppose hypothetically that a state public utilities commission utilizes its authority to maintain the safety and reliability of a state's electricity grid by raising electricity prices to retrofit electricity infrastructure—regulatory agencies still may face pushback about overstepping their bounds. For instance, in the hypothetical example, electric utility companies, interest groups affiliated with those electric utility companies, angry legislators, and even ordinary con-

---

ents) rather than policies affecting the internal organization of institutions (e.g., a state legislature creates a novel committee or adopts a novel rule on how bills can be considered). An interesting extension of the project pursued in this book would be to investigate factors driving invention and borrowing with respect to policies that change the internal structure or organization of institutions.

5. For example, the Internal Revenue Service could allow for the online submission of tax returns in order to streamline the receipt and processing of tax returns.

6. A classic example from public utilities commissions involves the setting of electricity rates, as public utilities commissions were originally explicitly set up to be impartial electricity rate arbiters (Besley and Coate 2003; Parinandi and Hitt 2018; Troesken 2006). In the RPS space, public utilities commissions generally manage and enforce state RPS programs (e.g., they communicate with electric utility companies about RPS program stipulations and enforce compliance with RPS programs). By virtue of overseeing electric utility companies' participation in states' electricity sectors and also managing the maintenance of those electricity sectors, public utilities commissions conceivably have the authority to adopt RPS policy. Furthermore, even in states where legislatures have adopted the majority of state RPS policy, they appear to have not clearly enumerated what public utilities commissions cannot do, thereby creating the possibility that public utilities commissions across the states have the opportunity to adopt RPS policy.

7. Taken to the extreme, some have argued that the lack of strong references to the bureaucracy in the U.S. Constitution suggest that regulatory agencies should not exist within the United States (American Bar Association 2018).

sumers can take umbrage with the public utilities commission's behavior and claim that the regulatory agency went beyond its purview. This same assortment of disaffected actors need not stop there and could use the claim of the regulatory agency acting outside of its purview to make the job of the agency much more onerous: these actors could utilize legislative and judicial hearings, for example, to consume the time and resources of regulators and sow doubt about the ability of regulators to act as impartial executors.[8] The point here is to emphasize that regulatory agencies must exhibit caution when adopting policy in order to try to minimize accusations of overstepping their executive role.

Trying to minimize accusations of overstepping bounds plausibly matters in explaining why state public utilities commissions have invented RPS policy less than state legislatures. Invention is by definition novel in the sense that it has not yet been tried across the states. Given that regulatory agencies seek to avoid appearing to overstep their bounds, they may shy away from adopting policy that as a result of being novel may elicit such an appearance.[9] In contrast, as actors of the chief policy-making branch, legislatures are expected to seek out policy solutions and arguably (relative to their regulatory agency peers) need not shy away from inventing due to the fear that they will be accused of overstepping their prescribed governmental role, as legislatures are widely recognized to possess the authority to adopt policy and as invention falls under the archetype of adopting policy. This is not to say, of course, that legislatures are frequent inventors of policy: if the RPS policy area explored prominently in this book is any guide, legislatures invented 169 times but borrowed 357 times, implying that invention represented roughly 32% of legislative policy adoption. Invention does not have a different definition for legislatures (e.g., it is still

---

8. Legislators, of course, can also face pushback for the policy-making actions that they take. However, the pushback in this case is generally directed at how legislators voted rather than debating whether legislators have the authority to craft policy in the first place. Even when the judiciary has struck down a particular policy, it has not challenged the ability of legislative bodies to adopt policy. Challenges to policy adopted by regulatory agencies, however, almost invariably include accusations that the regulatory agencies stepped outside of their executive authority.

9. Using our working hypothetical example, suppose that the public utilities commission issuing a price increase to retrofit electricity infrastructure is the first governmental body to do this across the U.S. states. The observation that an executive body adopted an unprecedented policy may invite criticism that the executive body is overstepping its bounds. The line of attack here would parallel the claim that a body that is purportedly executive in character has limited business adopting policy that has never been vetted in any state let alone the state in question.

characterized by its novelty), and the fact that candidates for invention have not been vetted across other states may partly account for why invention occurs less frequently than borrowing, even for legislatures. However, even accounting for the fact that invention is not especially common, the greater legitimacy given to the role of legislatures as policy adopters arguably creates increased permissiveness for legislatures to invent vis-à-vis regulatory agencies, which might help explain the higher incidence of RPS invention among legislatures compared to public utilities commissions.

The same difference in view about the primary job responsibility of legislatures versus regulatory agencies—where legislatures adopt policy while regulatory agencies execute it—also potentially explains why legislatures have been more frequent borrowers of RPS policy than have public utilities commissions, as borrowing also represents policy adoption. At the same time, it is possible that borrowing may be less likely to precipitate accusations of regulatory agencies overstepping their bounds than inventing based on the idea that many in the public may be more accepting of regulatory agencies adopting tested and vetted policy compared to adopting novel and unprecedented policy, leading regulatory agencies to borrow more than they invent.[10] In short, at least in the RPS policy area, the belief that it should mainly be the purview of legislatures to adopt policy along with the belief that it should mainly be the purview of regulators to execute policy may shed light on why legislatures have been more prolific policy adopters than regulatory agencies.[11]

Ultimately, the existence of legislative and regulatory RPS invention, even acknowledging the possibility that legislatures tend to invent more due to their position as the chief policy-making branch, implies that legislatures and regulatory agencies matter as sources of RPS policy inven-

---

10. There is empirical support in the RPS policy area for this possibility, as public utilities commissions borrowed more often than they invented (54 times versus 36 times). Of course, these numbers for borrowing and invention pale in comparison to analogous numbers produced by legislatures (357 times for borrowing and 169 times for inventing).

11. While both of the policy areas analyzed in this book—RPS, which is featured prominently through most of the book, and abortion, which is explored near the end of the book—exhibited predominantly legislative policy adoption, it is worth exploring whether certain policy areas are more amenable to regulatory policy adoption than others. At the federal level, for example, it is possible that issues that have a higher potential to cause direct physical harm to the public, such as policy related to pharmaceutical drug approval, might have higher levels of regulatory agency policy adoption relative to legislative policy adoption compared to other policy areas. I discuss this possibility further in the conclusion.

tion and further suggest that we explore when these two institutions are more receptive toward enacting novel policy in what has emerged as one of the preeminent methods through which the United States has pursued renewable energy development and attempted to deal with climate change. Given that the two institutions are conceivably able to invent RPS policy, what factors influence when the actors within each institution do so? If we take seriously the idea that classic views about how legislatures and regulatory agencies should behave with respect to policy adoption actually shape how these institutions behave when inventing, then the explanation that I have offered for why legislatures invented more than public utilities commissions regarding RPS policy might provide clues as to what motivates RPS invention within legislatures and public utilities commissions. I now turn to discussing this topic as a prelude to the fuller theoretical and empirical conversation that will occur over the next two chapters.

How Job Responsibility Difference Explains Legislative and Regulatory RPS Invention

If the notion that the core job responsibilities of legislatures and regulatory agencies should affect the relative frequency with which these two institutions invent RPS policy, then these same job responsibilities may shed light on when legislatures and regulatory agencies invent RPS. In this section, I discuss how the view of legislatures as chief policymakers and the view of regulatory agencies as mainly executive in nature creates potential possibilities for understanding when legislatures and regulatory agencies might invent. I sketch out what these possibilities might be in order to set the stage for the next chapters, and I cover legislatures and regulatory agencies in turn.

In the previous section, I talked at length about how the legislative branch enjoys broad legitimacy to adopt policy but did not talk about how the nature of legislative service can influence the kinds of policy adoption (and ultimately invention, as it is a form of adoption) that are likely to occur within legislatures. Those serving as legislators are not only empowered to adopt policy but do so on behalf of voters who entrusted them with this responsibility (Pitkin 1967). In serving voters, legislators are also trying to *lead* them; legislators are telling voters that they possess the tenacity and know-how to bring voters a vision of the world that voters ostensibly want. A big part of leading voters involves building an identity that allows legislators to claim that they represent a vision that voters might want. The identity not only functions as a form of communication between legislators and voters but enmeshes legislators within an ecosystem of ideas that the legislators can use as the basis for making policy. For example, a legislator who proclaims herself as a liberal not only sends a signal to voters about what direction she purports to lead those voters (here, in a liberal direction) but also is likely exposed to and espouses policy ideas that will lead society in a liberal direction.

Having broad legitimacy to make policy, combined with being exposed to and espousing policy ideas comporting with one's ideological affiliation, suggests that a legislator is likely to advocate for adopting policy that comports with their ideological affiliation. This not only makes sense at the micro (legislator-specific) but also at the macro (legislature-specific) level, suggesting that as a legislature takes on a particular ideology, that legislature should be more likely to advocate for adopting policy comporting with its particular ideology. Even though many states adopting RPS programs have had conservative bona fides, the fact that RPS sits within the universe of energy and environmental regulation suggests that legislatures should be more likely to advocate for the adoption of RPS policy as they become more liberal in character. On its face, this might not seem all that surprising, but distinguishing invention from borrowing allows us to discern whether the ideological comportment of a legislature has a differential relationship with respect to inventing and borrowing. In the next chapter, I argue and show using statistical analysis that increases in government liberalism more meaningfully account for RPS invention compared to RPS borrowing.[12] I offer that this discrepancy may potentially be attributable to the idea that greater ideological extremism (here, in the liberal direction) makes legislatures more apt to ignore or overlook a lack of evidence when adopting policies that align with their ideological agenda, which would explain the link between government liberalism and RPS invention given that RPS is within the liberal paragon of policies. While increased government liberalism admittedly should also increase the probability that legislatures borrow RPS policy, the quality of already

_____

12. As I more thoroughly show in the next chapter, greater governmental liberalism (the scores of which correspond heavily to legislative actors, as I also discuss in the next chapter) relates statistically with an increased likelihood of RPS inventing but not RPS borrowing.

having been tested brings a wider ideological spectrum of legislatures on board with borrowing, thereby leading to a weakened association between government liberalism and borrowing. In the eighth chapter of the book, I show that this same pattern occurs with respect to legislatures' level of conservatism when considering the conservative policy area of restrictions toward obtaining abortion.

When deliberating about why the ideological orientation of a legislature has such influence on the adoption choices made by that legislature—increased liberalism in a legislature has greater statistical association with RPS invention than with RPS borrowing even though both forms of adoption are positively correlated with rising liberalism, and increased conservatism in a legislature has greater statistical association with anti-abortion invention than anti-abortion borrowing even though both forms of adoption are positively correlated with rising conservatism—it seems important to reiterate that "taking a view" in terms of staking one's ideological ground is part and parcel of the task of legislating. Insofar as ideology informs the lens through which legislators perceive the world and identify policies to work toward their worldview, it is perhaps not surprising that ideological extremism should lead to an increased willingness to disregard evidence in policy adoption.[13]

Another hallmark of the job of legislating is that those serving in legislatures are subject to electoral accountability and that legislative impressions of electoral danger may influence RPS invention and borrowing. Brandeis's comment in *New State Ice Company versus Liebmann* (285 U.S. 262) about a "single courageous state" attempting "novel social and economic experiments without risk to the rest of the country" implies that the novel or untested nature of inventing carries some risk for any state government undertaking inventing.[14] At the same time, Brandeis's comment

---

13. It is an open question about how legislative invention and borrowing should work in a "moderate" policy area. While it is easy to say that "moderate legislatures should be more likely to invent moderate policy," the unidimensional (left-to-right or right-to-left) nature of ideology measures suggests that there might be no statistical association between the ideological orientation of a legislature and moderate policy invention. At the same time, borrowing has been shown to be amenable to ideologically broad sets of lawmakers in left-leaning (RPS) and right-leaning (anti-abortion) policy, suggesting that it might also be amenable (and nonsignificant statistically given unidimensional ideology measures) to ideologically broad actors in moderate policy. One challenge in testing this possibility would be to identify and then collect subpolicies from a "moderate" area, and I discuss this in the conclusion of the book.

14. Of course, this implication does not preclude state governments from inventing, as those

also implies that this same risk is less pronounced for borrowing based on the logic that state governments can observe the experimentation of other states with respect to borrowing.[15]

Brandeis's comment potentially has implications for how electoral accountability may affect legislative inventing and borrowing. Given the novelty of invention, one may be tempted to see it as being akin to a last ditch effort or "Hail Mary pass" that lawmakers pursue when they believe there is a credible possibility that they could lose office. However, one may also be tempted to conclude in the opposite direction that the novelty of invention makes it something that lawmakers tend to pursue when they believe that their hold on their positions is secure. The known or tested quality of borrowing also has a possible link to electoral accountability. Since a policy candidate to be borrowed has occurred elsewhere, it is conceivable that lawmakers may tend to borrow when they want to be able to show skeptical constituents evidence that their policy ideas have a chance of working. The desire among lawmakers to allude to such evidence may increase when lawmakers believe that there is an anti-incumbent mood among constituents.

In analyzing the relationship between legislative electoral vulnerability and RPS invention and borrowing, I fail to find a statistically meaningful relationship between legislative electoral vulnerability and RPS invention. This is perhaps somewhat reassuring on normative grounds, as it suggests that at least in the area of RPS, lawmakers are not subjecting constituents to novel policy choices out of desperation to hold on to power. It is perhaps also normatively reassuring with the same token that lawmakers do not subject constituents to novel policy choices when those lawmakers believe that they are electorally secure, as one might wonder why lawmakers must feel that they should be secure before adopting an untested policy. Legislatures with higher levels of electoral vulnerability are more likely to borrow RPS policy. This finding could also be regarded as normatively good insofar as lawmakers are responding to the fear of losing office by embracing tested and vetted best practices, suggesting that in the case

governments may believe that inventing addresses a need that is unmet through borrowing. This is probably normatively a good thing, otherwise it would be much more difficult for novel policy choices to enter the system of policy choices that have been made across the states.

15. This is not to say that borrowing is free from risk, as a state could borrow a policy from another state that is "the wrong fit." However, with borrowing, states can at least observe the experiences of other states while with inventing, they cannot.

of RPS, electoral accountability of lawmakers produces evidence-based policy-making.

Since RPS is the central policy area studied in this book, I devote the space above to discussing linkages between legislative electoral vulnerability and RPS invention and borrowing. Recall though that in the eighth chapter of the book, I evaluate legislative inventing and borrowing with respect to the conservative area of anti-abortion policy. This evaluation includes interrogating how legislative electoral vulnerability affects anti-abortion inventing and borrowing, and I ultimately find that legislative electoral vulnerability in this area has a statistically meaningful relationship with invention (where greater vulnerability corresponds to a higher likelihood of invention) but not borrowing. In terms of explaining my rationale for this finding, I draw a distinction between policy areas that tend to be viewed within a strictly moral "right-versus-wrong" prism (such as abortion, as is documented in Mooney 1999 and Kreitzer and Boehmke 2016) and policy areas that may be less likely to be viewed as purely good or evil propositions (RPS may fit the bill here, as RPS policies appear to have a greater diversity of purpose than do anti-abortion policies, which all seek to restrict abortion access).[16] Evidence may matter less in moral policy areas considering that voters might interpret such areas through intrinsic references to right versus wrong. At the same time, voters caring about such issues may look favorably upon invention, as adopting unprecedented policy (here, unprecedented anti-abortion policy) may be a signal to these voters about legislators' commitment to their cause. As legislative electoral vulnerability increases, legislators may feel emboldened to invent moral policy to showcase their commitment to voters caring about moral policy. In contrast, where evidence is in play (e.g., policy areas that relative to abortion are less likely to be seen purely through the prism of right-versus-wrong, such as RPS), legislative electoral vulnerability drives an emphasis toward tested or vetted policy-making.

The differential results of how legislative electoral vulnerability works with respect to RPS and anti-abortion policy have potential normative implications if one thinks that there *should* always be a relationship between legislative electoral vulnerability and invention. Specifically, if the result concerning the anti-abortion area is any guide, then changing the perception of a policy area so that it is viewed through a binary moral lens

---

16. I discuss my logic about this in greater detail in chapter 8.

may be a way to spur a link between legislative electoral vulnerability and invention. The problem with this approach, again if the anti-abortion area is any guide, is that it may obviate linkages between legislative electoral vulnerability and borrowing. More study is ultimately warranted to better understand how legislative electoral vulnerability may influence invention and borrowing across a host of policy areas arrayed on the basis of the degree to which those policy areas are interpreted as binary moral issues. Although it has been quite labor intensive and time consuming to operationalize my framework across the RPS and anti-abortion areas, in the conclusion of the book I propose how scholars may be able to systematically measure the degree to which a policy area is considered to be moral, and I then detail how my framework can be extended to incorporate a wider range of policy areas.

Of course, leaving aside the two factors discussed here—lawmaker ideology and electoral vulnerability—it is possible that *other* factors could affect legislative RPS invention and borrowing such as the resource capacity that a legislature possesses or the per capita income of a given state. I control for these and other possibilities in the fuller legislative RPS analysis displayed in the next chapter.[17] Having remarked about how important within legislature variation could impact RPS invention and borrowing, I next turn to exploring how the core job responsibility of regulatory agencies might shed light on when public utilities commissions invent RPS policy.

In my discussion of regulatory agencies earlier in this chapter, I not only described a classic view positing that regulatory agencies should serve mainly as executors of policy, but I also parlayed this into the possibility that regulatory agencies might shy away from inventing due to the fear of being accused of veering from their mainly executive nature by not just merely adopting policy but adopting policy that is novel and has not been tested elsewhere. Going one step further, it is possible that the same logic might help us illuminate when public utilities commissions (an example of a regulatory agency) are more likely to invent with respect to RPS policy. One thing that stands out from the idealized view that regulators should

---

17. Chapter 8 is a replication and extension of a paper on anti-abortion policy adoption by Kreitzer and Boehmke (2016). There, I utilize one model where I add key explanatory variables to the same set of variables used by Kreitzer and Boehmke, and I utilize another model where I add key explanatory variables and state-specific spatial and temporal measures of invention and borrowing to the variables used in the original paper.

strive to behave as fair policy arbiters is that regulators may generally exhibit conflict avoidance. Regulators may seek to limit facing scrutiny from other actors (e.g., regulated entities, legislators, and the court system) since such scrutiny can cast doubt on the ability of regulators to function as fair policy arbiters.[18]

The possibility that regulators demonstrate conflict avoidance has implications for when public utilities commissions may be more likely to invent with respect to RPS. Perhaps *the* most interested observers of regulatory agency behavior are the regulated entities that are not only monitored by regulatory agencies but also subject to regulatory agency-based policy-making. In the RPS space, regulated entities typically refer to electric utility companies that distribute (and in many cases, also generate) electricity to end-use consumers. Electric utility companies include well-known behemoths of industry such as American Electric Power, Consolidated Edison, and Xcel Energy, and these companies seek to earn profit as well as safeguard the drivers of their own profitability. It does not require a leap of faith to believe that electric utility companies vociferously defend their interests to the public utilities commissions that govern them.

RPS policy generally imposes costs on electric utility companies—many of which are *entrenched* in the sense that they possess near-monopolistic control of electricity provision under sectoral regulation or had near-monopolistic control prior to deregulation—by asking them to change how they procure electricity, and RPS invention does so in a way where electric utility companies cannot turn to the experiences of companies in other states to get a sense of how the policy might impact them.[19] Knowing that electric utility companies will generally dislike uncertainty in an area (RPS) where the electric utility companies are potentially being asked to substantially change their electricity procurement practices, public utilities

18. Although RPS policy invention by public utilities commissions is not as common as it is by legislatures, it does happen, suggesting that regulatory conflict avoidance does not completely eliminate the occurrence of regulatory RPS invention. On occasion, regulators may find RPS invention to be valuable (to use a stylized example, they may want to enact novel policy to increase the diversity of sources utilized in a state's electricity grid to reduce the possibility that shocks to supply and demand in a monocultured electricity grid can disrupt service), and I am deciphering when regulators may feel more comfortable to invent.

19. While electric utility companies all ostensibly desire profitability, they do *not* like uncertainty since this makes it difficult for them to plan for the future (Lagerberg 2015). By virtue of not having been vetted elsewhere, invention carries greater uncertainty than borrowing and may have less support among electric utility companies compared to borrowing.

commissions may be more likely to invent RPS policy when they think that electric utility companies will be less likely to challenge such policy-making, and I argue that this situation is more common when a state has a deregulated electricity sector.

Prior to state electricity deregulation, entrenched electric utility companies had control over the procurement and distribution of electricity in their respective service areas. With electricity deregulation (Ka and Teske 2002; Borenstein and Bushnell 2015), these same entrenched electric utility companies lost monopolistic control over the procurement side of electricity—consumers could choose to purchase electricity from alternate electricity vendors—but retained control over the distribution or transmission of electricity over their grid infrastructure. Deregulation signifies that some control of electricity provision has been taken away from entrenched electric utility companies, and it may have the effect of influencing entrenched electric utility companies to be more pliant toward regulators out of a desire to preserve the control over electricity provision that they still possess. Public utilities commissions, for their part, are conceivably aware that deregulation imposes a demonstration effect on entrenched electric utility companies that reduces these companies' willingness to challenge regulatory policy-making.[20] In turn, this suggests that if public utilities commissions were deliberating about inventing with respect to RPS, they would be more likely to actually invent RPS policy when electric utility companies are less apt to challenge them, which is more likely under deregulation.

I find some evidence in chapter 6 that RPS invention is more likely given state electricity sector deregulation but fail to find a statistically meaningful relationship between deregulation and RPS borrowing. This does not mean that electric utility companies somehow love RPS borrowing or that public utilities commissions think that electric utility companies will never challenge RPS borrowing. Indeed, I find a positive (though not statistically significant) association between deregulation and RPS borrowing, which gives a weak measure of support for the idea that deregulation increases the probability of RPS borrowing. The nonsignificant relationship, however, provides less cover for the notion that public utilities commissions rely

---

20. This seems like a reasonable assumption to make considering that deregulation was heavily marketed as something that would transfer power from entrenched electric utility companies to end-use consumers (Borenstein and Bushnell 2015).

on the weaker position of electric utility companies afforded by deregulation to increase RPS borrowing, and a reason for this might be that firms accommodate borrowing more than they do invention since borrowing arguably creates a history that firms can access to study potential policy impacts.[21]

Ultimately, the finding linking electricity sector deregulation to increased regulatory RPS invention is promising in the sense that it gives us a clue as to where novel RPS policy-making by regulatory actors might occur but also limiting considering that a minority of states have deregulated electricity sectors.[22] The same finding begs the question of whether a relationship exists between giving regulatory actors greater voice to speak to the public and discerning an increased chance of novel RPS policy adoption. While a majority of states deem that public utilities commission members are chosen by elite-level actors (usually gubernatorial appointment subject to legislative confirmation), a handful of states specify that public utilities commission members be chosen through statewide vote (Besley and Coate 2003; Parinandi and Hitt 2018). The public utilities commissions across both cases generally have similar responsibilities (for example, regulating commerce related to electricity, gas, and water usage within their respective states) and have similar stated expectations about adhering to impartial regulatory roles.[23] However, in states where public

---

21. Given the importance that public utilities commissions give to reducing the chance of electric utility company pushback when adopting RPS policy, why don't legislatures give the same level of importance to electric utility companies? While it is far-fetched to say that legislatures do not care about electric utility companies, it is not far-fetched to say that legislatures are less concerned with pushback from electric utility companies compared to public utilities commissions. There are some possible reasons for this. First, regulatory commissions may worry more about facing accusations of bias compared to legislatures, which are almost expected to take a view and advocate for that view even if disproportionately impacts some groups over others. And, second, regulatory commissions have a narrower policy purview than legislatures (as Besley and Coate document in their 2003 piece, regulators have purview only over policy aligning with their regulatory area while legislatures have purview over a general basket of areas of which any one regulatory area is one specific item), implying that regulators may be more attuned to push back within their area compared to legislatures that deal with a broad range of areas.

22. In figure 8 in chapter 6, I provide a map of the states that have deregulated electricity sectors as of the end point of this study.

23. For instance, the mission statement of the New Mexico Public Regulation Commission (the state's elected public utilities commission) references "fair and reasonable" rate-setting as well as the "reasonable and adequate" provision of services to the public (New Mexico Public Regulation Commission 2021). The presence of words such as "fair" and "reasonable" implies an expected degree of neutrality in the commission's behavior.

utilities commissioners are selected through statewide vote, the ability of public utilities commissioners to frame regulatory issues as popular matters may provide the commissioners with some leeway to deviate from wanting to accommodate electric utility companies. That is to say, public utilities commissioners in states with direct election may be able to take their case directly to voters about why RPS policy-making is worthwhile and, in doing so, they may be able to create a cushion to downweight some of the worry about electric utility company pushback. This suggests that public utilities commissioners in states with direct election may be more likely to make RPS policy compared to appointed public utilities commissioners, who are arguably less able to take cases directly to the public.

Based on the idea that electric utility companies may generally be more amenable to borrowing than invention due to the tested nature of borrowing, it is possible that elected public utilities commissioners might find taking their case directly to the public to be especially valuable with respect to justifying novel RPS adoption. This would, if true, establish a key institutional pathway for regulatory RPS invention. As shown see in chapter 6, the benefit of direct election in terms of inducing regulatory RPS adoption is not exclusive to invention, as elected public utilities commissioners are more likely to invent as well as borrow RPS policy compared to their nonelected peers. Indeed, the likelihood of borrowing RPS policy given direct election is greater than the likelihood of inventing RPS policy, and this perhaps makes intuitive sense in light of the observations that borrowing may be more accepted by electric utility companies and that borrowing allows regulators to claim that they are pursuing results produced elsewhere.[24] As much of the mandate for this book revolves around conceptually separating invention and borrowing and then determining whether various factors differentially influence invention and borrowing, I give less centrality to the direct election regulatory finding even though direct election increases RPS invention and RPS policy adoption more generally.

---

24. Just because elected commissioners may be able to take issues to the public to cushion concerns of electric utility company challenge does not mean that they can ignore fears of such challenge; borrowing, by virtue of being tested, therefore still plays an important role in regulatory officials' RPS policy-making menus. Also, insofar as facing direct election makes public utilities commissioners accountable to voters, it is possible that commissioners may act like their legislative colleagues and borrow in hopes of credibly claiming that they are delivering results seen elsewhere. Both of these reasons together would help explain why direct election produces a greater magnitude of borrowing vis-à-vis invention.

A question worth asking is what the direct election result means normatively. The fact that direct election appears to spur regulatory RPS invention is good if one believes that regulators should play a direct role in adopting novel RPS policy and thereby injecting new policies into the system of policies used across the states. At the same time, the fact that direct election appears to produce more regulatory borrowing than invention may be reassuring for observers if they think that officials should exercise caution in exposing the public to untested policy-making. The broader finding linking direct election to greater regulatory RPS policy-making may itself be reassuring for some observers since it suggests that a lack of direct electoral accountability may restrain policy-making among non-elected regulators (which, of course, is in line with the classic view of regulators described earlier in this chapter). Yet practical recommendations from this finding may be somewhat limited. It is not easy to change a state's method of public utilities commissioner selection, and trying to do so for the sake of hopefully precipitating increased RPS policy-making may be a fool's errand. Moreover, a literature (Gormley 1983; Besley and Coate 2003; Troesken 2006; Parinandi and Hitt 2018) connecting the election of public service regulators to the diminished quality of electricity infrastructure—mainly through neglected upkeep sparked by a desire to maintain low prices—suggests that possible gains from enacting RPS policies may be offset by efficiency issues. While the direct election of regulators might admittedly provide diagnostic value as to where we might look to detect novel RPS policy-making, the jury is arguably out as to whether it is of great use prescriptively to induce such policy-making, especially given that regulatory RPS policy adoption is so much rarer than similar legislative action.

Another issue worth mulling over is debating whether and how much the belief systems of regulatory agencies influence their policy-making. It is reasonable to think that the ideological comportment of policymakers should influence their thoughts; whether it influences policy outcomes, however, may be dependent on the nature of institutional actors' job responsibilities. Earlier in this chapter, I described a link between government ideology and RPS policy adoption (and especially RPS invention), and I made the point that we should probably expect ideological comportment to affect legislator policy-making since an integral part of the job of legislators is to take a view and advocate for that view among constituents. Given that a classic view of regulatory agencies depicts these actors as fair policy arbiters, it is plausible that we should see less of an overt and more of a muted link between government ideology and regulatory RPS policy adoption. An obscure relationship between government ideology and regulatory policy action makes intuitive sense here, as an overt link would suggest that regulatory agencies are abrogating the fairness and impartiality that comprise a central aspect of their mission.

In the sixth chapter of the book, I include government ideology as a control variable and find no discernible link between government ideology and regulatory RPS borrowing but find a negative relationship between government ideology and regulatory RPS invention. The negative relationship stands out as anomalous, as it suggests that greater conservatism among regulators should lead to more prodigious levels of regulatory RPS invention (which is anomalous because conservatives generally favor lower amounts of energy regulation). In the sixth chapter, I make the case that the negative relationship between government ideology and regulatory RPS invention is an artifact of one conservative state (Arizona) featuring high levels of regulatory RPS invention. A major motivator behind Arizona's pursuit of RPS was the desire by its regulators to develop some of the country's most promising reservoirs of solar energy, and if I drop Arizona from the analysis (as I discuss in chapter 6), the anomalous finding linking conservatism in government ideology to increased regulatory RPS invention is no longer near statistical significance, giving heft to the idea that the result was an artifact rather than something systematic.

More generally, the finding with respect to government ideology draws attention to the difficulty of identifying and measuring the belief systems of state public utilities commissions. Many existing measures of government ideology are heavily modeled on legislative behavior.[25] And even if some public utilities commissioners take on partisan affiliations, many—such as those in Alaska, California, and Kentucky—are avowedly nonpartisan, meaning that using regulatory party affiliation as a measure of regulatory belief would create serious gaps in the data to be evaluated.[26] Moreover, even when party affiliation is present and even if regulators have previous histories in other branches of government, the job of the regula-

---

25. Even the Berry et al. measure from 1998, which makes space for a governor's ideology, bases the governor's ideology on same-party legislators. I discuss this in greater detail in the next chapter.

26. See the public service commissioner page on Ballotpedia: https://ballotpedia.org/Public_Service_Commissioner_(state_executive_office)

tor itself can potentially make those affiliations and previous experiences less informative. In the book's conclusion, I discuss how we might reliably measure public utilities commission ideology and use it within studies of energy policy moving forward.[27]

In sum, the picture of regulatory RPS invention that emerges here is one where the view of regulatory agencies as somewhat impartial policy arbiters potentially restricts the ability of public utilities commissions to invent RPS policy to instances where public utilities commissions can better handle pushback from electric utility companies. This opportunity can occur after sectoral deregulation, which arguably reduces the willingness of entrenched electric utility companies to push back on regulatory initiatives. This opportunity may also occur when regulatory commissioners are elected, as they may be able to take regulatory issues to the public to help buttress electric utility company pushback; direct election's RPS pro-adoption behavior is not limited to invention as it is in the case of deregulation, however. Of course, other factors (for example, whether state government is controlled by Democrats; whether a state legislature has term limits; a state legislature's level of professionalism; and a state's level of per capita wealth) could also influence regulatory RPS invention, and I control for these explanations in chapter 6. The story that I lay out here, however, provides a possible blueprint for where we may expect to see public utilities commissions take on the important task of adopting novel RPS policy.

Conclusion

The objective of this chapter has been to build context for the empirical chapters of the book by illustrating how the job responsibilities of legislatures and regulatory public utilities commissions potentially not only explain how much RPS policy adoption legislatures and public utilities commissions undertake but also help illuminate when legislatures and regulatory public utilities commissions tend to invent RPS policy. My focus on the core functions of institutions—and on the differences between the

---

27. That being said, I do not believe that incorporating the ideology of public utilities commissioners (were a sufficient measure of such ideology to be created) would invalidate the need for public utilities commissions to try to avoid occasions of conflict that could make them look unfair in the dispensation of their responsibilities.

core functions of institutions—is central to understanding when legislative and regulatory actors behave in accordance with Brandeis's vision that individual states add to the corpus of policy solutions that could be utilized across the states. Knowing that invention could have a different genesis across different institutions helps us determine what we expect from each institution with respect to RPS, and it may assist in future endeavors to make sense of legislative and regulatory policy adoption in a different policy area. I now turn to one of the book's key empirical chapters, where I flesh out greater detail about legislative invention and borrowing concerning RPS and provide empirical analysis.

CHAPTER 5

Liberal Ideology and Legislative Invention in Renewable Energy Policy

In the American political system, the legislative branch is the main governmental institution tasked with crafting and adopting laws. The Founders intended for the legislative branch to be the most important branch, and with rare exceptions, federal politics in the late eighteenth and nineteenth centuries revolved around powerful legislators articulating their policy positions in the halls of the national Congress (Elkins and McKitrick 1995; Cox and McCubbins 2005; Tulis 2017). Even as the nineteenth century gave way to a twentieth (and so far, a twenty-first century) typified by the emergence of a powerful administrative state (Wilson 1887; Lewis 2012; Potter 2019), the legislative branch formally retains the role of writing law and tasks the executive branch with enforcement.[1]

The role ascribed to the legislature in the above paragraph rings true for state legislatures. The American Congress was modeled on the workings of the 13 colonial legislatures, and the state legislatures in turn have been influenced by the workings of the American Congress (Squire 2017).[2] Inasmuch as the national legislature has served as the principal institution in charge of crafting laws at the national level, so too have state legislatures served as the principal institutions in charge of crafting laws at the state level. And as the states have taken on greater policy responsibility in recent decades (Peterson

1. An argument is emerging (e.g., Shane 2009) that increasing executive power is threatening the primacy of the legislative branch. I do not take a stance with respect to this argument in this book.

2. I am referring to the 13 colonies that eventually became the United States.

1995), state legislatures have arguably needed to exercise their lawmaking responsibility more often and on matters of increasing complexity.

Legislatures across the states have exercised their lawmaking responsibilities in myriad ways and have often adopted policies that are original in the sense that they have not been adopted previously in other states. For example, in 2013, the North Dakota legislature approved House Bill 1305 (2013). House Bill 1305 was first-of-its-kind across the states in that it banned abortion in cases where a fetus has genetic abnormalities (such as Down syndrome). While other states had already passed restrictions on when and how an abortion could be obtained, no state had banned the procedure on the basis of the detection of fetal genetic abnormalities. In justifying why the North Dakota legislature had done what no other legislature had done, Representative Bette Grande couched the bill's adoption in moral terms by saying that "the state has a compelling duty to find what is the potential life of a fetus" (quoted in Eligon and Eckholm 2013). An ally of Grande, Paul Maloney of North Dakota Right to Life, remarked that the "people of North Dakota thought, 'We have the kind of legislative body that would pass these kinds of pieces of legislation'" (quoted in Eligon and Eckholm 2013).

The North Dakota legislature invented by banning abortion related to genetic abnormality, and North Dakota's invention has since been borrowed (though unsuccessfully) by states such as Indiana and Ohio.[3] North Dakota's invention arguably represented a proverbial crossing of the Rubicon in the abortion policy domain, not only because it expanded the scope of conflict as predicted by classic political science theory (Schattschneider 1975), but also because it made a policy feature adoption that may have been considered (at least in some circles) as impossible become possible. In understanding what made the North Dakota legislature's adoption of this policy feature possible, Paul Maloney of North Dakota Right to Life highlighted some theoretical possibilities with his comment that the "people of North Dakota . . . have the kind of legislative body that would pass these kinds of pieces of legislation."

Maloney's comment about possessing the kind of legislature that would

---

3. At the time of writing, the North Dakota genetic abnormality restriction is the only one that has taken effect. Indiana adopted the same genetic abnormality policy feature in 2016 and Ohio did likewise in 2017 but the federal court system has either blocked or delayed implementation in these latter cases (Cha 2018). The Supreme Court's decision in *Dobbs vs Jackson Women's Health Organization* presumably will operationalize anti-abortion laws in a number of states.

push through novel or unprecedented legislation suggests, for instance, that a *united* legislature may be more likely to invent when adopting policy. Maloney's comment about the kind of legislature may also pertain to *government ideology*, or what members of the legislature generally believe on a liberal-to-conservative spectrum. If the typical member of a legislature is on average highly ideological in orientation (in either the conservative or liberal direction), then certain novel policies that would probably be overlooked by an ideologically moderate legislature may be adopted because the ideologically charged legislature believes that such policies are the "right" policies to enact. Maloney's reference to the "people of North Dakota" suggests that legislators may be responding to the wishes of voters and that electoral vulnerability could be causing invention (Pitkin 1967; Mayhew 1974; Ashworth 2012). Finally, Maloney's comment about the "kind of legislature" suggests that structural aspects of a legislature (such as the amount of resources or *professionalism* that a legislature possesses) might influence invention, as legislatures with greater resource availability may be able to invest in invention.

The question of what influences state legislatures to invent extends beyond abortion and into other policy areas. In 2011, the California legislature passed Senate Bill X1–2 and required retail electricity suppliers in the state to provide 33% of the electricity sold to consumers from renewable sources (Nahai 2011). California could have followed other states (such as Illinois and Oregon) in establishing mandatory standards specifying that utilities supply 25% of electricity sold to consumers from renewable sources, but the state's legislature instead chose a novel 33% standard. In endorsing the legislature's action, Governor Jerry Brown said that California's choice of the ambitious standard was no accident and was motivated by California's role as a trendsetter and force for good in the world: "It's about California leading the country" (McGreevey 2011).

Brown's comment mirrors those of Grande and Maloney, even if the policy domain of renewable energy regulation is different. Brown's comment also ignites the same questions about when a state legislature might invent. Could it be that California had a unified government where the majority of legislators as well as the governor belonged to the same political party? Could it be that members of California's legislature are predominantly liberal in ideological orientation and are more likely (compared to ideologically moderate or conservative legislatures) to be attuned to novel policy proposals championed by left-leaning policy advocates and to believe that those novel policy proposals are worth adopting? Could it be that California legislators are simply acting based on reelection desires and adopting a novel renewable energy standard in order to cater to the demands of voters? Or could it be that the California legislature's level of professionalism (which is very high, as evidenced by Kousser 2005; Squire 2007; Boushey and McGrath 2017; Arel-Bundock and Parinandi 2018; California Legislature 2018) played a role in that state's invention with respect to the novel energy standard?

The motivating examples of North Dakota and California display the promise of federalism as envisioned by Brandeis. Pioneering states adopt novel policies and in doing so create some policies that may be borrowed and co-opted by other states.[4] Policymakers in individual states can "customize" and choose policies that are best supported by their respective constituencies (Karch 2007; Ostrom 2008). Since legislatures are the primary institutions within the states tasked with adopting laws, it is worth exploring and uncovering the factors that contribute to legislatures inventing when they adopt policy. Are the factors that contribute to legislatures inventing the same as those that contribute to legislatures borrowing existing policy from other states? And what explanations are the most compelling in terms of predicting legislative invention?

Knowing the answer to the questions above is crucial, as this knowledge helps us determine how invention by legislatures occurs and how the causes of invention may be different from those that explain borrowing. In this chapter, I use the case of renewable portfolio standard policy adoption by state legislatures to discern the causes of legislative invention and borrowing. Studying legislatures is not only helpful because they are the main institutions tasked with crafting law; studying legislatures is also helpful because all legislators are elected, meaning that we can evaluate how changes in electoral vulnerability influence the relative likelihoods of state legislatures inventing and borrowing. Focusing on legislatures is addition-

---

4. Another benefit of invention occurs when an inventing state shows other states how *not* to act. For example, North Carolina invented when it adopted what is colloquially known as the "Bathroom Bill" in 2016. This law required that individuals utilizing public restrooms in that state use the restroom corresponding to the sex listed on their birth certificates rather than the gender with which they identify. The passage of the law sparked a national backlash and featured prominent business groups pulling out of the state in protest and was partially repealed (Domonske 2017). The renewable portfolio policy domain does not feature such a prominent and high-profile abandonment of policy, and I therefore do not focus on policy abandonment (or failure) in this book. However, it is important to note that a key benefit of invention is that one state's experience can show other states what not to do.

ally helpful since a systematic measure exists of how state legislatures differ from one another in terms of professionalism or resource capacity. In this chapter, I present a cogent analysis detailing how variation in key behavioral and institutional factors affects decisions by legislatures to invent or borrow when adopting policy. Understanding the potential implications of such variation is important, not just from an academic perspective but also because ongoing developments in the body politic may change the propensity of legislatures to invent. Looking at the renewable portfolio standard area, I ultimately show that greater governmental ideological liberalism influences invention but not borrowing. This finding matters because it shows which state legislatures are pushing novel advances in the important area of renewable energy policy and offers a starting point for a conversation about whether ideology influences state legislative invention more broadly (I revisit this issue in chapter 8 as well as the concluding chapter). I also find that electoral vulnerability influences borrowing but not invention, and this finding shows that electoral concerns have helped key renewable energy development policies spread across the states and similarly helps augur a conversation about how electoral vulnerability influences state policy-making more broadly (I also revisit this issue in chapter 8 and the concluding chapter).

I structure the rest of the chapter as follows. First, I briefly review extant literature on state legislatures and invention. Then, I theorize about explanations that could predict invention by legislatures and also theorize about how those explanations could differentially impact invention and borrowing. I combine my theorizing with a description of data and analytical results and close with implications about the role that legislatures play in advancing invention versus borrowing during RPS policy adoption.

Making Room for Inquiring about Legislative Invention and Borrowing and What Influences Them

Recall that what I refer to in this book as invention, or the adoption of a policy that is new to a system of actors by a member of that system of actors, builds on the work of Jack Walker (1969).[5] Walker is interested in determining what makes state legislatures "innovate" and defined innova-

---

5. Here, the system is the set of 50 American states and a member of the system is an individual American state.

tion as occurring whenever a state adopts "a program or policy which is new to the states adopting it, no matter how old the program may be or how many other states have adopted it" (Walker 1969, 881). Walker's own endeavor was motivated heavily by the work of Everett Rogers (1962), who determined that ideas and technologies (what he also termed "innovations") spread out or diffuse across a population or system of actors according to an S-shaped pattern. In the context of Rogers's diffusion theory, Walker wants to know why a state legislature would make an adoption that is new to that state regardless of where the adoption lies along the S-curve. My goal for the book in the context of Rogers's diffusion theory is to evaluate why a state would adopt a policy that has not yet been introduced along the S-curve for all 50 states; and an integral part of this goal centers on figuring out whether the factors predicting invention are the same as those that predict borrowing. My goal for this chapter in the context of Rogers's diffusion theory is to evaluate why a state *legislature* would adopt a policy that has not yet been introduced along the S-curve for all 50 states.

Although Walker studied innovation by legislatures rather than invention by legislatures, his outlining of factors is instructive and helps form the basis of how we might think about the causes of invention. Walker believed that high levels of per capita income, urbanization, and legislative professionalism could lead to high levels of innovation. The leading measure of legislative professionalism (Squire 2007) views Congress as the quintessential professionalized legislature and compares each state's legislature to Congress based on how each state's legislature approximates the professionalism of Congress based on the sum of three factors: the compensation of a state legislator; the length of a state legislative session; and the average number of staff available to a state legislator.

The common logic with respect to legislative professionalism, state per capita income, and a state's level of urbanization is that they reflect the idea that higher resource endowments correspond with a greater ability to find policy and marshal it through the lawmaking process, resulting in the greater adoption of new policies that are "new" to the states adopting them (Walker 1969). This idea is not limited to Walker's work and extends to other diffusion scholarship including Gray (1973), Berry and Berry (1990), and Shipan and Volden (2006). There is not ironclad evidence, however, that all factors corresponding to greater state resource endowments work in the same direction concerning innovation and that legislative professionalism relates positively with innovation. Using Walker's definition of invention, Boehmke and Skinner (2012) find that per capita income and urbanization correspond with greater innovation but find no effect for legislative professionalism; these findings are corroborated by Desmarais, Harden, and Boehmke (2015). Walker's belief linking greater resource capacity to state-level innovation has potential implications for state-level invention. Greater resources may enable state legislatures to identify and formulate novel policies to adopt and spark invention. However, greater resources may work in the opposite direction by introducing more scrutiny into the legislative process and leading to greater borrowing during adoption.

Scholarship utilizing Walker's definition of innovation also linked unified government to innovation. Unified government refers to the situation where one political party possesses control over the legislative and executive branches of government (Alt and Lowry 1994; Binder 2003). Arguments about how unified government relates to policy adoption embrace the view of veto player theory (Shepsle and Weingast 1987; Tsebelis 2002), where the ease with which policy change occurs relates inversely to the number of pivotal (or veto) actors participating in the policy-making process. A veto player can slow down the policy-making process by voicing displeasure with a policy proposal and can even block policy-making through using institutional powers to halt the advancement of policy. Having fewer veto players reduces the opportunity for any one veto player to slow down or halt policy-making and thereby increases the ease with which policy change can occur.

Similar to the logic above, some policy innovation and diffusion studies have shown that unified government corresponds positively with adoption by reducing the possibility that partisan gridlock could slow down or block adoption (see Berry and Berry 1990; Pacheco 2012). Even when unified government fails to attain statistical significance in adoption and diffusion studies (Volden 2002b; Shipan and Volden 2006; Volden 2006), the fact that this variable is repeatedly included in analyses on adoption and diffusion testifies to its theoretical importance. Just as unified government has been linked to policy innovation, it may also influence policy invention in the sense that lawmakers are more easily able to adopt novel policy when they face fewer roadblocks in policy-making.

Scholars have begun to tie government ideology to the diffusion of policy. Ideology describes how systematic one's beliefs are along a conservative-to-liberal spectrum and has emerged as a powerful predictor of whether policymakers support and try to advance the policy proposals that they do (Krehbiel 1998). Ideology was missing a role in Walker's story on legislative policy innovation in the states; one reason why is presumably that scholars had not yet devised a way to systematically measure ideological orientation within and across the U.S. states. In the intervening decades, scholars have engineered reliable measures of ideological orientation that allow for comparisons to be made within and across the states, with the result being an explosion in the use of ideology as an explanatory variable for a host of political and policy-specific outcomes.[6]

One measure of ideology—*government* ideology—captures the ideological comportment of state governmental officials on a conservative-liberal spectrum. Berry et al. (1998, 2010) construct a governmental ideology score for each state/year by assuming first that the ideological comportment of a state's legislators of a given party can be gleaned from the ideological comportment of that state's national legislators who belong to the same party.[7] The authors also assume that the ideological comportment of a state's governor can be gleaned from the estimated ideological comportment of a state's legislators who belong to the same party as that state's governor.[8] Lastly, the authors use a weighted sum combining the ideological scores of major and minor party delegations from each chamber of a state's legislature along with that of the governor to calculate a governmental ideological score for that state.[9] In figure 5,

---

6. The two most prominent and utilized measures of state-level ideology are those devised by Berry et al. (1998, 2010) and Shor and McCarty (2011). Since the Berry et al. measure covers the entire time span (1983–2011) I analyze in my study, is complete, and is utilized heavily in work on energy and environmental policy (e.g., Carley, Nicholson-Crotty, and Miller 2017), I use the Berry et al. measure in this book. I acknowledge that Shor and McCarty's measure is also a valuable tool for evaluating the role of ideology in influencing policy-making outcomes.

7. A state's national delegation of legislators is chosen because ideological scores exist for the national legislators that can be interpolated onto same-party state legislators. Another reason is that interpolation can be standardized within and across states (Berry et al. 1998).

8. The authors make this assumption because ideological scores do not exist for governors. The assumption is reasonable based on the idea that state legislators and a governor from the same party are probably working together to achieve a similar worldview. The fact that gubernatorial ideology is interpolated from estimates of state legislator ideology should ameliorate concerns that the inclusion of the governor in the Berry et al. measure disqualifies its use in a study on legislative invention and borrowing.

9. The score ranges from 0 to 100, with 0 being the most conservative and 100 being the most liberal. The formula for the weighted sum is that *Government Ideology*$_{i,t}$ = .25(*Democrat Share of Power in Lower House*$_{i,t}$*Average Ideology of Democrats in Lower House*$_{i,t}$ + *Republican Share of Power in Lower House*$_{i,t}$*Average Ideology of Republicans in Lower House*$_{i,t}$) + .25(*Democrat Share of Power in Upper House*$_{i,t}$*Average Ideology of Democrats in Upper House*$_{i,t}$ + *Republican*

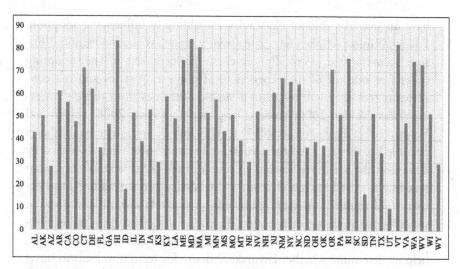

Fig. 5. Government Ideology
Source: Data on government ideology comes from Berry et al. (1998).

I plot a state's average government ideology calculated over the full time span of the study.

Figure 5 reveals observations that conform to conventional wisdom but also defy it. It is not surprising that Maryland and Massachusetts have liberal state governments or that Utah and Idaho have conservative state governments. However, California is not as liberal as one might expect, and West Virginia has historically had a very liberal state government.[10]

Using the Berry et al. measure (originally derived in 1998) and employing a logic emphasizing that ideologues want to adopt policies that fit with their worldviews, scholars have linked government ideology to adoption with respect to abortion (Kreitzer 2015), unemployment benefits (Gilardi 2010), and stringent renewable energy regulations (Carley and Miller 2012). However, policy adoption and diffusion scholars have not examined whether government ideology differentially impacts whether an adopting state legislature invents or borrows.

Recently, scholars studying the diffusion of policy across the U.S. states

---

*Share of Power in Upper House$_{i,t}$*Average Ideology of Republicans in Upper House$_{i,t}$) + .50(*Ideology of Governor$_{i,t}$*). Full details of the scoring procedure are available in Berry et al. (1998). Further, the scoring procedure has been validated against Shor and McCarty's alternate procedure (Berry et al. 2010).

10. California has had a history of electing conservative political officials. West Virginia, on the other hand, routinely elected descendants of the New Deal Democrats until the 2000s.

have uncovered a role for electoral vulnerability in influencing adoption. Policy diffusion scholars have consistently argued that a key reason diffusion occurs is that electorally vulnerable policymakers in later adopting states free ride off of the experiences of pioneering states and tell constituents that they will re-create desirable outcomes from those pioneering states (Volden 2006; Volden, Ting, and Carpenter 2008; Shipan and Volden 2014; Butler et al. 2017).[11] This line of argument establishes a possible link between electoral vulnerability and borrowing—which is by definition the act of replicating an earlier state's policy action—but what link might exist between electoral vulnerability and invention? Do electorally vulnerable lawmakers see invention as a "Hail Mary" and do so in hopes of rejuvenating their reelection chances? Evaluating whether electoral vulnerability differentially impacts invention and borrowing would help us determine whether lawmakers' desire for reelection leads to novel policy creation or the copying of existing policy.

Lastly, it is important to briefly revisit the topic of policy reinvention. While Walker (1969) focused on why innovation by legislatures occurs, Berry and Berry (1990) shifted the emphasis in political science to investigating why policies spread instead of investigating why states adopt "new" policies (Boehmke and Skinner 2012). Some scholars, however, did not turn to diffusion per se but investigated why states customize or reinvent policies during the diffusion process (Clark 1985; Glick and Hays 1991; Hays 1996; Mooney and Lee 1999; Karch 2007; Carley, Nicholson-Crotty, and Miller 2017).

While the scholars above did not systematically distinguish invention from borrowing by focusing on all categories of policy features within a policy domain, their work is instructive. Glick and Hays (1991), in the words of Mooney and Lee (1999), show that "reinvention may have a systematic impact on the content of a state's policy" (Mooney and Lee 1999, 82). Glick and Hays (1991) and Mooney and Lee (1995) also hint at the idea (though they do not state it explicitly since the concept of reinvention is slightly different from my concept of invention) that the creation of novel policy is a systemwide process, with later adopters making novel enhancements and modifications to the policy regimes of earlier adopters.

---

11. An example of such re-creating is the following: suppose California lowers its corporate income tax rate and experiences a surge of corporate investment. Washington may observe California and act likewise, hoping for the same outcome.

Clark (1985) and Hays (1996) hint at the idea that earlier adopters are the novel policy creators while later adopters mainly borrow with little modification. Karch (2007) argues that scholars do a better job of articulating that the causes of customization are internal while Carley, Nicholson-Crotty, and Miller (2017) point to the importance of recognizing that reinvention results from internal and external factors and that we should give coverage to both internal and external determinants in our analyses.

Although I do not study reinvention as it has been operationalized by the scholars mentioned above, my analysis of legislative invention and borrowing sheds light on questions that remain unanswered in the policy reinvention literature. The inclusion of time as a variable in my analysis can help adjudicate between the theories offered by Clark (1985) and Glick and Hays (1991). And my inclusion of internal and external variables can help determine whether legislative invention is driven by domestic rather than non-state-specific considerations. The analysis will aid us in determining how and when legislatures function as wellsprings of novel policy-making, and I now turn to the central explanation of the chapter.

The Roles of Government Ideology and Electoral Vulnerability in Legislative Invention and Borrowing

I make two main arguments in this chapter. First, I contend that government ideology corresponds with legislative invention more than it corresponds with legislative borrowing.[12] And second, I contend that electoral vulnerability corresponds with legislative borrowing more than it corresponds with legislative invention. I also evaluate whether legislative professionalism influences invention differentially from borrowing but fail to find meaningful evidence with respect to it mattering and therefore do not elaborate on this relationship outside of speculating as to why a negative finding might exist in the conclusion of the chapter.

Invention is by definition unprecedented and untested, and due to its novelty, I assume that most observers are unaware of the policy ideas that could be candidates for invention. This assumption is a reasonable one when applied to ordinary citizens, as an ordinary citizen may generally know about an untested policy idea but probably does not know about the

---

12. Much of this section draws on analogous work in Parinandi (2020).

particular policy features that could comprise the bill allowing for the general untested policy idea to be adopted (Parinandi 2020). This assumption is also reasonable to make with respect to lawmakers, who face constraints of resources and time that prevent open-ended exploration and studying of untested policy features that could be put into a bill (Kousser 2005; Arel-Bundock and Parinandi 2018). Although the assumption of knowing little is a reasonable one to make in regard to ordinary citizens and lawmakers, I do assume that lawmakers know more about potential candidates for invention than do ordinary citizens. Given limited time and resources, *something* must push legislators to devote their energies toward learning about untested policy ideas, and I submit that that "something" is interest or passion in a cause. Such interest, in turn, is highly predicated upon the ideological worldview of the legislator (Gilardi 2010; Kreitzer 2015; Carley, Nicholson-Crotty, and Miller 2017). Since greater interest can compel legislators to expend valuable resources learning about untested policy features and since ideological comportment corresponds with interest in particular issue areas or causes, it follows that government ideology should captivate legislators in a legislature to expend valuable resources to learn about and pursue untested policy features that are associated with causes that the legislators care about. In short, left-leaning legislatures have interest in pursuing left-leaning causes and are more likely (compared to non-left-leaning legislatures) to expend time and resources on learning about untested policy features that could help them advance those left-leaning causes. Analogously, right-leaning legislatures have interest in pursuing right-leaning causes and are more likely (compared to non-right-leaning legislatures) to expend time and resources on learning about untested policy features that could help them advance those right-leaning causes.

Yet simply knowing about an untested policy feature does not result automatically in legislative invention during policy feature adoption. Knowing about the existence of a novel green energy policy feature does not mean that a liberal legislature will invent that policy feature. It also matters that the legislature does not mind adopting the policy feature even though there is a lack of any evidence demonstrating how the feature will perform once adopted. Since invention means that an adopter cannot "free ride" on others' experiences (Volden, Ting, and Carpenter 2008), it also implies that an inventor chooses to adopt despite not having access to others' histories to get a semblance about the performance of a policy feature. I argue that an increase in ideological extremeness makes a legislature more likely to overlook, ignore, or dismiss evidence and support the adoption of an untested policy feature (or in other words, to invent) that the legislature believes comports with its own ideological worldview.

I elaborate on my claim by appealing to the burgeoning literature on ideological diffusion. Work on diffusion has revealed that governments are more likely to learn from and adopt policies when such policies have already been implemented by other ideologically similar governments compared to when such policies have been implemented by ideologically dissimilar governments (Grossback, Nicholson-Crotty, and Peterson 2004; Gilardi 2010; Carley, Nicholson-Crotty, and Miller 2017; Parinandi, Langehennig, and Trautmann 2020). In ideologically based diffusion, beliefs override evidence in the sense that a borrowing government pays attention to the source ("who adopts") rather than the message ("what is being adopted" (Butler et al. 2017). An untested or novel policy feature does not have analogues in other states, leading to the situation where an inventing government cannot observe other ideologically similar governments across the states to figure out whether to adopt a novel policy feature. But yet, with respect to invention, ideology can override evidence with regard to what is being adopted in the sense that different issue areas (or domains) of policy-making have different comportments ideologically. Regulations concerning abortion, for example, are associated with the ideological right (Kreitzer 2015) while regulations concerning clean energy are associated with the ideological left (Potrafke 2010). Compared to an ideologically moderate legislature, an ideologically extreme legislature may be more willing to overlook a lack of evidence and adopt a novel policy feature if that policy feature falls in a domain that is congruent with the more extreme legislature's worldview. Ultimately, while all legislatures at some point utilize cues in lieu of evidence to facilitate policy-making (Lupia 1994), ideologically extreme legislatures are more willing to rely on cues—in this case, cues about whether crafting policy in a particular domain corresponds to their ideological comportment—and ignore a lack of evidence during policy adoption than are their ideologically moderate peer legislatures.[13]

---

13. I make an assumption here that in more ideologically extreme legislatures, potential candidates for invention in a given policy domain generally advance the interests of the dominant ideological group that is typically associated with adopting policy in that policy domain. This is to say that in an ideologically conservative legislature, novel policy proposals dealing with abortion are typically going to represent the interests of the ideological right and restrict abor-

In sum, ideologically extreme legislatures are more likely to invent than ideologically moderate legislatures because ideology provides the spark (in the form of passion and motivation) to learn about novel proposals that could be adopted; and ideologically extreme legislatures are more likely to tolerate the risk of invention because they are predisposed to believe (based on congruence ideologically with a particular policy-making domain) that such features are worth adopting. In this book, I utilize data on RPS policy feature adoption to empirically validate theoretical claims. The concept of an RPS was a market-based libertarian idea and in fact, Texas has one of the most well-established RPS programs in the United States; however, RPS is an example of "green" energy related environmental regulation and conforms generally to a left-leaning ideological worldview (Rabe 2004; Rabe 2007; Hurlburt 2008). I therefore expect that increased liberal ideology in government makes a state legislature more likely to invent during RPS policy feature adoption.

Governmental Liberalism and Invention Hypothesis: A state legislature is more likely to invent during RPS policy feature adoption when state governmental liberalism increases.

And what of the relationship between government ideology (governmental liberalism in our case, since we are dealing with the RPS policy domain) and borrowing? I hypothesize that more extreme government ideology plays a less prominent role in influencing borrowing than it does invention. Unlike in the case of invention, borrowed policy features have a track record and that track record can be accessed in order to inform adoption decisions. Although the zeal of ideologically predisposed legislatures (liberal legislatures given that we are analyzing renewable energy

---

tion while in an ideologically liberal legislature, novel policy proposals dealing with renewable energy are typically going to represent the interests of the ideological left and expand the use of renewable energy. I make this assumption based on the logic that the typical legislator wants to get their novel policy feature proposal adopted and therefore will be less likely to introduce and spearhead candidates for invention that do not conform to the median ideological makeup of their state legislature. Hence, in ideologically conservative states, we should not see too many abortion-related novel policy feature proposals get advanced that seek to expand abortion access; similarly, in ideologically liberal states, we should not see too many renewable energy-related novel policy feature proposals get advanced that seek to restrict renewable energy use. It is possible, of course, that some novel renewable energy-related policy features get advanced that restrict renewable energy use, but these instances are far from typical and in fact are quite rare.

legislation) can lead to the ignoring of evidence during policy adoption, more moderate legislatures possess less zeal with respect to the cause of the policy and therefore will rely more heavily on evidence in guiding adoption decisions and may ultimately show a comparatively reduced preference for inventing during policy adoption. Additionally, compared to an ideologically liberal legislature, an ideologically moderate legislature will include more individual (e.g., in this case, conservative) legislators who may be predisposed against adopting RPS policy, and these individuals will give an especially important role to evidence in helping them potentially override their own predispositions against the policy domain and adopt RPS policy features (Butler et al. 2017). This suggests that ideological extremism (in this case, liberalism) should explain invention more than it explains borrowing, where the existence of a track record can ostensibly bring legislators of more diverse ideological persuasions into the policy-making enterprise.[14]

Governmental Liberalism Influences Invention More than Borrowing Hypothesis: While the increased left-leaning orientation of a state legislature positively influences the likelihood that the state legislature will invent during RPS policy feature adoption, it has less influence on the likelihood that the state legislature will borrow during RPS policy feature adoption.

The importance of an observable track record—in other words, evidence—to borrowing processes suggests how electoral concerns could relate to invention and borrowing during policy feature adoption. The typical member of a state legislature is accountable to the state's median voter and tries to show that he or she is acting in the interest of this voter. Legislative members seek reelection, and one way that legislative members signal that they are serving the median voter is by adopting policies—and *policy features*—that they claim best match the interests of the median

---

14. My point here is not to say that other states' policy-making experiences are the only factor motivating borrowing. Several other factors motivate borrowing, and I try to control for them in my analysis. Rather, my point is that borrowing affords policymakers the ability to utilize the experiences of other states in their policy-making should they so choose. This is valuable information that could potentially help would-be borrowers validate their own choices and benefit from the courage of inventors, as Brandeis would characterize it.

voter (Mayhew 1974).[15] In deciding to adopt a policy, a legislature pays attention to each possible policy feature that, taken together with all other policy features, makes up a policy, and the legislature can invent by adopting a novel policy feature or borrow by adopting a policy feature that already exists in another state.

I therefore assume that reelection-seeking legislators do not adopt a policy feature that they believe will not be supported by the median voter regardless of whether that feature is novel and borrowed. For legislators, however, an important criterion in choosing between invention and borrowing relates to how credibly the legislators can sell the projected benefits of a given action and how the median voter can credibly perceive of (or visualize) the projected benefits of that action. The capability of legislators to credibly sell policy benefits combined with the capability of the median voter to perceive them is something I refer to as *observability*.[16] While a less observable adoption has benefits that are harder to credibly sell to constituents and harder to credibly perceive for median voters, more observable adoptions have benefits that can more credibly be sold because they are more perceivable to median voters. Since borrowed policy features have an observable track record, they are on balance more discernible to the median voter than are untested policy features. This is the case since borrowing gives both legislators *and* the median voter a template—a state or states that already adopted the policy feature under consideration—that can be used to ascertain the possible benefits of adopting the already-tested policy feature (Volden 2006; Pacheco 2012). In contrast, no template exists for invention, suggesting that legislators will have greater difficulty credibly selling, and the median voter quickly perceiving, the possible benefits of inventing.

Adopting policy features whose benefits can easily be sold to the median voter is arguably especially important when legislators are vulnerable electorally. Increased electoral vulnerability may cause legislators to

15. Some may be concerned that the finding linking ideological extremism to invention complicates the notion that legislators cater to median voters. I am less concerned with this possible complication, as median voters still select legislators in instances where legislatures are ideologically extreme (there is no stipulation that median voters must be moderate).

16. This is a concept operationalized in Makse and Volden (2011) and tweaked in Parinandi (2020). Furthermore, I recognize that the concept is similar to that of "traceability" put forth in Arnold (1990). However, while traceability deals with legislators' desires to be linked to policymaking, observability deals with the ability of the public to perceive benefits associated with policy. Thus, observability is perhaps a first order condition for traceability.

believe that they are facing a more skeptical median voter. This will then compel legislators to adopt policy features whose benefits are immediately observable to the median voter so that the legislators can say that they are replicating "successes" adopted elsewhere (Gilardi 2016). Legislatures are therefore more likely to borrow during RPS policy feature adoption when the electoral vulnerability of members of those legislatures increases.

> *Borrowing during Electoral Vulnerability Hypothesis:* As the electoral vulnerability of members of a legislature increases, that legislature experiences an increased likelihood of borrowing during RPS policy feature adoption.

While I believe that increased electoral vulnerability leads to an increased likelihood of borrowing, I do not think that increased electoral vulnerability substantively influences invention. My claim linking observability to borrowing obviates the possibility that increased electoral vulnerability engenders increased invention, since vulnerable legislators would ostensibly find it difficult to sell novel and untested policy features to median voters that they consider to be skeptical. But at the same time, I do not think that electoral vulnerability necessarily decreases the likelihood of invention, and I defend this belief with one reason: even if electorally vulnerable legislators mainly borrow during policy adoption, some amount of "customization" or invention will naturally happen, thereby creating the possibility that invention may not decrease in any meaningful way (Karch 2007). Simply put, some invention occurs in the bill adoption process and may actually be expected to occur in a policy domain like RPS that deals with local sectoral energy regulation. We should therefore not infer that even electorally vulnerable legislators will invent less just because we expect that increases in electoral vulnerability will make legislatures borrow more.

One potential criticism is that voters and even politicians do not care about track records in policy-making and ultimately see invention and borrowing to be one and the same. The logic undergirding this criticism is that voters and even many politicians lack detailed knowledge about policy-specific issues (Converse 1964) and thus may care more that "something" is being done in a particular policy area rather than the novelty of what is being done. While this criticism merits consideration, I point to two important studies documenting that the distinction between invention and borrowing is indeed real. First, Volden (2006) and Shipan and

Volden (2014) reveal that policymakers are indeed aware of a track record and try to avoid risky ventures (which are presumably more likely in the absence of a track record). Second, a study by Kogan, Lavertu, and Peskowitz (2016) reveals that voters support policy decisions (in the form of school levies) partly on the basis of whether they think municipalities have documented evidence in terms of achieving favorable educational outcomes. These two studies taken together give some credence to the idea that invention is different from borrowing in the minds of policymakers and voters. As to whether my explanation of borrowing requires the public to possess sophisticated knowledge about policy, I say that it does not. The public only needs to be swayable to arguments pointing out borrowing, and I believe that lawmakers themselves could provide this information to constituents. Research (Pacheco 2012) has shown that the public is receptive to the concept of borrowing. Given that lawmakers are consummate Mayhewian actors, it is reasonable to expect that they would supply and advertise about something (borrowing) that they think the public is receptive toward. Suffice it to say that the story acknowledges that the public lacks savvy policy knowledge.

To recapitulate my claims, I first argue that ideological extremism and in particular governmental liberalism better explains legislative invention than it does legislative borrowing. And I next argue that electoral vulnerability better explains legislative borrowing than it does legislative invention. There is an important caveat worth discussing concerning these theoretical claims: namely, that the expectation that a factor will increase the likelihood of one type of policy feature adoption (e.g., invention) does *not* automatically imply that the same factor will decrease the likelihood of the other type of policy feature adoption (e.g., borrowing). This is because a state government's choice to invent with respect to one policy feature does not mean that it cannot choose to borrow with respect to another. Since state governments adopt multiple policy features to make their policy regimes (in this case, RPS programs) operational, a variable that influences one kind of policy adoption need not have the opposite effect on the other kind of policy adoption. My argument here is consequently that government liberalism and electoral vulnerability make invention and borrowing respectively more likely but not that they engender the opposite effect on borrowing and invention. I now turn to evaluating my hypotheses using the data on RPS policy feature adoption.

Evaluating Legislative Invention and Borrowing
Using RPS Policy Feature Adoption Data

I test my theoretical expectations by evaluating whether government ideology and electoral vulnerability differentially influence the likelihood that legislatures invent or borrow when adopting a policy feature or a combination of policy features. In chapter 3, I walked through how invention and borrowing are identified in policy-making documents and also described how invention and borrowing datasets (regardless of the institutional actor doing the inventing or borrowing) could be created and then analyzed through a pooled event history procedure (Boushey 2016). This means that I can extract all instances where *legislatures* invent (or alternatively borrow) along with corresponding instances of non-adoption for invention (or borrowing) of a given policy feature or combination of policy features by a given state. I extract instances of non-adoption so that the true probabilities of a legislature inventing or borrowing are reflected in the structure of the datasets. Having an event history data structure that accurately captures the probability of an event's occurrence—here, legislative adoption that can take two forms: invention or borrowing—is important since I adhere to convention within event history analysis and use a statistical technique called logistic regression to examine which independent variables make a given event more or less likely (Hosmer and Lemeshow 2000; Box-Steffensmeier and Jones 2004).[17]

---

17. Recall from chapter 3 that a state gains the opportunity to invent with respect to a policy feature (or combination of policy features) starting in 1983, when Iowa was the first state to adopt a proto-RPS program. A state loses the opportunity to invent with respect to a given policy feature (or combination of policy features) once it invents (meaning that it is either the first state to adopt a policy feature or combination of policy features or it does so by the next calendar year after the first state has done so) or if it fails to invent once two years have passed since the first state's adoption of the feature or combination (so if Ohio is the first state to adopt a feature in 2008, all states that have not adopted that feature lose the ability to invent it by 2010). States that do not invent with respect to a feature or combination gain the opportunity to borrow once two years have passed from the first state's adoption of that feature or combination (so in the Ohio example, all noninventing states gain the ability to borrow starting in 2010). A state that gains the ability to borrow a feature or combination only loses it once it has borrowed that feature or combination. The risk sets for inventing and borrowing are kept disjoint to reflect the idea that invention and borrowing have mutually exclusive definitions. Starting the opportunity for invention in 1983 and keeping the risk sets for invention and borrowing separate were recommendations made by reviewers for a companion piece to this book (Parinandi 2020), and

It is also worth reemphasizing in this chapter that a legislature in state *i* gains the opportunity to adopt a policy feature even if that feature was first adopted by another nonlegislative institutional actor (typically a public utilities commission) in state *j*. This reflects the common possibility that a legislature in one state could borrow from the decision-making of a public utilities commission in another state. It is also worth reemphasizing in this chapter that a legislature in state *i* loses the opportunity to adopt a policy feature if another institutional actor within the same state (again typically a public utilities commission) has already adopted the policy feature. This reflects the idea that a state's legislature cannot adopt a policy feature once that same feature has already been adopted in the state by another institutional actor.

Finally, it is worth reemphasizing why I focus on legislative decision-making by itself rather than comparing legislative invention and borrowing to that of state public utilities commissions. First, all legislators are elected and subject to electoral constraints, meaning that zeroing in on legislatures allows us to evaluate how changes in the amount of electoral vulnerability (in a population where everyone is theoretically exposed to some amount of electoral vulnerability) might differentially influence invention and borrowing. Many state public utilities commissioners are appointed rather than elected, meaning that including these officeholders alongside legislatures in our analysis precludes us from figuring out how changes in electoral vulnerability among a population that faces similar institutional constraints affects invention and borrowing. Moreover, even if some public utilities commissioners are elected, the nature of their electoral constraints is arguably vastly different from that of legislators for two reasons: first, since the commissioners are selected on the basis of their stewardship of utility-related regulatory issues while legislators are selected on the basis of their stewardship of a "basket" of issues of which utility regulation is just one component (Besley and Coate 2003); and second, because elected commissioners not only create but also execute regulatory policy, meaning that they can electioneer in a way that is not open to legislators since legislators do not also possess executive power (Parinandi and Hitt 2018). Therefore, focusing on legislatures allows for the determination of how electoral vulnerability affects invention and borrowing in a

---

I retain those changes in this book to help build interchangeability and consistency with the companion piece.

situation where the population under investigation faces a similar kind of electoral constraint.[18]

A second reason for focusing on legislatures is that doing so allows for us to evaluate whether governmental resource capacity differentially influences invention and borrowing. Legislatures vary tremendously in terms of their professionalism, and this variance has been measured successfully and validated in scholarly work (Squire 2007). No analogous measure of resource capacity exists for public utilities commissions and, furthermore, no attempt has been made to create a measure of resource capacity that could span both legislative and regulatory actors. Additionally, one wonders whether it is possible to create such a measure of resource capacity given the stark differences in job responsibilities between legislators and regulatory actors. Therefore, I refrain from comparing legislatures to regulatory actors and instead analyze legislatures alone.

Finally, I focus on legislatures because doing so allows for the best test of how elite-level ideology may differentially influence invention and borrowing. Although Berry et al. (1998) describe their measure as *government ideology*, it is constructed from the behavior of elected officials and best captures legislative ideology. The same is true for the other leading measure of elite-level ideology used in American politics research (Shor and McCarty 2011). This suggests that extant measures of government ideology probably do not adequately reflect the underlying worldview of public utilities commissioners and that comparing the behavior of legislatures to public utilities commissioners would distort the true effect of government ideology on legislative activity.

I now describe my empirical testing. I have two dependent variables, *legislative invention* and *legislative borrowing*, that map onto each of the respective legislative inventing and legislative borrowing datasets. I use logistic regression to determine which independent variables make the dependent variables more likely, and there are two independent variables in the analysis: a state's current year *government ideology*, which is taken from Berry et al. (1998), and the *median incumbent vote share* of a legisla-

---

18. Besides the fact that commissioners have different responsibilities from legislators, comparing legislators directly with commissioners would give us the unenviable task of defining electoral vulnerability across two very different types of elected official (legislators and the minority of commissioners who are elected). In the next chapter, I evaluate how the presence or absence of electoral vulnerability in the same kind of actor (public utilities commissioner) influences invention and borrowing.

tor in a state's legislature in the most recent election. The median incumbent vote share variable captures electoral vulnerability based on the idea that a lower vote share implies greater anti-incumbent mood among the electorate and hence greater electoral vulnerability.[19]

I also include a host of control variables and describe the most important ones here. *Legislative professionalism* captures the resource capacity of a state's legislature in a given year and comes from Squire (2007); I include this variable to test whether legislative resource capacity differentially influences invention and borrowing. Other noteworthy controls include a state's *per capita income* (measured here as the fraction of state income against the federal baseline where the baseline is set to 100); the *price of energy* in a state (measured in 2011 dollars per million British Thermal Units); a state's percentage of energy that is produced from *fossil fuel sources*; a state's *citizen ideology* (where the ideology of a state's citizens is measured on a 0–100 scale by Berry et al. where 0 is perfectly conservative and 100 is perfectly liberal); and whether or not a state has *unified Democratic government*. As noted, I utilize separate logistic regressions for each dependent variable and cluster standard errors at the state level to reflect the idea that decisions within a state are correlated. In table 3, I display regression results for the variables described above.[20]

Results from table 3 indicate how a given independent variable relates to legislative invention and borrowing. The critical values or thresholds (denoted by asterisks) in the table are used to indicate the certainty of estimated relationships, or the probability that the associations shown in

---

19. A handful of state legislatures utilize multimember districts. This measure also takes multimember districts into account based on the logic that the occupants of these seats too would pay attention to anti-incumbency trends. I utilize a different measure in the book's appendix.

20. In addition to the variables described in table 3, I include the following control variables in regression models pertaining to both legislative invention and borrowing: the percentage of a state's population that is urban; a state's change in unemployment; whether a state has a deregulated electricity sector; whether the political party dominating a state's government is in decline; the fraction of RPS policy features that have been adopted previously by a state's geographic neighbors; the fraction of RPS policy features that have been adopted previously by a state's ideological neighbors; and the amount of time that has elapsed since an RPS program was first adopted in 1983. For the model pertaining to legislative invention, I also include a control variable capturing the fraction of prior instances of invention that have occurred in the state in question; and for the model pertaining to legislative borrowing, I include control variables capturing (1) the fraction of prior instances of borrowing that have occurred in the state in question and (2) the number of years that have elapsed since a particular policy feature was first adopted across the states. In table A4 of the appendix, I show results for variables not displayed in this chapter.

TABLE 3. Ideology and Electoral Vulnerability on Legislative Invention and Borrowing (Selected Variables)

Variable	Legislative Invention	Legislative Borrowing
Government Ideology	0.014**	0.011
	(0.007)	(0.010)
Median Incumbent Legislator Vote Share	−0.007	−0.022***
	(0.005)	(0.007)
Legislative Professionalism	−0.566	0.385
	(1.254)	(1.673)
State Per Capita Income	−0.190	0.003
	(0.155)	(0.165)
Price of Energy	−0.082	−0.037
	(0.051)	(0.062)
Fossil Fuel Sources	−0.002	0.001
	(0.003)	(0.004)
Citizen Ideology	0.019	0.029**
	(0.014)	(0.013)
Unified Democratic Government	−0.487	0.016
	(0.389)	(0.514)
Observations	182,984	47,433
	(169)	(357)

*** = critical value of 0.01; ** = critical value of 0.05; * = critical value of 0.10

the estimated relationships were determined through chance. A few points are worth mentioning. First, the positive association between government ideology and legislative invention lends support for the claim that greater governmental liberalism corresponds with an increased likelihood of invention in RPS policy-making.[21] Second, the more certain positive association between government ideology and invention compared to the association between government ideology and borrowing gives support for the claim that governmental liberalism among lawmakers does a better job of explaining invention in RPS policy-making than it does borrowing. And, third, the finding of a statistically significant (or more certain) negative association between median incumbent legislator vote share and borrowing along with the lack of a statistically significant association between median incumbent legislator vote share and invention suggests that legislator electoral vulnerability matters more with respect to borrowing than it does with respect to invention.

21. Recall that increased values in the government ideology variable (Berry et al. 1998) correspond with greater government liberalism.

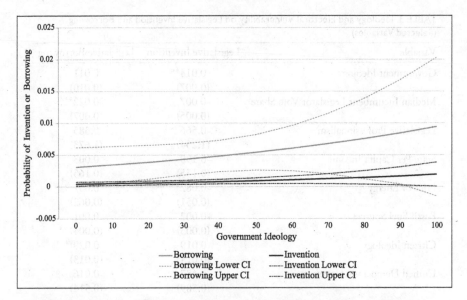

Fig. 6. Comparison of Government Ideology on Legislative Invention and Borrowing
Source: Data on government ideology comes from Berry et al. (1998). Data on state RPS adoption primarily comes from the Database on State Incentives for Renewables and Efficiency.

The results depicted in table 3 only show general associations and not effects. Figure 6 provides a graphical comparison of the effects of government ideology on invention versus borrowing. In order to display sensible results, I hold dichotomous variables to their most common values and hold continuous variables at their means.

In figure 6, solid lines refer to the main predicted probabilities of legislative invention and borrowing as the level of government ideology varies.[22] Dashed lines of the same color refer to corresponding upper and lower bound predicted probability estimates based on a 95% confidence interval. It is perhaps unsurprising that increased governmental liberalism should drive greater RPS-related invention *and* borrowing by legislatures since the policy domain of RPS is largely liberal in ideological character. However, predicted probabilities related to invention are more certain than those related to borrowing, as is reflected in the observation that the

---

22. The minimum and maximum values of government ideology for states in figure 6 are 0 and 97.9, respectively. The corresponding mean and median values of government ideology are 51.9 and 53.3, respectively.

lower bound predicted probability curve with respect to invention does not cross zero while the analogous curve with respect to borrowing does. This gives us some assurance in saying that support exists for the claim that increased governmental liberalism does a better job of predicting legislative invention than it does of predicting legislative borrowing. Looking at the curves of invention and borrowing, it appears as if the slope of borrowing rises at a steeper clip than that of invention. This is partly an artifact of placing invention and borrowing on the same scale: since the invention dataset contains fewer instances of invention but more opportunities to invent than the borrowing dataset (which contains more instances of borrowing and fewer opportunities to borrow), invention appears to rise more gently. A useful way to compare slopes here would be to calculate the percentage rise in predicted probability values for invention and borrowing across the full range of the government ideology variable. Over this range, the predicted probability value for invention increases in size by almost 350% (roughly 343%) while the predicted probability value for borrowing increases in size by a little over 200% (roughly 204%).

In figure 7, there is clear evidence that electoral vulnerability influences borrowing more than it does invention, and this evidence can be seen in comparing how the predicted probability of borrowing quickly decreases as median incumbent vote share increases while the predicted probability of inventing only gradually slopes downhill as median incumbent vote share increases.[23]

One potential issue with my dichotomization of invention and borrowing is that I might use too permissive a definition of invention. The potential trouble with my definition of invention is that it is designed to identify novelty but does not make adjustments for whether the novel policy feature only represents a marginal change over what has already been adopted, either in the state adopting the novel feature or in some other state. For example, New Hampshire's legislature invented when the state became the first to require that 23.8% of electricity sold to consumers be derived from renewable sources in 2007 (New Hampshire General Court 2007). New Hampshire's policy adoption is a case of invention in the sense that no state had adopted this same threshold prior to it (and indeed, no

---

23. The minimum and maximum values of government ideology for states in figure 7 are 0 and 97.9, respectively. The corresponding mean and median values of government ideology are 51.2 and 52.9, respectively.

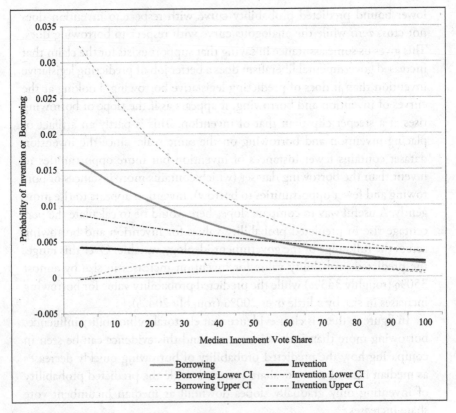

Fig. 7. Comparison of Median Incumbent Vote Share on Legislative Invention and Borrowing
Source: Data on electoral vulnerability comes from Klarner et al. (2013). Data on state RPS adoption primarily comes from the Database on State Incentives for Renewables and Efficiency.

state has adopted the same threshold in the time since). However, it may only represent a marginal rather than significant invention in the sense that a number of states—California, Hawaii, and Nevada—had already adopted provisions requiring that utilities procure 20% of electricity sold to consumers from renewable sources years before New Hampshire's adoption. Is a required 23.8% threshold really all that different from a required 20% threshold, and if it is not, are results from the empirical analysis an artifact of having too many marginal cases of invention in the dataset?

I account for the issue described above in a supplemental analysis by considering all thresholds of the same type (e.g., required versus voluntary) that fall within the same decile or bandwidth to be classified as the

TABLE 4. Ideology and Electoral Vulnerability on Legislative Invention and Borrowing Combining Similar Rates/Thresholds (Selected Variables)

Variable	Legislative Invention	Legislative Borrowing
Government Ideology	0.016**	0.011
	(0.007)	(0.010)
Median Incumbent Legislator Vote Share	−0.007	−0.021***
	(0.006)	(0.007)
Legislative Professionalism	−0.624	0.489
	(1.287)	(1.714)
State Per Capita Income	0.011	−0.012
	(0.016)	(0.013)
Price of Energy	−0.086	−0.035
	(0.053)	(0.062)
Fossil Fuel Sources	−0.001	0.001
	(0.003)	(0.004)
Citizen Ideology	0.018	0.031**
	(0.016)	(0.013)
Unified Democratic Government	−0.598	0.035
	(0.379)	(0.524)
Observations	152,718	40,597
	(147)	(371)

*** = critical value of 0.01; ** = critical value of 0.05; * = critical value of 0.10

same policy feature. This means that all instances of a state requiring that a utility generate anywhere between 20% and 29.9% of electricity sold to consumers from renewable sources are considered to be examples of adopting the same exact policy feature. This also means that all instances of a state requiring that a utility generate anywhere between 10% and 19.9% of electricity sold to consumers from renewable sources are considered to be examples of the same policy feature, and it means that all instances of a state giving a utility the voluntary option of generating anywhere between 10% and 19.9% of electricity sold to consumers from renewable sources are considered to be examples of the same policy feature. Using the decile or bandwidth definition of invention with respect to thresholds alleviates the marginal invention problem by assuming that features of the same type within the same bandwidth are functionally if not exactly similar. Regression estimates shown in table 4 show that the substantive results are unchanged.[24]

---

24. I include the same variables that I use in table 3. Also, like table 3, I only show results from selected variables for visual appeal.

I include several supplemental analyses for robustness that can be seen in the appendix of the book. First, I account for whether allowing for policy to be adopted via direct ballot initiative changes results; as seen in table A5, results are unchanged. In table A6, I use mean incumbent vote share rather than median incumbent vote share, and I find that the inclusion of this variable does not affect substantive results.[25] In table A7, I include legislative term limits in the analysis and find results unchanged.

Other robustness or sensitivity analyses address the concern that empirical results may be an artifact of certain kinds of features—say, combinations of policy features—dominating the dataset. In table A8 of the appendix, I drop combinations of policy features from the analysis and find that substantive results are unchanged. In table A9 of the appendix, I drop rates or thresholds from the analysis and still find that substantive results are unchanged.

There is qualitative support for the argument raised in this chapter as well. Consider the renewable portfolio policy feature adoption experiences of two states: Illinois and Indiana. I compare these states more fully in chapter 7 but distill main themes here. These neighboring Midwestern states have much in common: they are both key agricultural states with important agricultural lobbies, ranking sixth and tenth respectively in terms of total cash receipts from all agricultural commodities in 2017 (United States Department of Agriculture Economic Research Service 2018). Importantly, both states rank among the nation's largest corn producers, which matters since corn is a key feedstock for biomass and biofuel-based renewable electricity (National Corn Growers Association 2018). And, furthermore, both states are home to the same declining but still important fossil fuel industry (coal), which matters since the shape of both states' renewable portfolio regimes will be affected by the need to accommodate fossil fuel interests (United States Energy Information Administration 2018).

Both Illinois and Indiana adopted renewable portfolio standard policy regimes, and both did it through legislative action. However, the content of each state's regime has been quite different. Illinois has invented repeatedly, and in the span from 2007 to 2011, chose four novel policy

---

25. I also evaluated an alternative formulation using the percentage of a state's legislative races in the most recent electoral year that had a victory margin of less than 10 percent. This formulation fails to achieve statistical significance.

features.[26] Indiana, on the other hand, has been a consummate borrower and adopted a renewable portfolio standard regime in 2011 that almost consists entirely of borrowed policy features.[27] The factors uncovered quantitatively can help articulate why the Illinois and Indiana legislatures embraced different levels of novelty in their RPS regimes. First, the Illinois legislature is quite liberal in ideological comportment and has had ideological scores ranging from 92.3 to 86.8 during the 2007–2011 interval (recall that 50 is the most ideologically neutral or moderate score in Berry et al.'s scale). The liberal nature of Illinois's legislature presumably helped give its legislators greater motivation and willingness to seek out and adopt novel policy features in the state's RPS program and made more ambitious policy-making conceivable. In contrast, Indiana's legislature has been one of the most conservative in the nation and garnered a score of 3.8 (out of 100) in 2011. Generally composed of legislators who are presumably not predisposed to ambitious renewable energy, it is perhaps not surprising that the Indiana legislature largely shied away from inventing in crafting its RPS regime.

In terms of electoral vulnerability, Indiana legislators were definitely more vulnerable than their Illinois counterparts in the sense that the median incumbent vote share in the most recent election for the Indiana legislature was 64.72% while it was in the range of 100 to 73.73% for the Illinois legislature in the 2007–11 period.[28] Although Indiana's median incumbent vote share may seem high, it is lower than the state's own median value for this variable (67.46) and lower than the overall 50 state median value for this variable (71.65). Given legislators' overwhelming focus on working toward reelection and their adeptness at securing it (Mayhew 1974), it is possible that the Indiana legislators may have interpreted recent incumbent electoral margins (e.g., being more vulnerable than what is typically the norm in their own state or across states) as a sign of weakness and consequently sought out greater observability in

---

26. These were requiring that electric utilities procure 25% of electricity sold to consumers from renewable sources, and three instances of adopting policy features in specific combinations that had not been adopted before.

27. The only invention in Indiana's RPS regime was that Indiana adopted a mix of policy features that had never been combined together before. Unlike Illinois, all of the individual constituent policy features in Indiana's regime have been borrowed.

28. Recall that electoral vulnerability does not relate systematically to legislative RPS invention. It is advisable therefore to not draw a connection between Illinois's higher level of invention during adoption and its low level of electoral vulnerability.

their policy adoption choices, leading to an RPS regime consisting almost chiefly of borrowed policy features. In sum, Indiana's dearth of invention is due in part to its legislative ideology—and particularly its conservatism, given that clean energy is within the liberal ideological worldview—and its borrowing is due in part to having a level of electoral vulnerability that is greater than typical within-state or across-state levels.[29]

Conclusion

The central goal of this chapter has been to uncover reasons why state legislatures would invent novel policy, why they would borrow existing policy, and whether the factors influencing invention and borrowing are different from each other. My inquiry and subsequent analysis using state renewable portfolio policy adoption data demonstrates that more extreme (in this case, liberal) state legislatures are more likely to invent than their moderate counterparts and that increases in legislative electoral vulnerability increase the likelihood of borrowing in the RPS area.

The results shown here have great importance for our understanding of how new policies are adopted by the chief institutions—legislatures—tasked with policy-making in the states.

Invention driven by more extreme ideological orientation among legislatures may be beneficial for public policy in the sense that fewer roadblocks exist in getting novel policy ideas translated into concrete policy than would ostensibly be the case if legislatures were more ideologically heterogeneous in orientation. This means that we can expect state legislatures with greater ideological dispositions to serve an important role of introducing novel policies to the 50-state federal system, and this role is valuable to the system insofar as some of those novel policies diffuse and become mainstays across the states. Of course, while ideology may be beneficial for public policy in terms of introducing novel policy features into the corpus of policy features that could diffuse across the states, it may simultaneously be bad for public policy if ideologically extreme legislators

---

29. Indiana's low level of invention can also be contrasted with the experiences of two other neighboring states: Ohio and Michigan in 2008. That year, legislatures in both states adopted RPS regimes and included three inventions each in their respective regimes. Ohio had a government ideology score of 65.1 in 2008, and Michigan had a score of 81.8 that same year.

willfully ignore evidence and subject constituents to potentially risky policies that have never been tried or vetted in other states.

Ideology's role in fostering legislative invention is also noteworthy because other factors that at first glance would appear to influence legislative invention do not. Far from causing legislators to seek out novel policy solutions, electoral vulnerability in the RPS area has no noticeable connection to legislative invention and actually encourages borrowing. And while it is in certain respects desirable that electoral vulnerability does not influence invention, the lack of a link between electoral vulnerability and invention is potentially problematic for public policy if the scale of a policy challenge—such as mitigating the consequences of climate change or devising a more effective way to regulate the burgeoning market for recreational drugs—is so large that it requires novel policy-making.[30]

Ideology's role is also noteworthy when considered alongside the lack of a finding connecting legislative resource capacity or professionalism to increased invention. Giving legislators more resources does not translate into increased invention. One reason why this may be the case is that legislators may not use the added resources from professionalism to search for and learn about policy ideas that could be operationalized into novel policy features. Another reason why this may be the case is that additional resources are not a substitute for interest in a particular policy area.

Ideology also appears to trump unified partisan control, as greater liberalness in government ideology predicts legislative invention while unified Democratic government does not. This result may seem surprising at face value but makes intuitive sense given that each of the two parties is not a homogeneous monolith but actually contains significant within-party ideological diversity (Aldrich 2011). By way of example, one of the most consistently Democratic states during the 1983–2011 time frame of this study has been Arkansas. Arkansas had unified Democratic government for 17 out of the 28 years of the study period. However, Arkansas never invented with respect to an RPS policy feature or even adopted an RPS policy regime in spite of the Democratic Party having controlled

---

30. The lack of a link between electoral vulnerability and invention is desirable in that legislators do not needlessly subject voters to the risk inherent in invention—that the policy feature has never been adopted before—based on hopes of improving their own electoral fortunes. The reverse issue, of course, is that electoral accountability does not motivate legislators to tackle large-scale challenges that may best be solved by novel policy-making.

its government for the bulk of the nearly three-decade period examined here. One reason why Arkansas did not behave like some other largely Democratic states—such as Hawaii, which was under unified Democratic control for 20 out of 28 years of the study's time period and invented five times with respect to RPS policy features—is probably that Arkansas's government has been less liberal than that of Hawaii, even when both states' legislative and executive branches were controlled fully by the Democratic Party. In 2011, a year in which both states had unified Democratic government, Arkansas had a government ideology score of 57.3 while Hawaii had a corresponding score of 93.9. The comparison, though anecdotal, demonstrates that a more pronounced or extreme government ideology score captures a unanimity of purpose that same party affiliation does not.

To be sure, there are limits to the analysis conducted here. One such limit concerns the potential uniqueness of the results to the RPS policy domain. RPS represents a fairly technically complex policy domain, and the complexity of the domain may influence findings. For example, the null link between electoral vulnerability and invention may become positive in a different policy domain—say, the conceptualization and installation of early warning systems to communicate about the dangers of wildfires—where legislators may believe that voters will be able to visualize the observability of benefits from inventing due to that domain being less complex.

Another limit concerns the possibility that results may be different in a policy domain that is considered to be a more classical exemplar of "moral" policy-making than is RPS (Mooney and Lee 1995, 1999). While climate change (along with the policies devised to deal with it) is increasingly being viewed as a moral issue with overtones of right and wrong (Adger et al. 2017), it takes a greater leap of faith to say that RPS policies, perhaps especially given their complexity and the perceived indirect nature between RPS policy-making and carbon production, inspire feelings of morality among the public.[31] Indeed, one recent study indicates that the general public's concerns about RPS policies are primarily financial rather than moral (Stokes and Warshaw 2017). I do not expect the finding linking government ideology and legislative invention to differ substantially

---

31. The indirect nature that I am referring to is that RPSs lower carbon production through utility companies increasing the share of renewable sources used for electricity generation and procurement.

if more classically moral policy-making (such as a policy domain dealing with environmental justice and the eradication of health disparities among individuals owing to exposure to toxins) were analyzed, since legislatures that are more ideologically extreme should display a greater willingness than moderate peers to seek out and adopt novel policy features from policy domains that conform to that ideological worldview.

However, the importance of observability in linking electoral vulnerability to legislative policy feature adoption could change when moral issues are considered. Specifically, observability may matter less to voters when moral issues are concerned since voters may have convictions about the "right" and "wrong" courses to take regarding such issues and may care less about the track record of a particular action and more about whether lawmakers are "doing something" to address an issue that is viewed in moral terms (Ryan 2017). This potentially suggests that electoral vulnerability could relate positively with legislative invention, as lawmakers try to show voters that they are taking action to ameliorate the perceived wrong that is being addressed through the morality policy. This also potentially suggests that in terms of morality policy, which is generally less complex than the RPS policy analyzed here (Mooney and Lee 1999), electoral vulnerability may not relate systematically with borrowing insofar as observability is not an issue for morally charged voters.

While the vast majority of the book deals with the RPS policy area, in chapter 8 I utilize my framework to study state legislative invention and borrowing in another area: that of anti-abortion policy. While the anti-abortion area notably involves federal intervention (typified by the *Roe v. Wade* decision), the states have been given tremendous latitude to craft their own anti-abortion restrictions short of banning the procedure unconditionally (Kreitzer and Boehmke 2016). Investigating the determinants of legislative invention and borrowing in anti-abortion policy provides a first-cut answer to the moral policy issue I raised above and could motivate future research into comparing policy experimentation across moral and less moral areas (which is something that I take up in the conclusion).

The inclusion of the anti-abortion area also provides a conservative policy to analyze. Even though RPS began as a libertarian concept (Wiser et al. 2007), and conservative states like North Dakota and Utah have adopted RPS policy regimes, and research demonstrates that conservatives are amenable to RPS (Hughes and Lipscy 2013; Brown and Hess 2016; Hess et al. 2016), RPS generally lies within the realm of liberal policy-making

(Neumayer 2004; Gromet et al. 2013). Anti-abortion policy, which seeks to restrict the availability of abortion, is decidedly conservative in ideological orientation (Kreitzer 2015), and studying it not only allows us to see how some of the explanations outlined in this chapter with respect to RPS function in a conservative direction but also helps lay ground for future investigation into state policy experimentation across more areas.

In closing, while the legislative branch has played an outsized role in adopting RPS policy, it is not the only institution that has done so, as state public utilities commissions have also invented and borrowed RPS policy. Public utilities commissions are regulatory in nature and have different missions from legislative actors: for starters, most of them are not elected and their central task is to serve as arbiters who manage how electric utility companies interact with the public. This central task of public utilities commissions arguably makes them sensitive to the wider regulatory structures in which they operate and aware of potential grievances from regulated entities as the commissions try to maintain stewardship of state electricity systems. Studying whether variation in the regulatory structures faced by commissions influence their own RPS invention and borrowing activity is important in terms of sketching out how renewable energy policy-making is occurring in the regulatory realm and is the main enterprise of the next chapter.

CHAPTER 6

Regulatory Invention and Deregulation

Even though America's state legislatures are prominent policy creators, state regulatory agencies also play a role in crafting novel policy. State regulatory agencies are part and parcel of the large and professionalized administrative edifice that characterizes modern American government (Wilson 1887; Van Riper 1983; Potter 2019). Although regulatory agencies are perhaps best known for simply being the executors or implementers of existing policy, they also routinely craft their own policies. For example, Boushey and McGrath (2017) found that state regulatory agencies adopted 292,568 policies over a 20-year (1990–2010) span. While the authors do not distinguish the invention of novel policy from the borrowing of existing policy, one can surmise from the sheer number of policies adopted that regulatory agencies most likely invented a sizeable proportion of these policies. Concrete examples of inventing by state regulatory agencies exist, including in renewable energy policy, where state regulatory agencies invented several policy features (Parinandi 2020). Examples exist in other policy areas as well. In the area of legalized marijuana, the Colorado Department of Revenue's Marijuana Enforcement Division, the entity responsible for regulating the recreational marijuana industry in the state, has invented numerous policy features related to how this new industry should be structured (Pardo 2014).

While it seems reasonable and defensible to claim that state regulatory agencies are key actors in the invention of policy, the "policy innovation" literature in political science is primarily legislature-centric (e.g., Kousser 2005; Shipan and Volden 2006; Boushey 2010), and appears to have sidestepped the investigation of how regulatory agencies invent novel policy.

The legislative focus not only encompasses seminal work on diffusion (Berry and Berry 1990) but also includes earlier work on policy reinvention (Glick and Hays 1991; Hays 1996) and recent work on policy reinvention in the renewable energy policy space (Carley, Nicholson-Crotty, and Miller 2017).[1] It is easy to understand why scholars would give more attention to legislatures. First, legislative action arguably represents where the high drama of policy-making occurs, suggesting that accounts of legislative activity may be more compelling to broad audiences. Second, legislatures are the main institutional actors tasked with adopting law, which could impart a bias toward studying legislative activity. And third, state legislative acts—which are typically published as session laws—may be systematically easier to locate compared to state regulatory decisions.

Whatever the reason for the lack of focus on regulatory agencies, ignoring an investigation of the conditions under which regulatory agencies invent policy would produce a glaring gap in our knowledge of how the creation of novel policy occurs across the states. This is not only because regulatory agencies adopt so many policies (Boushey and McGrath 2017) but also because they are in a position to adopt so many policies: regulatory agencies serve as mediators between the entities that they regulate and the public and therefore have considerable power to craft policy pertaining to how entities interact with the public.[2] Given that regulatory bodies play such a prominent role in organizing modern life that modern government itself has been referred to as "the regulatory state," understanding when regulatory agencies invent policy sheds light on a crucial pathway (regulatory agency decision-making) through which new policies can be introduced to the system of policies generated as a result of experimentation across the states (Glaeser and Shleifer 2003).

In this chapter, I exploit data on RPS policy feature adoption by state

1. Admittedly, some scholarship (Volden 2006; Parinandi 2013) investigates bureaucratic *diffusion*. However, the issue of novel policy creation by regulatory agencies appears to be ignored.

2. The idea that regulatory agencies mediate the relationship between regulated entities and the public is arguably the purpose for the existence of regulatory agencies. In the marijuana example, the Colorado Department of Revenue's Marijuana Enforcement Division mediates (in terms of setting purity standards) what marijuana retailers can sell to the public; in the area of air pollution, the federal Environmental Protection Agency mediates (in terms of setting toxic gas standards) what factories can spew into the air the public breathes; and in the area of renewable energy portfolio standards examined in this chapter, state public utilities commissions mediate (in terms of dictating that utilities procure renewable sources of energy) how electric utility companies obtain electricity that is then consumed by the public.

public utilities commissions to examine when regulatory agencies invent. The RPS data is useful because it captures multiple instances where a state's public utilities commission was the first actor in any state to adopt a particular policy feature (thus making the analysis of regulatory invention possible) and because a broad set of states have invented policy through regulatory action, thereby allowing us to examine how variation in the regulatory environment across the states influences the likelihood that state regulatory agencies invent. Using the pooled event history analysis technique employed in the last chapter and investigating public utilities commission policy feature adoption over the 1983–2011 span, I ultimately find that deregulation facilitates inventing. Specifically, public utilities commissions in states with deregulated electricity sectors are more likely to invent compared to public utilities commissions in states with regulated electricity sectors.

I argue that this is the case because deregulation disrupts the ability of entrenched electric utility companies to challenge attempts by public utilities commissions to adopt novel regulation.[3] Inventing represents unprecedented adoption—not just in Walker's (1969) sense of being new to the state adopting it but also being new across the system of all states—and entrenched electric utility companies might find unprecedented regulation to be particularly nettlesome because they are uncertain about how such regulation will affect their finances and cannot use firm experiences in other states to make inferences about financial impacts (as could conceivably be done in borrowing). Therefore, public utilities commissions operating under sector deregulation (where entrenched electric utility companies are less well positioned to challenge policy development by the commissions) may be more likely to invent novel regulation compared to commissions operating under sector regulation (where entrenched electric utility companies are in a stronger position). This finding comports with

---

3. By "entrenched electric utility companies," I am referring to investor-owned-utility companies that have essentially had (or have, if deregulation has not occurred in a state) vertically integrated monopolistic control over electricity provision in their respective service areas under sector regulation. Under deregulation, "entrenched electric utility companies" refers to investor-owned-utility companies that lost vertically integrated monopolistic control over electricity provision in their respective service areas when the respective states in which they operate transitioned to sector deregulation. Entrenchment therefore implies that a company has (or had, if deregulation has occurred) vertically integrated monopolistic control over electricity in a state. As we will see, the act of deregulation can induce entrenched companies to behave differently vis-à-vis regulators compared to how they behaved prior to deregulation.

the view dating back to the Weberian ideal (Constans 1958; Walton 2005; Gualmini 2008) and reiterated in literature on regulation (West 2005; Dal Bo 2006; Braithwaite 2008; Kettl 2008; Carrigan and Coglianese 2011) that regulatory agencies act as self-preservationists. Part of acting out of self-preservation also entails that regulatory agencies are strategic about *when* they seek to enact novel regulation that could stoke opposition from entrenched electric utility companies: regulatory agencies adopt such regulation when they think that entrenched electric utility companies are less likely to challenge them, and this condition is more likely to obtain under sector deregulation as opposed to regulation.[4]

The finding sheds light on when we may see public utilities commissions invent RPS policy. Moreover, to the extent that the regulatory dynamics captured here extend to other areas—and I believe strongly that regulatory agencies in other areas also act as self-preservationists with respect to entrenched regulated entities—then this finding provides scholars with a useful lens to assess how regulatory invention could unfold in new areas of regulatory policy-making such as the crafting of recreational marijuana safety standards (Pardo 2014) or rules concerning road usage by autonomous vehicles (Fleetwood 2017). This chapter proceeds as follows. I first provide background into how public utilities commissions regulate the electricity industry and discuss the deregulation of state electricity retail markets that largely took place in the late 1990s and early 2000s (Ka and Teske 2002). I then explain why public utilities commissions would be more likely to invent RPS policy under deregulation. I conclude by discussing implications and set the stage for the case study analyses in the next chapter.

---

4. One important point to emphasize is that in the RPS space, public utilities commissions have adopted policies that impose limits on how electric utility companies can procure electricity, meaning that these policies can incite opposition from electric utility companies due to the possibility that the companies will face compliance costs from the policies. Indeed, this is a big reason why electric utility companies have emerged as key players in attempts to abolish RPS programs (Stokes 2020). It is possible for a public utilities commission to invent in a way that entirely assists an electric utility company; hypothetically, the Colorado Public Utilities Commission could invent if it were the first policy-making body across the states to give perpetual electricity distribution and transmission rights to an electric utility company operating in that state. However, I do not find examples of such egregious acts of "pro-utility" (Parinandi and Hitt 2018) policy-making in the regulatory RPS policy adoption data, suggesting that this study focuses on cases of regulatory invention where regulated parties are more likely to oppose than favor the policy-making outright. In the conclusion of this chapter, I highlight how scholars might investigate classically "pro-utility" regulatory inventing.

Public Utilities Commissions and the Regulation of Electric Companies

State public utilities commissions emerged in the early twentieth century as an institutional answer to the issue of ensuring that electric utility companies retain financial viability without gouging consumers (Troesken 2006).[5] When electric utility companies first emerged and constructed electricity generation and distribution infrastructure to supply electricity to consumers, oversight of the companies was practically nonexistent; municipal governments had entered into "franchise contracts" with electric utility companies but lacked authority to compel electric utility companies to treat consumers fairly, owing to the belief among state governments that electricity service regulation was not an "essential" function of municipal government (Gormley 1983; Troesken 2006). A consequence of this lack of oversight was that electric utility companies faced few constraints on the prices they could charge consumers and charged consumers exorbitantly high prices for electricity service. A solution to this problem was to allow municipal governments to regulate the activity of electric utility companies, and several states—including California, Florida, and Ohio—enacted laws permitting municipal governments to directly regulate the activity of electric utility companies operating within municipal boundaries.

Direct regulation of electric utility companies by municipal governments ameliorated the problem of companies charging exorbitant prices for electricity service but created the countervailing problem of placing electric utility companies at the mercy of politically minded municipal governments (Troesken 2006). Municipal politicians ran for election promising low electricity prices to voters and would then set low electricity prices once in office, even if the prices were set far underneath the break-even point for electric utility companies (Troesken 1996; Neufeld 2008). Setting artificially low prices is problematic not only for the financial viability of the electric utility companies that are the objects of such regulation but also because artificially low prices can influence the quality of service provision adversely by reducing the monies that electric utility companies have available to maintain and upgrade their electricity infrastructure (Guthrie 2006).

The creation of state public utilities commissions was a compromise

5. Consumers are called "consumer-voters" in some of the regulation literature (for example, see Besley and Coate 2003). To increase readability, I avoid overly technical jargon and use "consumers" rather than "consumer-voters."

solution aimed at balancing the demands of electric utility companies and consumers (Troesken 2006; Parinandi and Hitt 2018). Indeed, in some states (such as Illinois, as relayed in Troesken 2006), electric utility companies themselves clamored for state-level regulation, hoping that placing regulatory authority in the hands of multimember state-level commissions would reduce opportunities for pandering compared to when such regulatory authority is wholly in the hands of municipal governments.[6] While electric utility companies recognized that they would face some amount of regulation from state-level commissions, the companies believed that they would receive fairer treatment at the hands of state commissions rather than municipal governments and the regulation of electric utility companies by state-level public utilities commission has persisted into the twenty-first century (Knittel 2006; Neufeld 2008).

Today, state public utilities commissions possess regulatory authority over electric utility companies operating in their states, retain considerable power over the prices that are charged by electric utility companies to consumers—by approving prices directly in regulated states, by setting price caps (which were in place for the bulk of the later part of the time period of this study) and still approving distribution prices in deregulated states, and by controlling access to electricity retail markets in their states.[7] State public utilities commissions typically set policy with the goals of balancing electric utility company and consumer price demands while also ensuring access to "safe and reliable electricity" as well as preparing for "the future of the electricity system" in terms of readying electricity infrastructure to meet anticipated changes in demand and the energy mix used to derive

---

6. There is an active and ongoing debate in the regulation literature about how much pandering occurs among state public utilities commissions, especially because many states allow for the direct election of their public utilities commissioners, suggesting that the opportunity for pandering may still exist (Besley and Coate 2003). I do not enter into this debate but do control for whether a state's public utilities commission is elected or appointed in the analysis. One could surmise that the type of pandering described by Troesken (promising voters unreasonably low prices) occurs less among state public utilities commissions than municipal governments, not only because state regulation has been a stable institutional arrangement (lasting several decades now) but also because it is unresolved whether direct election of commissioners even leads to pandering on price, as several observers (Stigler 1971; Laffont and Tirole 1991) hypothesize that the low salience of these elections among voters might actually benefit electric utility companies.

7. The regulatory authority of state public utilities commissions pertains to the retail electricity market, not the wholesale electricity market, which spans state lines and is regulated by the Federal Energy Regulatory Commission (Allison and Parinandi 2020). The federal government has not adopted any policy resembling an RPS.

supply (Nanavati and Gundlach 2016, 6–7). State public utilities commissions are also considered widely to be experts in the area of electricity regulation and enjoy latitude to set their own policies regarding the regulation, maintenance, and upgrade of electricity service provision (Byrnett and Shea 2019).

Even though state public utilities commissions have latitude to set policy regarding electricity service provision, it is important to note that commissions are expected to chiefly serve as neutral arbiters of electric utility company and consumer interests and are further expected *not* to overly disadvantage companies or consumers in commission decision-making (White 2018). This expectation of neutrality—which is important so that public utilities commissions have legitimacy with *both* the companies they regulate and consumers at large—arguably may account for the rareness of regulatory policy feature adoption concerning RPS (since adopting an RPS policy feature opens up commissions to charges of being biased against electric utility companies). It may also account for why public utilities commissions are more likely to invent novel RPS policy when companies are in a less fortuitous position to challenge them.[8] Many state public utilities commissions have utilized their regulatory authority and adopted RPS policy features—inventing several of these by making their states the first to adopt them—on the pretext of providing efficient access to electricity and planning for possible disruptions to the supply of energy.[9] In table 5 below, I provide a list of states that adopted RPS policy features via public utilities commission rulemaking along with the percentage of a state public utilities commission's adoptions that are examples of inventing.

The table displays significant breadth across the states in terms of regulatory adoption, with at least one state in each region of the United States adopting a RPS policy feature through public utilities commission decision. The table also shows that most of these states' public utilities commissions invented *and* borrowed when adopting their respective RPS policy

---

8. In statistical analysis, I control for consumer opinions about regulation with a citizen ideology variable. I focus on electric utility companies because these generally oppose RPS policies (Stokes 2020) and because these have been shown (Olson 1965) to more effectively challenge public utilities commissions compared to consumers at large.

9. Disruptions could include events like increases in the cost of inputs such as petroleum (Welch and Barnum 2009) or the urgent need to replace aging plant, which introduces considerations about the cost effectiveness of alternative versus traditional forms of energy (Gruenspecht 2019).

TABLE 5. States with Regulatory Adoptions, with the
Percentage of Those That Are Inventing

State	Regulatory Adoptions That Are Inventing (%)
Arizona	45
Maine	33
Massachusetts	80
Michigan	50
Nevada	33
New Jersey	50
New Mexico	26
New York	29
North Carolina	50
North Dakota	0
Pennsylvania	50
Rhode Island	50
Texas	66
Vermont	16
Washington	50
Wisconsin	66

features. Similar to the strategy used with respect to legislatures in the last chapter, here we can compare how variables relate to regulatory inventing and borrowing and ultimately uncover factors that have unique resonance in explaining when regulatory agencies invent.[10] Before doing this and specifically before articulating why sector deregulation corresponds uniquely with regulatory inventing, I review what sector deregulation is and what it has entailed for state public utilities commissions.

Electricity Sector Deregulation

The deregulation of the electricity sector describes a process that occurred across many of the states in the 1990s and early 2000s (Ka and Teske 2002). With deregulation of a state's electricity sector, the vertically inte-

10. Just as was the case in the last chapter, some factors may produce both inventing and borrowing. These factors are obviously important, and I control for them; however, such factors are not the main emphasis of my analysis since they do not inform us about the unique drivers of inventing. Being able to identify the unique drivers of inventing is a key reason for distinguishing inventing from borrowing in the first place.

grated and quasi-monopolistic positions of electric utility companies were broken up, and new entrants were allowed to sell electricity to that state's consumers. Prior to deregulation, an electric utility company would typically control all phases of the production and distribution of electricity to its consumers; that is, the same company would be responsible for procuring, producing, and transporting electricity from generation to final use by a consumer. Furthermore, in a regulated system, an electric utility company essentially had monopolistic power within its service area, and this monopolistic power was established through agreement with a state's public utilities commission.

Under deregulation, the electric utility companies that previously had a vertically integrated monopoly over the electricity supply chain lost this control. Specifically, entrenched electric utility companies—the companies that previously exercised monopolistic control under a regulated sector—lost control over much of their generating infrastructure (sometimes through forced divestment, as is discussed in Kwoka et al. 2010) and had to compete with new entrants that could sell electricity directly to final users (Borenstein and Bushnell 2015). While the entrenched electric utility companies retain full control over distribution infrastructure (distribution refers to delivering electricity to the final user), they have to allow other firms to have access to that distribution infrastructure. This combination of losing control of much of their generation capacity along with needing to accommodate other producers in their distribution networks is what exposed entrenched electric utility companies to retail competition over electricity but not the distribution of it (Borenstein and Bushnell 2015). In fact, under deregulation, a final user might pay two monthly bills for their electricity usage: one to a new entrant firm for the electricity itself, and one to an entrenched electric utility company for distributing the electricity to the final user.[11] In the event where an entrenched electric utility company does not have enough generating capacity on hand to meet the demands of consumers—which has occurred commonly in several deregulated states in cases where entrenched electric utility companies lost much of their generating capacity through divestment but only lost small numbers of consumers to other firms—the entrenched electric utility company will

---

11. In regulated states, a final user would pay one bill to an entrenched electric utility company for the generation and distribution of that electricity.

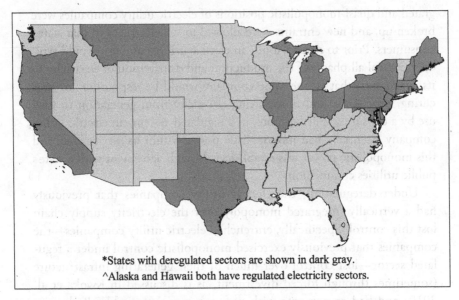

*States with deregulated sectors are shown in dark gray.
^Alaska and Hawaii both have regulated electricity sectors.

Fig. 8. Deregulated States, as of 2011
Source: Data on market deregulation comes from Magali Delmas, Michael Russo, Maria Montes-Sancho, and ElectricChoice.com

need to procure or purchase the demanded electricity from other firms and distribute it over its own network to its consumers.

In figure 8, I show a map of the continental United States in which states are grouped according to whether or not they have deregulated their electricity sectors by the end of this study.[12] While deregulation seemed like the wave of the future in the 1990s, it has largely stopped diffusing across the states and is concentrated in the Northeast, the West Coast, Texas, and the Great Lakes region (Delmas et al. 2007; Borenstein and Bushnell 2015). California's experience with severe electricity blackouts in the early 2000s concerned officials in some other states about the reliability of electricity service under deregulation (Borenstein and Bushnell 2015). Nonetheless, a sizeable number of states have pursued and retained deregulated electricity sectors as of the end point of this study. Several of these states (e.g., Texas, New York, Illinois, Pennsylvania, and Ohio) are among the most populous in the United States, suggesting that many Americans receive electricity from deregulated sectors. Moreover, deregulation is

---

12. In addition, Alaska and Hawaii both have not deregulated their electricity sectors.

probably here to stay given that many states are nearing their third decades under deregulation. While the jury is out in terms of how deregulation has impacted electricity prices (Borenstein and Bushnell 2015), it has arguably influenced how public utilities commissions approach inventing. Understanding how regulatory RPS invention activity differs across states with deregulated versus regulated sectors is consequently worth exploring since it sheds light on how the regulatory environment faced by public utilities commissions can influence policy adoption behavior.

Regulators Invent More under Deregulation

Deregulation of the electricity sector did not just introduce new entrants into a state's retail electricity market; it has also made public utilities commissions more likely to invent novel RPS policy features. To see why this might happen, it is important to explore two issues: first, why entrenched electric utility companies might oppose RPS policy (and especially oppose novel RPS policy); and second, how electric utility companies in states with regulated sectors could be better positioned to challenge regulatory attempts to promulgate novel RPS policy compared to electric utility companies in states with deregulated sectors. The end result is that public utilities commissions are more likely to invent when the ability of entrenched electric utility companies to challenge their action is comparatively weaker.

Entrenched electric utility companies have generally taken a dim view of RPS programs (Stokes 2020). A key reason why is that these companies incur financial costs in complying with RPS programs. This simply means that entrenched electric utility companies will incur some financial cost to switch from fossil-fuel-based sources to renewable sources to meet an RPS mandate. Scholars (Kim et al. 2016; Greenstone and Nath 2019) have shown that renewable energy is more expensive to produce than fossil-fuel-based energy.[13] Given that the price of electricity is an important aspect of energy policy to consumers (Besley and Coate 2003), and given that a major element of the popularity of RPS programs among consumers is that the programs are imposed on electric utility companies rather than directly on consumers (Äklin and Urpelainen 2018), such as an individual

---

13. It should be noted that some analyses (Ram et al 2018) are now showing that renewable production is cheaper than fossil fuel production.

carbon tax would be, entrenched electric utility companies will likely face some financial impact in complying with RPS obligations.[14] Moreover, entrenched electric utility companies in both regulated and deregulated settings face the financial impacts (Kim et al. 2016): while entrenched electric utility companies in regulated settings may have to upgrade their own infrastructure to comply with RPS obligations, entrenched electric utility companies in deregulated settings (to the degree that they no longer own generation facilities) may have to negotiate costly procurement deals with new suppliers to obtain the renewable energy needed to meet RPS obligations.

While the financial costs associated with complying with RPS obligations have made most entrenched electric utility companies skeptical of RPS programs, I argue that these companies might oppose *novel* RPS policy features more than they oppose features that have already been adopted in other states. The reason why is that entrenched electric utility companies could be exposed to greater uncertainty in estimating how novel policy will impact them financially relative to the uncertainty they face in estimating the financial impact of a policy that has already been adopted in another state. A novel policy has never been adopted before, meaning that an entrenched electric utility company cannot use the experiences of other electric utility companies operating under the policy to make opinions about the policy. In contrast, a borrowed policy has been adopted before, meaning that an entrenched electric utility company can draw upon the experiences of other electric utility companies operating under the policy to help form its own judgments about the policy.

Having more information at their disposal about how a policy works in practice matters for entrenched electric utility companies so they can adequately negotiate with public utilities commissions for assistance in defraying *some* of the cost associated with complying with RPS obligations. Although RPS programs have imposed added costs onto entrenched electric utility companies, public utilities commissions have recognized that entrenched electric utility companies cannot shoulder all of the financial burden of transitioning to the new RPS regulatory regime. Therefore, public utilities commissions have implemented social benefits charges

14. This is not to say that consumers pay *no* cost associated with RPS programs, as we will soon see that social benefits charges (Rabe 2008) use consumer fees to cushion some of the RPS-related cost faced by electric utility companies. Rather, the point is that consumers expect that utility companies will at least pay part of the cost associated with RPS mandates.

(Rabe 2008) that ameliorate the impacts faced by electric utility companies by making consumers give a subsidy (in the form of the charges) to the electric utility companies. Entrenched electric utility companies have an incentive to not only stretch the amount that this subsidy will cover but also reduce the possibility that unanticipated side effects of RPS policy could harm them financially.

Entrenched electric utility companies may believe that they are better able to pursue both incentives when a policy under consideration for adoption has actually been tested before compared to when the policy under consideration is novel and has never before been adopted. This is because with a borrowed policy, an entrenched electric utility company can use the experiences of how other utility companies fared under the policy to inform its own strategy about how to prepare for the adoption of that policy. Even if an entrenched electric utility company in a state considering whether to borrow a policy faces different challenges from those that were faced by other utility companies in state(s) that have already adopted the policy, the entrenched electric utility company can still extrapolate and exploit lessons from the other companies' experiences to help it prepare for the policy's arrival. Assume, for example, that an entrenched electric utility company in a state considering whether to borrow an RPS policy feature has a higher level of fossil fuel utilization compared to the level utilized by utility companies operating in state(s) that already adopted the policy feature when those respective state(s) adopted the policy feature. The entrenched electric utility company in the state considering whether to borrow the policy feature can use its higher utilization level to clamor for a more generous social benefit charge; and it can also use its higher utilization level to more aggressively implement a cost-cutting strategy to transition to the new regulatory environment. The point is that the company in the state considering whether to borrow the policy feature can use other firms' experiences as reference points to help in formulating its own plans; even if the company does not follow the other firms' actions, it can still consult those actions and experiences for guidance.

In contrast, with novel policy, the entrenched electric utility company has no other firm-specific reference points it can use to guide its planning and is arguably largely on its own in terms of anticipating how the policy could affect it. This impacts the company by raising uncertainty about whether its chosen strategy could backfire upon adoption of the policy. The company, for example, could advocate for a certain social benefits level but would be doing this without being able to benchmark its strategy against the experiences of firms in other states and might fear that it could incur unanticipated losses as a result. Similarly, the company could employ cost-cutting measures but would be doing this without being able to benchmark its strategy against the experiences of firms in other states and also might fear that it could incur unanticipated losses as a result.[15] Ultimately, not being able to benchmark plans against the experiences of peers might increase feelings of uncertainty among company executives and lead to a situation where executives believe that they are unable to effectively manage or adapt to the policy under consideration for adoption. This feeling of a loss of control can generate opposition among company executives toward invention, as executives believe that their companies are being made the objects of regulatory experimentation. Company executives' dislike of uncertainty (and by extension, of novel regulatory attempts that have not even been tried elsewhere) is not conjecture. A 2015 survey of global business executives by the firm Grant Thornton revealed that executives prefer higher taxes to greater uncertainty in regulation (Lagerberg 2015); this finding is corroborated by academic research (Baker and Raskolnikov 2017) showing that companies generally oppose uncertainty.

Public utilities commissioners ostensibly know that companies oppose invention, and this might explain why regulatory invention is so rare (with only 36 instances of it occurring in the time period analyzed). Despite the rarity of regulatory invention, however, I argue that public utilities commissions are more likely to invent under sector deregulation compared to regulation. There are arguably two reasons for this. First, in states with regulated sectors, entrenched electric utility companies possess vertical integration along with a monopoly over electricity provision in their respective service areas. Having singular control over the entire electricity provision process may put utility companies in states with regulated sectors in a comparatively strong position to challenge RPS policy invention. This is because full control over the entire supply chain gives companies an ability

---

15. My point here is not to say that these events *do not* occur under borrowing, as they definitely can occur. However, being able to benchmark one's decisions against the experiences of peers—even if one does not follow those experiences—can lead to greater feelings of certainty and control along with the belief that the policy under consideration can be managed if adopted. When one cannot benchmark one's decisions against the experiences of peers, in contrast, one may have comparatively reduced feelings of certainty and control along with reduced expectations that a policy under consideration to be adopted can be managed.

to more authoritatively speak to how the novel policy will adversely impact their assets. For example, a utility company in a state with a regulated sector could use the fact that it controls its own generation to pinpoint how the novel RPS policy (through requiring a greater procurement of electricity from renewable sources) impacts its own generation infrastructure. Being able to pinpoint effects might give companies greater clarity in their own arguments and consequent confidence to oppose the novel RPS policy.

In contrast, in states with deregulated sectors, entrenched electric utility companies do not have singular control over the entire supply chain and particularly do not have full control over generation, as many utility companies procure electricity in the wholesale market and then distribute it to end-use consumers. This lack of full control may limit the ability of entrenched electric utility companies in states with deregulated sectors to speak authoritatively about how novel RPS policy could adversely impact them. For example, an entrenched electric utility company in a state with a deregulated sector could be told by regulators to simply search for new wholesalers if the company argues that the novel policy will substantially raise costs with its current wholesalers. And regulators may be making this suggestion out of the belief that entrenched electric utility companies are desirable purchasers of electricity (by virtue of still possessing a monopoly on the distribution of electricity) and should be able to negotiate favorable terms with wholesalers even in the presence of the novel regulation. In this deregulated scenario, having the choice or flexibility to purchase its own electricity arguably diminishes the ability of an entrenched electric utility company to authoritatively advocate for how novel RPS policy could impact them adversely and suggests that peer utility companies in regulated states (who possess singular control over vertically integrated structures) may comparatively be able to more effectively push back against novel RPS policy.

There is a second reason why entrenched electric utility companies in deregulated states may be less willing to push back against novel regulatory invention, and it boils down to the idea that entrenched electric utility companies in deregulated states have already lost monopoly power and adopt a conciliatory approach vis-à-vis regulators to preserve the advantages that they still retain. Losing much of its generation assets, for example, may make a formerly monopolistic electric utility company engage in loss prevention to reduce other threats to its dominance. For instance, a formerly monopolistic electric utility company may still want to be declared the default electricity provider within its service area.[16] Furthermore, the same entrenched electric utility company may want to preserve its control over the distribution of electricity. Given its desire to forestall future losses to its position, the entrenched electric utility company might act in a conciliatory manner toward regulators to build a positive reputation among those regulators. One manifestation of this conciliatory approach could be reduced opposition toward novel regulatory policy-making.

Under sectoral regulation, on the other hand, an entrenched electric utility company might believe that opposition is a better option than conciliation. This opinion is not just because of the argument that I put forth earlier—that monopolistic control of the entire supply chain places entrenched electric utility companies in regulated states in an advantageous position from which to challenge novel regulatory policy attempts. Rather, it is also because entrenched electric utility companies operating in regulated settings could think that losing their status through something like deregulation is extremely unlikely, thereby leading the companies to believe that challenging novel regulatory policy is a worthwhile strategy.

One explanation for why the practice of allowing an electric utility company to acquire vertical integration over the electricity supply chain and then granting that company a monopolistic presence over a geographically defined service area has endured for so long over a majority of the American states is that this arrangement provides for regulatory simplicity and gives the affected companies ample opportunity to build clout. By regulatory simplicity, I am referring to the idea that regulators might have fewer firms to oversee under sector regulation compared to deregulation. This is because restrictions to competition under sector regulation reduce (compared to deregulation) the number of firms with which regulators must interact. Working with a smaller number of firms could allow regulators to spend more time with each firm and could represent a strength of sector regulation (from a regulatory standpoint) insofar as regulators may be able to avoid overextending themselves across a large number of firms.

The other aspect of sector regulation is that it allowed for electric utility

---

16. In deregulated states, consumers have the opportunity to shop around for their electricity provider. However, if consumers choose not to shop around, a company is typically chosen by regulators to be the *default* provider of electricity. Formerly monopolistic entrenched electric utility companies may want to be designated as default providers in hopes that consumers would be less likely to switch providers once they start receiving service.

companies to amass a sizeable amount of influence in their respective states of operation. Companies not only received exclusive authorization to be the sole purveyors of electricity in their service areas but were also typically granted this authorization several decades ago (Troesken 2006). Not having to share the spotlight with rival firms as a consequence of being the sole purveyor of electricity, combined with having the opportunity to broadcast their interests over a long span of time, arguably gave electric utility companies broad influence with stakeholders in their respective states of operation. These companies, for example, created long-standing working relationships with regulators and may have enjoyed increased influence with regulators as a result of having formed such working relationships (Stigler and Friedland 1962; Olson 1965; Stigler 1971; Dal Bo 2006; Stavins 2006; Thornton et al. 2008). These companies further had ample opportunity to cultivate influence with members of state legislatures, and they also had ample opportunity to communicate directly with consumers in hopes of convincing the latter that company and consumer interests are congruent.

The point is that electric utility companies operating under sectoral regulation were able to develop substantial influence and consequently may have come to believe that losing their structural advantages via deregulation was unlikely. The expectation among firms that accumulated influence with stakeholders should help protect the firms against drastic losses to their market positions is central to economics and political science and forms much of our understanding of why firms try to build influence in the first place (Leech 2010). It is not unreasonable to further assume that companies operating under sector regulation—which due to a lack of competition enjoy the ability to advocate for their own interests without worrying about the arguments made by rival firms, and which have also had ample time to build networks of influence—might think that they have relatively unfettered access and influence among stakeholders that gives added protection against moves like deregulation, which would result in losses in market position. These companies' capacity to use their advantages under sector regulation to amplify arguments against deregulation— that it introduces added complexity for regulators, that it could lead to disruptions in electricity service, and that it could lead to volatility in electricity pricing (Smith 2002)—may augment their belief in their ability to forestall deregulation.

If electric utility companies believe that deregulation is unlikely, they might feel emboldened to oppose attempts by regulatory agencies to adopt novel policy. This is because freedom from the fear of deregulation arguably opens up avenues of action that may be closed absent such freedom. This suggests that electric utility companies that operate under sector regulation and believe that deregulation is unlikely—which may predominantly be the case for companies operating under sector regulation given their opportunity to cultivate clout—may be willing to oppose novel regulatory action. This is less likely to be the case for entrenched electric utility companies operating under sector deregulation. These firms lost their vertically integrated positions, must now compete with potential rivals for the attention of stakeholders, and could deduce that maintaining a conciliatory approach with regulators is an effective way to preserve their market power.

Regulators are adept at navigating the power dynamics in their relationships with other actors (Potter 2019) and seek to minimize conflict with the companies they regulate, not only to avoid expending energy dealing with conflict that could be spent attending to other aspects of their work but to also reduce the chance that they could face accusations from the companies and affiliated interests of overstepping their bounds by crafting novel regulation rather than engaging in implementation. Regulators ostensibly prefer to avoid facing such accusations, as accusations can bring unwanted attention upon regulators and lead to demands to investigate regulatory behavior, change regulatory personnel, and even redefine regulatory responsibilities (McCubbins and Schwartz 1984). Insofar as regulatory agencies contemplate adopting novel regulation, they are consequently more likely to do so when electric utility companies are less willing to challenge the adoption, which is more likely to occur under sector deregulation. This expectation is formalized in the following hypothesis.

> *Deregulation Invention Hypothesis:* Public utilities commissions are more likely to adopt novel policy if they are operating under sector deregulation compared to sector regulation.

One question that might remain pertains to why electric utility companies operating under sector regulation might not challenge regulatory borrowing to the extent they challenge regulatory invention. My answer for why this is the case centers on the idea that even under sector regulation, electric utility companies need to foster some level of cordiality with regulators and therefore will not challenge everything that regulators attempt to do. The relationship between regulators and regulated entities is not one-off but rather iterative. An implication of the iterative nature of this relationship is that electric utility companies have to deal with regulators in the future and therefore do not want to overly antagonize those regulators. This means that electric utility companies need to pick and choose when to challenge regulators. Electric utility companies operating under sector regulation will choose to challenge more uncertain novel policy more than they challenge borrowed policy. In contrast, entrenched electric utility companies operating under sector deregulation will be hard-pressed to challenge regulatory policy-making regardless of whether it is invention or borrowing.

Evaluating Regulatory Invention and Borrowing
RPS Policy Feature Adoption Data

Here, I test my theoretical expectation by evaluating whether public utilities commissions are more likely to invent with respect to RPS policy features under sector regulation compared to sector deregulation. Although regulatory invention is the main theoretical focus, it is important to also explore regulatory borrowing so that we can see how variables may differentially influence regulatory invention and regulatory borrowing. While my strategy in chapter 5 was to extract all instances where state legislatures invent or borrow policy features and then combine these instances with state nonadoption of policy features to formulate the datasets used to evaluate the likelihood of legislative invention and borrowing, my strategy here is to extract all instances where *state public utilities commissions* invent or borrow policy features and combine these instances with state nonadoption of policy features to formulate the datasets used to evaluate the likelihood of *regulatory invention* and *regulatory borrowing*. As is discussed in chapter 3, here a state public utilities commission does not have the opportunity to adopt a policy feature—and hence, invent or borrow—if another institutional actor in the same state has already adopted the same policy feature. Similarly, a state public utilities commission loses the opportunity to invent with respect to adopting a policy feature once two years have passed since the policy feature was first adopted by any of the U.S. states (regardless of the institutional actor doing the adopting); and a state public utilities commission only gains the opportunity to borrow with respect to adopting a policy feature once two years have passed since the policy feature was first adopted by any of the U.S. states (again regardless of the institutional actor doing the adopting). Also consistent with the discussion put forth in chapter 3, state public utilities commissions gain the opportunity to invent with respect to policy feature adoption starting in 1983, when Iowa was the first state to adopt a prototypical RPS program.

My dependent variables of interest are *regulatory invention* and *regulatory borrowing*. As in the previous chapter, I employ logistic regression to determine what makes regulatory invention and regulatory borrowing more likely. My main independent variable is *deregulated*, which is a binary variable that takes a value of 1 if a state has restructured its electricity market to allow new entrants to sell electricity to consumers in the retail sector and a value of 0 otherwise. Importantly, this variable takes a value of 1 if a state allows for electricity providers to compete in the retail sector by selling electricity to any combination of commercial, industrial, and residential consumers; I make this modeling choice to reflect the idea that mobilization among any of these three kinds of consumer—commercial, industrial, or residential—could have caused a state to embrace sector deregulation. The identities of states that have deregulated or regulated their retail electricity sectors (based on a given state-year) come from Delmas et al. (2007) with supplementation from www.ElectricChoice.com, a website set up to facilitate shopping for electricity providers in states that have undergone deregulation. Since this variable is captured at the state-year level, it also accounts for states that chose to deregulate only to later fully reregulate.

I account for a number of competing possibilities by including several control variables. The most prominent control variable is whether a state's public utilities commissioners are directly *elected* by voters or instead appointed by a governor subject to legislative confirmation. Much of the work about electing public utilities commissioners (Primeaux and Mann 1986; Boyes and McDowell 1989; Kwoka 2002; Besley and Coate 2003; Gormley and Balla 2018; Parinandi and Hitt 2018) focuses on the idea that voters take minimal interest in regulatory issues while regulated entities (e.g., here, electric utilities companies) take great interest in regulatory issues. The differential interest showed by voters compared to regulated entities concerning regulatory issues opens up the possibility that elected public utilities commissioners might be less willing compared to appointed colleagues to challenge regulated entities through adopting RPS policy features. Alternatively, direct election may give commissioners the leeway to challenge electric utility companies by allowing the commissioners to sell policy proposal ideas directly to the public (Alessina and Tabellini 2008). Appointees, on the other hand, are accountable to governors and legislative leaders and may be considered to be overstepping their role if they sell policy proposal ideas directly to the public (Weingast 1984; McCubbins et al. 1987; Epstein and O'Halloran 1999; Huber and Shipan 2002; Volden 2002a; Miller 2005; Parinandi 2013). The same appointees, moreover, may even choose to limit how much they sell policy proposal ideas to governors and legislative leaders in order to avoid being accused of being unfavorable toward regulated entities by legislators (and potentially even governors) whose interests are aligned with the regulated entities. This suggests that elected commissioners may be more likely to adopt RPS policy features compared to their appointed colleagues.

I include the *price of energy* (measured in 2011 dollars per million British Thermal Units) to account for the possibility that energy pricing trends could spur regulatory policy adoption. I also include a state's average annual *daily solar radiation level* (measured by the National Renewable Energy Laboratory and in units of kilowatt-hours per square meter per day); I include this variable since some of the states (e.g., Arizona and New Mexico) that have been prolific regulatory adopters of RPS policy features have high solar energy potential, which could have spurred policy feature adoption.[17] As in the previous chapter, other notable controls include a state's *per capita income*; a state's percentage of energy that is produced from *fossil fuel sources*; and a state's *citizen ideology* (where, like before, the ideology of a state's citizens is measured on a 0–100 scale where 0 is perfectly conservative and 100 is perfectly liberal).[18]

---

17. When a state encompasses areas that receive different levels of direct solar radiation, I use the level corresponding to the largest metropolitan area in that state. While I do not include this variable in the analyses performed in chapter 5, including it does not change the results displayed in that chapter.

18. As in the previous chapter, for the sake of brevity and visual appeal, I only discuss certain control variables within the main text of this chapter and in associated table 6. However, the models estimated to obtain the results displayed in table 6 and figure 9 also include the following variables not discussed in the main text for both regulatory invention and borrowing: the percentage of a state's population that is urban; a state's change in unemployment; a state's level of legislative professionalism (as measured in Squire 2007); the fraction of RPS policy features that have been adopted previously by a state's geographic neighbors; the fraction of RPS policy

I also include four variables for both the regulatory invention and regulatory borrowing models that capture how conditions across the other institutions of a state's government might influence regulatory decision-making. *Unified Democratic government* is a binary variable that could influence when regulators feel more comfortable adopting RPS policy features. *Government ideology* comes from Berry et al. (1998) and captures whether regulators are operating in conservative versus liberal arena (where conservatism to liberalism is measured on a 100-point scale, where 0 denotes pure conservatism while 100 denotes pure liberalism).[19] *Legislative term limits* is a binary variable receiving a value of 1 if a state imposes term limits on its legislators (it is possible that term limits reduce legislative capacity and thereby make regulatory policy adoption more likely).[20] Finally, I include legislative *median incumbent vote share* from the most recent election (analogous to what was included in the previous chapter) to capture the possibility that regulators could be influenced by the anti-incumbent mood displayed toward legislators.[21] As in the previous chapter, I utilize separate logistic regressions for each dependent variable and cluster standard errors at the state level to reflect the idea that decisions within a state are correlated.[22]

---

features that have been adopted previously by a state's ideological neighbors; and the amount of time that has elapsed since an RPS program was first adopted in 1983. For the model pertaining to regulatory invention, I also include a control variable capturing the fraction of prior instances of invention (regardless of the institutional actor) that have occurred in the state in question. For the model pertaining to regulatory borrowing, I include control variables capturing (1) the fraction of prior instances of borrowing that have occurred in the state in question (regardless of institutional actor) and (2) the number of years that have elapsed since a particular policy feature was first adopted across the states, again regardless of institutional actor. In table A10 of the appendix, I display results for variables not shown in this chapter.

19. Recall that the *government ideology* variable is constructed out of legislator behavior and thus only indirectly captures regulatory preferences. Moreover, since many public utilities commissioners have prior backgrounds in politics and serve across multiple legislative sessions, the government ideology variable may only poorly capture regulators' actual beliefs, which may largely be hidden and unrevealed (White, personal communication, 2018).

20. I included the *legislative term limits* variable in the regression analyses conducted and discussed in chapter 5 in table A7. Including this variable in those analyses does not change the substantive results concerning either legislative invention or legislative borrowing.

21. For those public utilities commissioners that are elected, I am unable to find complete and systematic information about the electoral results of these offices. The website Ballotpedia.org has some coverage of these contests but is far from having complete coverage. I substitute mean incumbent vote share and the percentage of a state's legislative races in the most recent electoral year that had a victory margin of less than 10 percentage points and find results unchanged.

22. One potential concern is that I have not accounted for when state public utilities commissions receive discretion to adopt policy features. In my reading of state legislative and regula-

TABLE 6. Deregulation on Regulatory Invention and Borrowing (Selected Variables)

Variable	Regulatory Invention	Regulatory Borrowing
Deregulation	1.021**	0.318
	(0.487)	(0.835)
Elected	1.618**	2.246***
	(0.674)	(0.670)
Price of Energy	−0.109	−0.283*
	(0.124)	(0.154)
Daily Solar Radiation Level	1.101***	1.909***
	(0.311)	(0.354)
State Per Capita Income	−0.008	−0.009
	(0.029)	(0.029)
Fossil Fuel Sources	−0.018**	−0.027**
	(0.007)	(0.010)
Citizen Ideology	0.068***	0.145***
	(0.023)	(0.041)
Unified Democratic Government	0.695	−1.178
	(0.589)	(0.891)
Government Ideology	−0.024**	0.003
	(0.011)	(0.016)
Legislative Term Limits	−0.794	−0.757
	(0.717)	(0.685)
Legislative Median Incumbent Vote Share	−0.002	−0.0008
	(0.010)	(0.010)
Observations	182,851	47,130
	(36)	(54)

*** = critical value of 0.01; ** = critical value of 0.05; * = critical value of 0.10

Results in table 6 reveal preliminary support for the Deregulation Invention Hypothesis, as the deregulation variable is positively and statistically significantly associated with regulatory invention. A reason for this could be that deregulation disrupts the ability of entrenched electric utility companies to fight back, leading to a scenario where public utilities commissioners are more likely to adopt novel RPS policy under deregulation compared to sector regulation. That the same result in terms of statistical significance and magnitude does not carry over to regulatory borrowing suggests that public utilities commissions operating in regulated and deregulated settings approach borrowing in the same way.

Moving to some of the controls from table 6, results regarding the

tory RPS documents, there did not appear to be a clear indication where legislatures authorized regulators to adopt specific policy features (regulators were largely authorized to enforce compliance but this is different from adopting policy). Moreover, both legislatures and public utilities commissions could claim jurisdictional authority to enact policy governing the electricity sector, which opens the door to both institutional actors adopting policy.

elected variable are worth discussing. Recall that the elected variable captures whether commissioners are selected by voters or through gubernatorial appointment subject to legislative confirmation and oversight. The positive association between election and regulatory invention is fascinating since it suggests that being free from gubernatorial and legislative oversight gives commissioners the ability to take policy-making proposals directly to voters, a path that is arguably closed to appointees, who potentially may be castigated by governors and legislative leaders sympathetic to electric utility company interests. At the same time, the even larger association between the elected variable and regulatory borrowing suggests that, like their legislative counterparts, elected public utilities commissioners may also emphasize the *observable* aspects of policy insofar as they can credibly tell voters that they are trying to replicate successes seen elsewhere (Kogan, Lavertu, and Peskowitz 2016). Another implication that can be drawn out from the elected variable is that appointees are less likely to either invent or borrow. A takeaway from this is that we should perhaps not expect invention to come disproportionately from appointees.[23]

---

23. One control result that is worth discussing concerns the price of energy variable, which is associated negatively with both regulatory invention and borrowing but achieves statistical significance with respect to borrowing. It is important to emphasize that no presumption is made about whether invention is a more versus less expensive policy option compared to borrowing: both are examples of policy-making that could increase operating costs on companies and plausibly should relate negatively to the price of energy, which they do. The presumption that was made, which has support in business survey results (Lagerberg 2015) as well as academic research (Baker and Raskolnikov 2017), is that firms generally dislike uncertainty, which extends—given the definitional difference between invention and borrowing—into a potentially greater dislike of invention compared to borrowing. While I do not dispute the presumption (upheld in Lagerberg 2015 and Baker and Raskolnikov 2017) that firms dislike uncertainty and certainly do not think that electric utility companies would clamor for added regulations in the form of invention or borrowing, it is possible that at least under high energy prices—which are calculated by the U.S. Energy Information Administration in the form of total end-use prices, implying that consumers already pay a high amount for energy and that public utilities commissions could be hard-pressed to shift regulatory costs onto consumers—electric utility companies might oppose known (e.g., policy that has already been adopted somewhere) drivers of regulatory cost increase much more than they would under lower prices due to the fear that they will have to absorb a higher share of the increase. Remember that a benefit of regulatory borrowing for firms is that they can use the experiences of other firms to make informed arguments about how they should be treated by regulators concerning regulatory cost relief; if regulatory cost relief is off the table due to high energy prices, then firms may be less tolerant of regulatory borrowing than they would otherwise be under lower prices. This decrease in tolerance given high energy prices with respect to regulatory borrowing, especially if accompanied by a smaller decrease in tolerance with

Another result worth discussing concerns the government ideology variable. Recall that this variable captures the broader governmental ideological environment in which regulators operate, as the variable is derived from legislator behavior. The negative and statistically significant relationship between government ideology and regulatory invention warrants explanation, and here, I believe this finding is an artifact of sizeable regulatory invention activity that took place in the state of Arizona. During the 1983–2011 time span of this study and based on mean government ideology scores, Arizona has been one of the most conservative states in the United States (with a mean government ideology score of 27.89, where 0 denotes pure conservatism while 100 denotes pure liberalism).[24] Despite the state's conservative profile, Arizona's public utilities commission—officially called the Arizona Corporation Commission—invented with respect to adopting several RPS policy features and did so out of an attempt to capitalize on the state's ample solar energy potential.[25] This is confirmed by the Arizona Corporation Commission's decision in 1996 to adopt an RPS program dedicated wholly to developing the state's solar electricity industry (Arizona Corporation Commission 1996).[26]

Dropping observations corresponding to Arizona and re-estimating the analysis removes the association between government ideology and regulatory invention, providing a measure of support for the idea that the finding linking conservative government ideology to regulatory invention was driven partially by invention on the part of Arizona.[27] The possibil-

respect to regulatory invention (say, for example, that firms generally dislike uncertainty across a broad range of energy prices) could produce the results seen here.

24. In fact, during the year in which Arizona regulators adopted the most inventions (1996), the state had a government ideology score of 1.8.

25. According to average daily solar radiation data from the National Renewable Energy Laboratory, Arizona receives (along with California, Nevada, and New Mexico) the greatest amount of sunlight of any state in the United States. Further, of those four states, a greater extent of Arizona's geography appears to be saturated by high levels of sunlight (National Renewable Energy Laboratory Resource Assessment Program, year unknown).

26. Other sources were later added to a revamped RPS program, but the decision to at first exclusively create an RPS program dedicated to solar energy underscores Arizona regulators' intent when launching the program.

27. The relationship between government ideology and regulatory invention without Arizona has a coefficient value of –0.021 and a standard error value of 0.017 (with an associated critical or "p" value of 0.213). Given that the relationship between these two variables in the dataset including Arizona yields a coefficient value of –0.024 and a standard error value of 0.011 (with an associated p-value of 0.029), the change in our expectation that the association between gov-

ity that the finding linking government ideology to regulatory invention is uninformative—not only because government ideology is constructed from legislator behavior and does not map neatly onto regulatory behavior, but also because the result could be driven by regulators in a conservative state (Arizona) inventing to take advantage of solar energy potential—raises the issue of how much we should even expect the ideology of public utilities commissioners (to the extent that this can actually be measured) to play an influential role in commissioner decision-making. The nature of the work that public utilities commissions perform—managing the relationship between electric utility companies and rate-paying consumers to make sure that the interests of both sides are represented fairly in decision-making—militates against ideology playing an overt role in public utilities commission decision-making. The Arizona Corporation Commission, for example, publicly states that a central goal in its oversight of utilities operations involves trying "to balance the consumers' interest in affordable and reliable utility service with the utility's interest in earning a fair profit" (Arizona Corporation Commission 2020).

Insofar as a pure liberal regulatory agenda would entail adopting more regulations to constrain firm behavior while a pure conservative regulatory agenda would entail removing regulatory constraints on firm behavior (Potrafke 2010), public utilities commissioners are limited in terms of how much they can infuse ideology into their decision-making while still conforming to their roles as arbiters of firm and consumer interests. If a public utilities commission of a liberal orientation (assuming that the ideologi-

---

ernment ideology and regulatory invention was obtained through chance increases by 0.18 (or 18%) when Arizona is dropped. The finding of a nonsignificant association between government ideology and regulatory borrowing does not change based on the inclusion of Arizona. I should add that the relationship between deregulation and regulatory invention goes from having a coefficient value of 1.021 and a standard error value of 0.487 (with an associated p-value of 0.036) with Arizona included to having a coefficient value of 1.043 and a standard error value of 0.671 (with an associated p-value of 0.120) with Arizona dropped, corresponding to a change in our expectation that the association between deregulation and regulatory invention was obtained through chance of 8.4%. Although the deregulation variable loses significance when Arizona is dropped with respect to regulatory invention, it is important to remember that the deregulation variable *barely* loses significance, with a p-value lying just outside of the conventionally accepted standard of 0.10. The fact that the p-value lies so close to a conventionally accepted standard suggests that the deregulation variable retains a measure of explanatory power when Arizona is dropped. It is less likely that government ideology retains explanatory power when Arizona is dropped considering that its associated p-value falls far (over 10%) from conventionally accepted standards.

cal comportment of public utilities commissioners can actually directly be measured) were to aggressively embrace a pro-regulatory agenda, it could expose itself to being accused by firms of not upholding its regulatory mission. Similarly, if a public utilities commission of a conservative orientation were to aggressively embrace an antiregulatory agenda, it could expose itself to being accused by consumers of not upholding its regulatory mission. Inasmuch as a public utilities commission wants to avoid facing such accusations—which is likely considering that the commission must expend time and energy defending itself, may need to respond to litigation, and may even face calls for its powers to be modified—that commission will strive to appear neutral in decision-making, and this striving for a neutral appearance should temper the role that ideology plays in regulatory decision-making.

The same desire for conflict avoidance compels public utilities commissions to pay attention to power asymmetries vis-à-vis regulated electric utility companies in the rare event that commissions invent with respect to RPS policy features. Sector deregulation matters in this context since entrenched electric utility companies are in a weak (compared to companies operating under sector regulation) position to challenge regulatory invention, suggesting that commissions in deregulated settings might be better able to invent without facing protracted conflict over the policy change.

In figure 9, I display the difference in the predicted probability of regulatory invention when a state's electricity sector is regulated compared to deregulated. When calculating predicted probability, I set continuous variable controls at their medians and set binary variable controls at their most frequently occurring values. The large dots correspond to the "main" predicted probabilities while the smaller dots correspond to the upper (if above) and lower (if below) bound predicted probabilities based on a 95% confidence interval. The main takeaway from the figure is to notice that the predicted probability of regulatory invention occurring in a state with a deregulated electricity sector is almost three times higher (0.0002691 for a deregulated sector versus 0.0000972 for a regulated sector) than the predicted probability of regulatory invention occurring in a state with a regulated electricity sector. One explanation for the difference in the predicted probabilities between regulation and deregulation offered here is that a public utilities commission, whose mission requires that it not discriminate against electric utility companies in its decision-making, is more

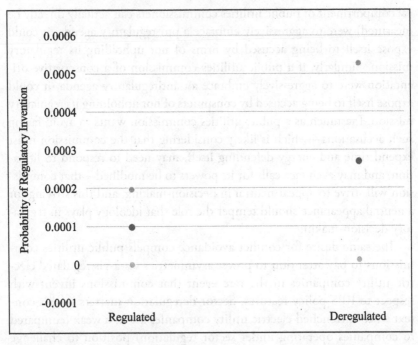

Fig. 9. Deregulation and Regulatory Invention
Source: Data on market deregulation comes from Delmas, Russo, and Montes-Sancho (2007), and ElectricChoice.com. Data on state RPS adoption primarily comes from the Database on State Incentives for Renewables and Efficiency.

likely to adopt novel RPS policy when electric utility companies are less willing to claim that they are the targets of discrimination. This behavior by public utilities commissions comports with the idea that regulators primarily see themselves as administrators and referees rather than lawmakers, and this behavior harkens back to the Weberian ideal (Weber 1978) in which regulators derive legitimacy from being seen as impartial in their decision-making. Inventing when firms are less willing to challenge policy is thus a way for commissions to reduce appearances of partiality.

Similar to the previous chapter, I also show results where similar rates and thresholds have been combined; these results, shown in table 7, substantively mirror the results in table 6.[28] I include other robustness checks

---

28. I use the same variables used in table 6. As with table 6, I only show results of selected variables for purposes of visual appeal.

TABLE 7. Deregulation on Regulatory Invention and Borrowing Combining Similar Rates/Thresholds (Selected Variables)

Variable	Regulatory Invention	Regulatory Borrowing
Deregulation	0.853*	0.308
	(0.489)	(0.828)
Elected	1.489**	2.353***
	(0.654)	(0.675)
Price of Energy	−0.083	−0.311*
	(0.106)	(0.159)
Daily Solar Radiation Level	0.888***	2.066***
	(0.295)	(0.404)
State Per Capita Income	−0.022	0.006
	(0.029)	(0.025)
Fossil Fuel Sources	−0.015**	−0.029***
	(0.006)	(0.010)
Citizen Ideology	0.050**	0.153***
	(0.021)	(0.043)
Unified Democratic Government	0.823	−1.182
	(0.628)	(0.857)
Government Ideology	−0.020*	0.001
	(0.011)	(0.016)
Legislative Term Limits	−0.544	−0.865
	(0.794)	(0.654)
Legislative Median Incumbent Vote Share	−0.005	0.003
	(0.009)	(0.010)
Observations	152,600	40,286
	(29)	(60)

*** = critical value of 0.01; ** = critical value of 0.05; * = critical value of 0.10

in the analysis. In table A11 of the appendix, I include a variable accounting for whether a state allows for policy to be adopted via direct ballot initiative and find that substantive results do not change. Similarly, in table A12 of the appendix, I substitute mean incumbent vote share for median incumbent vote share and find that substantive results do not change.[29] In tables A13 and A14, I respectively drop combinations and drop rates or thresholds from my analysis. In each of these analyses, the deregulation variable is no longer statistically significant, although it retains a larger influence with respect to invention compared to borrowing when rates

29. While I do not display these results, I additionally substitute using the percentage of a state's legislative races in the most recent electoral year that had a victory margin of less than ten percentage points. Using this variable does not change results.

or thresholds are dropped from the analysis. One thing to bear in mind is that dropping combinations results in an extremely low number of cases of regulatory invention (16), representing a more than 50% reduction in the number of cases of regulatory invention (36) appearing in the main regulatory invention dataset.

Conclusion and Discussion

In this chapter, I eschew the traditionally legislature-centric focus of U.S. state-level studies of policy-making and instead use the RPS policy experiences of state public utilities commissions to evaluate when regulatory agencies are more likely to invent novel policy during policy feature adoption. State regulatory agencies are key players in crafting and managing policy environments in their respective areas of jurisdiction; omitting an analysis of their policy adoption activity would lead to an incomplete picture of when state governments are likely to invent.

What emerges is a view of regulatory behavior that is perhaps best characterized as cautious. Not only is engaging in policy feature adoption (and even more so, invention) scarce among public utilities commissions, but invention tends to occur when commissioners face a lower probability that the objects of regulation (here, entrenched electric utility companies) will attempt to challenge regulatory action. Regulators appear to take seriously their role as arbiters and executors of policy and sparingly advance new policy directives when they believe that they can do so safely from the vantage point of not inviting unwelcome attention from the targets (as well as allies of the targets) of those new policy directives.

There are two broader takeaways from this finding, and each takeaway has different implications based on what one believes regulatory agencies should do with respect to inventing policy. If an observer believes that regulatory agencies should serve primarily as the managers of existing policy rather than the wellsprings of new policy-making, that observer might find reassurance in the sparseness of regulatory policy feature adoption and especially regulatory invention. While the same observer might find discomfort in the idea that public utilities commissions are more likely to invent new policies when electric utility companies have lost vertically integrated monopolistic power, the very fact that commissioners must take the power of such companies into consideration in choosing to invent suggests that regulatory agencies face limits on their authority and that they are not subjecting their respective states to copious inventing.

On the other hand, if a different observer believes that regulatory agencies have an obligation to use their managerial "on-the-ground" position to craft myriad novel solutions to a whole host of pressing social challenges, that different observer might find disappointment, not only in the scarcity of regulatory invention but also in the revelation (based on the sector regulation versus deregulation finding here) that invention may not take place in large areas that could benefit normatively from it.[30] The behavior of state public utilities commissioners regarding RPS policy feature adoption suggests that those desiring greater invention perhaps should not look to regulatory rulemaking to serve as a substitute for legislative decision-making. In the next chapter, I move on to case studies that further explore the dynamics discussed in this and the previous chapter.

---

30. The "large areas" here refers to states with regulated electricity sectors, and the "normative benefit" refers to a greater use of renewables combined with a concomitant decrease in fossil fuel utilization.

CHAPTER 7

Case Studies of Legislative and Regulatory RPS Invention

In the previous two chapters, I offered detailed and heavily quantitative analyses of legislative and regulatory invention with respect to RPS. In this chapter, I supplement those analyses with case studies focused on two pairings of states. In the first pairing, I look at two states that predominantly adopted RPS policy through legislative action—Illinois and Indiana—and revisit themes from the earlier legislative analysis to help explore why the Illinois legislature invented RPS policy much more frequently than did its counterpart in Indiana. In the second pairing, I look at two states that predominantly adopted RPS policy through regulatory action—Arizona and New York—and explore how the different regulatory structure across the two states impacted receptiveness toward RPS policy-making. The case studies not only buttress but build upon the main themes expounded in the book, and I now turn to each paired case.

Comparing Illinois to Indiana

Illinois and Indiana are not only neighboring states located in the Midwest but share a host of similar attributes. Both are states whose economies were heavily dependent on manufacturing (Matejka 1999; Turner 2016); both states were also impacted by deindustrialization in the late twentieth century (Matejka 1999; Turner 2016), arguably creating an opportunity to invest in technologies that could create employment prospects (renewable energy technology has often been billed in this manner). Both states are also appropriately described as agricultural titans: over the twenty-year span between 2000 and 2020, for example, Illinois and Indiana both ranked among the top five corn producing states in the United States (Crop Prophet 2021),[1] and large corn yields could create an opportunity for cellulosic-based renewable energy. At the same time, both states are important producers of coal: a National Mining Association brief from 2014, for example, lists Illinois and Indiana among the top 10 leading coal producers (National Mining Association 2014), and the existence of a powerful coal industry could militate against renewable energy investment.[2] In sum, the neighbors' parallel economic profiles and positions with respect to agriculture and industry suggest that their RPS development patterns might be similar to one another.

Even though the neighboring Midwestern states share many similarities and predominantly crafted their RPS programs through legislative action, the two states have taken different tacks with respect to how earnestly they have embraced new developments in RPS policy. Illinois has attempted to situate itself as a leader in RPS policy-making since the 2000s and invented four times over the final five years of the study (between 2006 and 2011). In contrast, Indiana was a latecomer to the RPS world, launched its RPS program in 2011, and included only one instance of invention within its program. Numbers alone do not do justice to how the invention behavior of Illinois differed from that of Indiana: while the Illinois legislature pursued instances of invention that pushed the envelope of RPS policy-making in an ostensibly pro-renewable-energy direction (mandating, for instance, that 25% of the electricity sold in the state be derived from renewable sources, and later proclaiming boldly that it would be a leader in wind energy), the Indiana legislature's invention was less pathbreaking, as it combined some decidedly nontraditional renewable energy features together (as an example, the state included a voluntary threshold alongside considering nuclear energy to be renewable). Indiana rather largely proved itself to be a consummate borrower in the RPS space, adopting policy features that had already been embraced elsewhere.

In terms of accounting for why Illinois has invented more than Indiana, the greater liberalism of Illinois's legislature comes to mind as a note-

---

1. Illinois is ranked at two while Indiana is ranked at five.
2. Illinois is ranked at five while Indiana is ranked at eight.

worthy factor. It is one thing to compare the ideology scores of Illinois and Indiana lawmakers—over the last five years of the study, the Illinois legislature had an average ideology score of 87.85 while the Indiana legislature had a much more conservative score of 20.9—but is instructive to remember that these scores suggest that the preferences of Illinois lawmakers are different from those of Indiana lawmakers and that the Illinois lawmakers might tolerate more novel policy-making in an ostensibly liberal area (RPS) compared to their Indiana counterparts.

One way beyond ideology scores to see how the preferences of Illinois lawmakers may be different from those of their Indiana counterparts is to compare the ratings given to the two sets of lawmakers by key environmental advocacy organizations. Two key environmental advocacy groups in particular, the Illinois Environmental Council and the Hoosier Environmental Council, share similar planks: the Illinois Environmental Council describes itself as "a group of dedicated grassroots environmentalists" and has goals to "maximize environmental protection," "hold decision makers accountable for their votes," and "ensure favorable legislative and rulemaking decisions" (Illinois Environmental Council 2020a). A goal of the group with respect to energy is to continue Illinois's "emergence as a leader of the clean energy economy" and ultimately achieve "100% clean energy in Illinois" (Illinois Environmental Council 2020b). The Hoosier Environmental Council refers to itself as "the voice of the people for the environment in Indiana" and has goals to promote a "sustainable economy," "environmental health and justice," and "water and wilderness protection" (Hoosier Environmental Council 2021a). In terms of energy, the Hoosier Environmental Council is clear in its desire to make Indiana "a sustainable energy leader in the U.S." and reduce the state's "carbon footprint" (Hoosier Environmental Council 2021b). The two groups therefore have overlapping agendas, and these agendas are appropriately described as liberal insofar as they seek to use government action to increase clean energy utilization. Given the ambitious nature of the two groups' agendas, it is reasonable to think that both groups would be supportive of novel action undertaken to bolster a state's renewable infrastructure.

Both groups offer ratings of state legislators in their respective states, and the ratings are instructive about how far legislators might be willing to go (including adopting novel and untested policy) in order to make their states clean energy leaders. Ratings range from 0 to 100, where 100 denotes full agreement with either of the two advocacy organizations.

If we compare the ratings of the Illinois Environmental Council of Illinois lawmakers who served in a sponsorship or cosponsorship capacity on Illinois's marquee RPS bill adopted in 2007 with the ratings of the Hoosier Environmental Council of Indiana lawmakers who served in a similar capacity on Indiana's adopted 2011 RPS bill, we find wide disparities in the level of endorsement given to the subsets of lawmakers from each state.[3] While the median endorsement rating given to the Illinois legislators by the Illinois Environmental Council was 90, the median endorsement given to the Indiana legislators by the Hoosier Environmental Council was a paltry 25.[4]

The difference in endorsement level not only suggests that the preferences of the groups of lawmakers shepherding RPS bills in each state are probably different—if they were not different, one would expect the ratings given to each state's group of legislators by advocacy groups with overlapping platforms to be similar—but also suggests that what each state's legislators want out of RPS legislation will be different. The Illinois legislators are more likely to be in line with and attuned to the objective of making their state a clean energy leader and may embrace novel RPS policy-making out of a belief that doing so is a worthwhile endeavor (in other words, they recognize that making Illinois a leader in clean energy requires the state to lead on renewable policy-making). Judging by the ratings given to them by the Hoosier Environmental Council, Indiana lawmakers on the other hand do *not* appear to aspire to make their state a national clean energy leader and consequently may be less receptive toward advancing novel RPS policy as a way to build the state's renewable energy

---

3. The 2007 reference to Illinois is the Illinois Power Agency Act (Senate Bill 1592) while the 2011 reference to Indiana is Senate Bill 251.

4. The ratings were accessed through Votesmart. For Illinois, legislators identified as being sponsors or cosponsors were Gary Forby, William Haine, John Sullivan, James Clayborne Jr., Deanna Demuzio, Michael Frerichs, Carol Ronen, M. Maggie Crotty, Edward Maloney, William Delgado, Antonio Munoz, Ira Silverstein, Don Harmon, Mattie Hunter, George Scully Jr., Bill Mitchell, John Bradley, Barbara Flynn Currie, Harry Osterman, Jim Watson, Greg Harris, Dan Reitz, Brandon Phelps, Patrick Verschoore, Michael Smith, Thomas Holbrook, Daniel Beiser, Robert Flider, Jay Hoffman, Lou Lang, Lisa Dugan, Naomi Jakobsson, Richard Bradley, William Davis, Mary Flowers, Constance Howard, LaShawn Ford, Wyvetter Younge, Al Riley, Esther Golar, Charles Jefferson, Monique Davis, Kenneth Dunkin, Careen Gordon, Robert Rita, David Miller, Eddie Washington, Sara Feigenholtz, Paul Froehlich, Elga Jefferies, Annazette Collins, Deborah Graham, Marlow Colvin, and Arthur Turner. For Indiana, legislators identified as being sponsors or cosponsors ("authors," using the state's terminology) were David Long, Beverly Gard, Jim Merritt, Brandt Hershman, Phil Boots, L. Jack Lutz, and Robert Behning.

reputation, preferring instead to adopt existing policies that imply that the state supports some renewable energy investment but does not want to jeopardize its fossil-fuel-driven industry.[5]

Written accounts corroborate this comparison of Indiana and Illinois legislators. Writing in the *Indianapolis Star*, three supporters of Indiana's RPS bill—Republican state legislators Beverly Gard, Brandt Hershman, and Jim Merritt—emphasized that their bill represented a prudent middle ground of where Indiana's clean energy footprint should be. Castigating those who call for "Indiana" to "abandon coal . . . as a principal fuel source and resort almost exclusively to renewable sources such as wind, solar, and hydro" as well as those who claim that "renewables are unreliable, too costly, and inappropriate for large commercial consumers," the legislators argue that their solution is emblematic of "good public policy" that is situated in "the center and not at the polar extremes" (Gard et al. 2011). The insinuation that their bill is prudent and modest arguably fits with how we would expect conservative legislators to advocate for a bill in a liberal area such as RPS. Compared to liberals, conservative legislators may see novelty as inherently reckless vis-à-vis moderation and may consequently desire to temper the boldness of RPS policy.

Indeed, voting patterns for Indiana Senate Bill 251 comport with the story laid out above. The bill passed the Indiana Senate with largely Republican support (the bill passed 31 to 19, with 29 Republicans voting "yes" while 11 Democrats voted "no"). Similarly, the bill passed the Indiana House with largely Republican support (the bill passed 62 to 34, with 56 Republicans voting "yes" while 32 Democrats voted "no") (LegiScan 2022). The bill also garnered the support of key energy players within Indiana, such as the American Energy Alliance, which advocates for free market energy solutions (American Energy Alliance 2011). In looking at how the bill could attract the support of those who would probably not be described as ardent enthusiasts of green energy, one explanation that makes sense is that waiting to see the fruits of other states' experimentation made aspects of renewable energy regulation more palatable to Indiana lawmakers. One example of such experimentation was Ohio's 2008 decision to incorporate nuclear energy within its RPS. Ohio's decision has received coverage and notoriety in renewable energy policy circles

---

5. Indeed, the word *sustainable* appears in Illinois's 2007 legislation seven times but never appears in Indiana's 2011 legislation.

(Heeter and Bird 2012), and the incorporation of nuclear energy became the lodestar of Indiana's RPS program. Given Indiana's lengthy border and overlapping energy landscape with Ohio (for example, American Electric Power, a major investor owned utility, has operations in both Ohio and Indiana), it is perhaps not coincidental that Indiana policymakers would know about Ohio's design choice and use it to soften their own RPS plan. In fact, the Indiana bill specifically evolved during the amendment process to more clearly showcase its commitment to including nuclear energy as a legitimate renewable resource. Part of that showcasing may have been intended to assuage conservative voters regarding the aggressiveness of an RPS, but part of it may have been intended to help Indiana lawmakers signal their cautious and careful bona fides in case the occasion arises where they might need to do so.

In contrast, the laudatory messages given to Illinois legislators by key environmental groups in the state suggest that the goal in Illinois was not moderation but rather to create a splash and make Illinois a trendsetter in the renewable energy landscape. In a column written in the *Rockford Register Star* in 2012, Kevin Borgia, then policy manager for an organization promoting wind energy use called Wind on the Wires, praised the gumption of Illinois officials, claiming that "forward thinking policy" has "made Illinois a national leader in wind energy" (Borgia 2012). In a similar vein, commenting in 2007 on how many in Illinois's government have become supportive of clean energy, Jack Darin, then director of the Illinois chapter of the Sierra Club, said that Illinois "sets an example for America to follow as Washington prepares to debate future energy policies for our nation" (Renewable Energy World 2007). The verbal vote of confidence from major Illinois environmental groups about Illinois officials paints a picture of officials who are not willing to wait on RPS and instead endeavor to create policy that sets a precedent for other states to follow. Considering that RPS is a liberal policy area, officials are more likely to behave in the manner outlined by Darin of the Sierra Club when they are ideologically liberal in orientation. Indeed, one of the major champions of Illinois's RPS program, now State Senator (and Senate president) Don Harmon, garnered a 100% voting record from the Illinois Environmental Council in 2005 as well as environmental leadership awards from the same group in 2010 and 2013 (Illinois Senate Democratic Caucus 2021); Harmon, who represents a Chicagoland district, also has a thoroughly liberal reputation (Hinz 2004).

The votes supporting Illinois's invention largely occurred along party lines (with Democrats in support and Republicans against), which, given the more liberal bent of the Democratic Party, comports with the idea that Illinois lawmakers would seek to establish the state as a renewable energy leader. Unlike Indiana's experience, Illinois's experience during bill amendment was not revolved around a showcase attempt (in Indiana's case, incorporating nuclear energy into the renewable lexicon) to borrow other states' policy-making. Moreover, Illinois's bill was opposed by large Illinois electric utility companies, such as the firm Ameren, which called Illinois's legislation "unconstitutional" (Ameren 2007). When contrasted with the support that Indiana's legislation received from key utility firms and their allies (e.g., laudatory support from the American Energy Alliance), Illinois's experience in garnering the opposition of utility firms suggests that the state's legislation intended to push the envelope on novel policy-making, establishing Illinois as a renewable energy trendsetter. In contrast, the three Indiana legislators who authored the *Indianapolis Star* article are conservative Republicans with an average rating from the Hoosier Environmental Council of 41.6 (Votesmart 2021), suggesting that we should not expect them to share the environmental leadership aspirations of their counterparts in Illinois.

The emphasis by the Indiana lawmakers on careful deliberation also may corroborate the link between electoral vulnerability and borrowing. In the year before Indiana adopted its RPS in 2011, the state's legislators faced a somewhat skeptical electoral environment, with the median vote share earned by an incumbent in state legislative races being 64.72%, representing a nearly 20 point decrease from a couple of elections prior.[6] If Indiana legislators believed that they faced potential skepticism from voters—and the recent drop in vote share suggests that this could have been the case—then those legislators may have tried to project themselves as meticulous analysts who chose wisely from a menu of existing options during the policy adoption process. In the case of Indiana, a state whose population is conservative with a nonetheless sizeable group of moderates who may be drawn to renewable energy due to issues of energy self-sufficiency and environmental conservation, lawmakers would ostensibly try to craft the

---

6. By way of comparison, Illinois lawmakers enjoyed incumbent vote shares hovering at 100 during the second half of the 2000s and remaining almost 10 points higher following the 2010 election. Of course, it is important to remember that there is no statistical relation between electoral vulnerability and invention.

state's RPS to include traditional renewable sources while also protecting the state's nonrenewable energy supply. Indiana lawmakers did just that and constructed an RPS program that was almost entirely borrowed: traditional renewable energy key features, including allowing for wind and solar thermal electric to be renewable, had first been adopted in other states decades before (initially in Iowa and then elsewhere; Iowa legislature 1983), but other less common features—including a voluntary 10% retail standard—also already had been adopted by other states (for example, this already appeared in both North and South Dakota; see House Bill 1506 of the Legislative Assembly of North Dakota in 2007; House Bill 1123 of the South Dakota legislature in 2008). Even Indiana's signature decision to include nuclear energy within its program had already been pioneered three years before in neighboring Ohio (see Substitute Senate Bill 221 of the Ohio General Assembly in 2008).

Although the Indiana lawmakers spearheading the 2011 RPS do not identify potential source states by name, their article in the *Indianapolis Star* emphasizes caution and a thorough survey of existing terrain, which suggests a borrowing-centric adoption strategy. Legislators Gard, Merritt, and Hershman mention "approaching" their RPS bill "from all sides of the energy debate," reference having "listened to . . . disparate opinions," and speak of wanting "balance" in their policy (Gard et al. 2011). Further, they intone against "dictating" solutions to their constituents—which could be interpreted as a criticism of the aspirational policy formulation occurring in states such as Illinois and Massachusetts—and instead advocate letting their constituents choose from a "menu" of practices (Gard et al. 2011). In sum, the language expressed in the *Indianapolis Star* article stresses predictability and routineness in its description of Indiana's RPS program. It is not far-fetched to believe that such language belies a policy adoption process that leaned heavily on borrowing existing features from the programs of other states.

In looking at why the legislators authoring the *Indianapolis Star* article would pen a piece in the newspaper serving the state's largest metropolitan area in which they harness a message of prudence and deliberation to push forth a program that has largely been modeled on the features of other states, one explanation that stands out relates to potential election concerns. The Indiana lawmakers, it appears, are striving to avoid creating the impression that they are subjecting their constituents to undue experimentation but rather seek to cultivate the impression that they are looking after their constituents through careful scrutiny. The careful scrutiny argument could serve to ameliorate potential skepticism among some voters, and this line of attack dovetails nicely with the fact that Indiana's RPS program was overwhelmingly borrowed. If the Indiana lawmakers were pushed to explain their policy choices in more detail, which could happen in encounters with interest groups and voter forums, they could point to the adoptions in North and South Dakota and Ohio as proofs of concept; all three states have cultural and political similarities to Indiana and thus might make ideal proofs of concept. Even if the Indiana lawmakers do not mention these other states specifically, it is not unreasonable to think that the other states' trials could serve as a form of internal vetting that the lawmakers use to try to reduce the chance that their policy choices could hurt them or their legislative allies electorally. This scenario seems plausible, especially given that the legislators behind Indiana's 2011 RPS effort built their expertise around energy issues and ostensibly knew about RPS developments occurring elsewhere.

Ultimately, the Indiana and Illinois comparison reveals that states in similar locations that have similar renewable energy development potentials can take different paths in constructing their RPS programs based on the ideological preferences of legislators as well as possible concerns of legislators regarding vulnerability come election time. The results suggest that observers of renewable energy policy not look at RPS policy-making deterministically, and that they not assume that states with similar locations and resource profiles will embrace similar RPS policy regimes. At the same time, the results help us recognize where leadership in RPS policy might originate at the state level and how ideological differences can drive heterogeneous policy development in spite of similar location and resource profiles.

Comparing New York to Arizona

The second paired comparison in this chapter looks at the RPS policy-making experiences of New York and Arizona. Both states have been erstwhile pioneers in RPS policy development and have also interacted with the RPS space through regulatory policy-making via their public utilities commissions, with New York spearheading its RPS in the early 2000s while Arizona made a foray into solar energy development in the mid-1990s. However, while New York has continued along a path of serving as a leader in the renewable energy policy space, Arizona regulators have faced significant pushback and pressure to dial down and even abandon their RPS program. One key distinction between New York and Arizona is that the latter has had a regulated electricity sector in which entrenched firms—such as the Arizona Public Service Corporation—have been able to utilize their influence to exert pressure on regulators. In New York, on the other hand, entrenched utility companies have largely served as partners of state regulators. The ability of entrenched utility companies to apply pressure on regulators under market regulation may be why Arizona regulators have faced calls to retreat to their RPS and why novel regulatory RPS policy-making has been so rare in states with regulated electricity sectors.

New York has long been a key producer of renewable energy policy advances. Blessed with ample hydroelectric power including one of the world's first hydroelectric generation plants engineered by Nikola Tesla at Niagara Falls, New York adopted its RPS program in 2004 (Lawson 2012; Allison and Parinandi 2020). New York's RPS program was spearheaded by state's Public Service Commission and has been a paragon of invention since its formation. State regulators not only pushed forward a 24% required target rate as well as incorporating distributed generation (or consumer-sited) based electricity within their RPS in 2004 but further pushed to combine solar water heat within their ambitious program several years later (New York Public Service Commission 2004, 2010). Observers such as analysts at Pace University in New York (Morris et al. 2013) unabashedly claim that "New York is a leader in promoting renewable electricity generation"; further, New York's own Energy Research and Development Authority—an agency created to deal with reducing the state's dependence on petroleum following the global 1970s oil crises—describes New York as having a "leading" position with respect to clean energy (New York State Energy Research and Development Agency 2020). A similar view was expressed by the New York Public Service Commission, which upon adopting the state's RPS mentioned that it had an obligation to "build new industries . . . based on clean, environmentally responsible energy technologies" (New York Public Service Commission 2004).

Interestingly, major New York electric utility companies have embraced the state's ambition to be a renewable energy trendsetter. Consolidated Edison, a large company that delivers electricity to the New York City metropolitan area, mentions that it "is committed to leading and delivering the transition to the clean energy future," writes of working "with government," and openly touts a goal of achieving "100% clean energy by 2040" (Consolidated Edison Company of New York 2020b). Consolidated Edison's enthusiasm is not a recent development, either. Indeed, in a 2004 brief written alongside New York's other major electric utility companies ("the Joint Utilities"), Consolidated Edison and its peers "support prompt implementation" of the state's RPS and argue that they "are in harmony" with the state's governing authorities regarding the RPS (Joint Utilities 2004). By 2006, less than two years after the adoption of New York's RPS, Consolidated Edison proclaimed in its annual report that "we support New York's Renewable Portfolio Standard" (Consolidated Edison Company of New York 2006).

While I do not doubt the sincerity of Consolidated Edison with respect to its claim that it supports New York's RPS program, one reason for this support may stem from Consolidated Edison having lost its vertically integrated monopoly and wanting to appear compliant in the eyes of New York regulators to preserve its hold on electricity distribution. New York regulators embraced deregulation in the mid-1990s, and the major goals of regulators in spearheading deregulation included "moving to a more competitive structure" and amplifying "consumer choice of service and pricing options" (First 2002; Nordlander 2002). New York regulators proceeded to "thoroughly examine" the state's old regulated electric utility model (First 2002) before cashiering it and replacing it with a deregulated system where new entrants on the generation side could sell electricity directly to consumers.

In New York's new regulatory environment, entrenched firms like Consolidated Edison gave up vertically integrated monopoly and only retained full control over distribution. Entrenched firms like Consolidated Edison understood that they were forfeiting a substantial share of market power and filed suit against New York regulators, charging that the latter lacked the authority to restructure the state's electricity marketplace; the ruling was not a success for the entrenched firms and established that "the agency had authority to order the utilities to take the actions envisioned" in the state's deregulation plan (Nordlander 2002). A group of consumers, who may have been affiliated with the entrenched firms, appealed the ruling only to be dismissed for lack of standing (Nordlander 2002).

Court losses arguably represented a crossing of the Rubicon for New York's entrenched electric utility companies. Deregulation would commence forthwith, and the entrenched and soon-to-be formerly vertically integrated electric utility companies would be better served by working with New York state regulators rather than against them. Working with regulators would allow entrenched utilities to fend off challenges to their monopoly on distribution—which is the last bastion of largely uncontested market power that the entrenched utilities possess—and obtain favorable concessions from regulators. One example of the benefit of this strategy pertains to the issue of distributed, or customer-sited, electricity generation. Customer-sited generation threatens to upend the business model for utility companies by potentially taking the need for distribution away from utility companies and giving it to local producers, who can then send electricity themselves to local consumers. Utilizing customer-sited generation has long been a desire among renewable energy advocates (Cleary and Palmer 2020), and in 2004, New York regulators invented by explicitly incorporating customer-sited generation within the state's RPS program. However, the way in which New York regulators incorporated customer-sited generation into the state's RPS program has been to make local producers use the state's entrenched electric utility companies—such as Consolidated Edison—to distribute electricity to local consumers (Consolidated Edison Company of New York 2020a).

This design move reinforces the centrality of entrenched electric utility companies to the state's electricity infrastructure and arguably was made easier by the support shown by firms like Consolidated Edison toward the policies put forth by state regulators. One could possibly intuit that regulators would have taken a different view toward the role of entrenched utility companies in the state's customer-sited scheme (perhaps choosing to let alternate distribution networks form) had the companies consistently opposed the efforts of state regulators. In the years since, New York's formerly vertically integrated electric utility companies have managed to safeguard their distribution stranglehold in spite of attempts by local advocates (such as New York City's Public Advocate Jumaane Williams) to do so, and this success in part probably stems from a collaborative relationship with state regulators (New York City Public Advocate 2021). Ultimately, the case of New York shows how electricity deregulation may foster regulatory invention by inducing affected electric utility companies to support regulatory policy-making. The next case—that of Arizona—shows what can happen when regulators push too far in policy-making and incur the wrath of powerful and entrenched interests operating in a regulated environment.

Similar to New York, Arizona has been blessed with ample potential to be a renewable energy powerhouse: while New York's initial strength lay largely in hydroelectric capacity (Allison and Parinandi 2020), Arizona is one of the sunniest states in the United States and has tremendous solar prospects (Perdana and Lopez 2020). Both states are also similar with respect to not being major producers of fossil fuels: in the last year of the study, according to the United States Energy Information Administration, New York registered no coal production while Arizona accounted for 0.7% of the United States total (United States Energy Information Administration 2021); the two states also had low shares of fossil fuel production as a percentage of total energy production (United States Energy Information Administration 2013), suggesting good environments for renewable energy development. Arizona regulators undoubtedly took the solar energy potential of their state into account when they invented by adopting Decision 59943 in 1996, which stipulated that 0.5% of retail electricity supplied in the state be derived from solar sources (Arizona Corporation Commission 1996). Four short years later, Arizona regulators built on this nascent solar legacy and invented by incorporating solar water heat into their RPS program (Arizona Corporation Commission 2000). One could reasonably conclude that at the turn of the century, Arizona had emerged as a hotspot of renewable energy policy-making.

The commitment by Arizona regulators to renewable energy development came around the same time that Arizona tried to dramatically transform the state's electricity market by embracing deregulation. The state began offering a form of deregulation to residential consumers in 1998 (Status of State Electric Industry Restructuring Activity 2003), and plans were made to substantially increase the scope of the state's deregulation and even force the state's large electric utility companies to divest from much of their generation. Unlike in the case of New York, though, Arizona's experiment with deregulation soon stalled. The experiences of neighboring California with respect to power outages and reliability gave pause to Arizona regulators regarding the merits of deregulation (PowerGrid International 2002). But the death knell to Arizona's attempt to deregulate occurred in 2004, when the Arizona Court of Appeals ruled in *Phelps Dodge v. Arizona Electric Power Cooperative* that Arizona regulators lacked the authority to break up vertically integrated electricity companies to foster electricity deregulation (Duda 2018). Arizona's large and vertically integrated electric utility companies—including Arizona Public

Service Corporation, which dominates the Phoenix metropolitan area—would continue to exist in their current form. Indeed, in the years since this ruling, Arizona still retains a regulated electricity sector and efforts to get the state to deregulate have not materialized.

Arizona's failure to deregulate arguably sent a message to firms like Arizona Public Service Corporation that their market position was safe, and the company spent much of the 2000s being quite vocal in its opposition to state RPS efforts. While Consolidated Edison of New York positioned itself as an ally of the state's renewable energy goals, Arizona Public Service Corporation took issue with Arizona's RPS and made its opposition known. In 2006, for example, Arizona regulators adopted Decision 69127 and invented by adding geothermal direct-use and solar light pipes to the state's RPS mix (Arizona Corporation Commission 2006). In testimony accompanying the decision, the Arizona Public Service Corporation directly challenged the ability of regulators to even take up the RPS issue and mentioned that "whether or not the Commission has the authority to promulgate the Proposed . . . rules is an unresolved issue of law as there are no cases on point" (Arizona Corporation Commission 2006, appendix B, 42). In other testimony opposing the same 2006 decision, the Arizona Public Service Corporation took issue with the definition of "renewable credits" (a way to track that renewable energy has been supplied to a consumer) and "proposed that the words `renewable electricity' . . . be changed to `electricity'" and that "it is not possible to explicitly assure that `renewable electricity' has been delivered to a customer" (Arizona Corporation Commission 2006, appendix B, 9). It is possible to infer from these statements that the Arizona Public Service Corporation was not only displeased with the state's RPS efforts but sought to torpedo the whole enterprise.

Much of Arizona Public Service Corporation's justification for opposing the state's RPS efforts touched on the issue of uncertainty. The company stated in 2006 that it had difficulty with being able to "reliably predict the availability or costs of renewable power for purchase" (Arizona Corporation Commission 2006, appendix B, 52). At the same time, it also stated that it "does not believe it is possible to evaluate the costs of addressing transmission expansion to meet" potential RPS obligations (Arizona Corporation Commission 2006, appendix B, 69). The Arizona Public Service Corporation's hostility toward perceived uncertainty in renewable energy technologies suggests that the company would frown upon efforts to make Arizona a national leader in renewable energy policy development, and that is exactly what transpired. After years of situating their state at the forefront of renewable energy policy-making in the late 1990s and early 2000s, Arizona regulators took a back seat in this area during the middle-to-late 2000s and early 2010s, borrowing a well-established 15% retail target rate in their 2006 decision and then flirting with repealing that target rate in 2013 (Luber 2013), in the process largely abandoning the state's former position as a renewable energy policy-making leader. Arizona regulators' declining commitment toward renewable energy policy leadership was conceivably influenced by the fact that the Arizona Public Service Corporation was secure in its market position and was less concerned than its New York peer (Consolidated Edison) with appearing to be supportive of possible regulatory initiatives.

The ability of the Arizona Public Service Corporation to unabashedly push for its own interests is probably facilitated by the fact that the company enjoys vertical integration in Arizona's electricity market. When the company was discussing the difficulty of predicting renewable energy costs, it was speaking from a position of controlling its own electricity supply chain and may have sounded more convincing than a company that did not control all of its supply chain. Further, vertically integrated electric utility companies do not have to share attention with potential rivals within their service areas and may be able to set the agenda about their own interests without interference from potential rivals. The Arizona Public Service Corporation has communicated relentlessly about issues of cost and reliability in its service area and even bankrolled a 2018 attempt to keep a renewable energy-related direct initiative off the ballot (Pyper 2018). The boldness of this action conceivably also represented a message to Arizona regulators to stay in line with Arizona Public Service Corporation's desires and arguably would be less likely to imagine in a state like New York where entrenched utility companies lost their vertically integrated positions and were ostensibly looking to be in the good graces of state regulators. The case of Arizona suggests that entrenched utility companies are more willing to challenge regulators in regulated as opposed to deregulated settings and that regulators are less likely to push for novel renewable energy policy advances under regulation, which resonates with the finding from the empirical analysis in chapter 6. Simply put, actually losing vertical integration appears to make entrenched electric companies more compliant toward regulatory dictates compared to not losing such vertical integration, which might explain why regulatory invention is more likely in deregulated settings.

The New York and Arizona comparison is fruitful because both states had ample renewable energy development potential, had divergent RPS development paths from the mid-2000s onward, and differed according to market deregulation status. However, the two states also differ in terms of regulator selection method (direct election versus appointment), raising the question of whether the divergent paths of the two states are due to regulator selection differences rather than differences of regulation versus deregulation. First, neither state's method of regulator selection changed throughout the period when both states tried to become key players in renewable energy policy: New York consistently appointed its regulators while Arizona consistently elected its regulators. What did change, however, was that Arizona stopped a tepid attempt at deregulation in 2004, which arguably emboldened the Arizona Public Service Corporation to push back on renewables in subsequent years. Arizona's divergence, however, started shortly after its failed attempt to deregulate, suggesting that differences in market regulation structure account to some degree for the divergence of Arizona and New York. Second, the explanation revolving around deregulation comports with empirical findings from chapter 6. Remember that direct election of regulators was associated with a higher likelihood of regulatory invention. Since direct election relates positively with regulatory invention, it cannot explain the divergence that occurred between New York and Arizona where New York continued on the trajectory of being a renewable energy trendsetter while Arizona did not. Finally, the deregulation argument makes sense in terms of how we might imagine that large and well-established companies—of which entrenched electric utility companies are a sterling example, considering that many have been around for several decades and over a century in some instances—would act if they were to lose a sizeable part of their business structure: while some companies may have previously exhibited a too big to fail mentality, they would probably attempt to appear supportive of regulators as a way to preserve their remaining business structure. Thus, deregulation is not only an important feature of state electricity policy but also explains regulatory invention in RPS.

There is more to briefly say about the Arizona and New York cases. Admittedly, the two states are different ideologically: Arizona remained conservative throughout the study period while New York drifted in a more liberal direction (Arizona has an average government ideology score of 27.9 over the study period while New York has a score of 65.5; lower scores denote greater conservatism, hence Arizona has been more conservative than New York). However, the ideological difference of the states does not entirely explain divergence in regulatory trends, as Arizona kept its conservative status when the state's RPS program was growing *and* when the program was facing pressure to downsize and New York's launch of its RPS program occurred prior to its move into ideologically liberal terrain. Notwithstanding the fact that the selection method of each state's regulatory commission is different, the career trajectories of commissioners in both states are roughly similar, as each state's commission heavily attracts former legislators and executive branch aides (Arizona Corporation Commission 2022a; New York Department of Public Service 2022). This gives credence to the idea that differences in background between the two commissions (insofar as commissioners in both states come from prior government service) are probably not driving differences in regulatory outcomes across the two states. Finally, in each state, the legislature largely stayed out of the way of regulators as they were designing their respective RPS programs. In Arizona, the state's constitution protects the Arizona Corporation Commission by enshrining commissioners with broad regulatory powers that exist independent of legislative or executive oversight (Arizona Corporation Commission 2022b). In the case of New York, regulators acted on the basis of an energy security plan that was implemented under the aegis of New York's executive branch (including its governor) with the goal of promoting self-sufficiency following the attacks of September 11, 2001 (State of New York 2002). Even though New York's governor supported the development of the state's energy plan and the legislature was aware of the plan, New York regulators shouldered the bulk of the responsibility in crafting and promulgating what would become the state's renewable portfolio standard. Regulators, for instance, not only initiated feedback with the public to gauge opinion about the standard but also conducted hearings prior to issuing their final policy-making decision. The preface to New York's 2002 energy plan does not even appear to mention the legislature, which gives heft to the idea that New York regulators possessed substantial autonomy in designing the state's RPS (State of New York 2002, sec. 1.1).

Conclusion

This case study chapter is meant to provide a less quantitative illustration of the factors influencing legislative and regulatory RPS policy-making and specifically invention. The Illinois and Indiana comparison reveals that liberal zeal among lawmakers can contribute to one state billing itself as a renewable energy leader while a neighbor embraces a much more modest position. The modest position may also suit lawmakers concerned about electoral vulnerability insofar as they can tell constituents that they are taking a careful and prudent tack on policy-making. The New York and Arizona comparison, on the other hand, reveals that a loss in vertically integrated structure may elicit firms to cooperate with regulators and make regulatory invention more likely than in the case where vertical integration persists intact. Both paired comparisons show just how institutional venue and characteristics of institutions can influence RPS policy development and invention and thus may have relevance in terms of suggesting that institutional venue and characteristics of institutions can affect invention as typified by Brandeis more broadly. The narrative also shows how four states with renewable energy potential can embrace different tacks on policy. Institutions, to put it mildly, matter, and institutional differences can lead to varying commitments in pursuit of renewable energy leadership. Giving the states more leeway by itself is not the answer to unleashing renewable energy policy development but also potentially requires certain legislative and regulatory characteristics, of which I have identified two.

This case study chapter and the chapters before it dealt with the issue of RPS policy adoption. While this is indeed a timely and pertinent issue given the enormous challenges of a warming climate as well as securing energy independence, RPS represents a relatively liberal policy area. How does state-level invention (and particularly legislative invention, given that the legislative branch is ostensibly the main law-crafting branch) occur in a conservative policy area? In the next and penultimate chapter, I provide a detailed walk through of state legislative invention in the area of anti-abortion policy. And in the conclusion of the book, I engage readers in a conversation about the book's takeaways and about how the line of inquiry developed here can be broadened.

CHAPTER 8

Extending the Legislative Analysis to Anti-Abortion Policy

Throughout this book, I have focused on utilizing data on RPSs to investigate factors influencing state policy invention. The choice to study RPSs was predicated on several important considerations. First, RPSs arguably are the preeminent way in which the United States has grappled with fostering investment in renewable energy and mitigating carbon production in its electricity sector, suggesting that examining RPSs could help us identify where advances in U.S.-based renewable energy policy are likely to originate moving forward. Second, RPS programs have been adopted across the majority of the U.S. states, meaning that findings regarding invention are not an artifact of a small number of states displaying policy-making in this area. Third, the RPS area exhibits variation in the institutions adopting policy, allowing us to examine how the drivers of invention may differ across institutional actors.

However, even accounting for the strengths of examining the RPS area, a possible concern is that I have selected an ideologically left-leaning area, thereby implying that we do not know whether policies with an ideologically conservative bent would produce results that are theoretically consistent with results produced using RPS data. While I would like to emphasize that it is debatable whether the RPS area is situated purely within the left-leaning or liberal end of the ideological spectrum considering that doggedly conservative states like North Dakota and Utah have adopted RPSs, the fact that RPS is a form of environmental regulation, which has been more likely to occur under the auspices of left-leaning governments

(Potrafke 2010), suggests that should also conduct my analysis in a conservative or right-leaning policy area.

In this chapter, I investigate whether findings gleaned from RPS extend to anti-abortion policy. Challenging the *Roe v. Wade* case that legalized abortion nationwide has long been a central goal of the modern conservative movement (Kreitzer 2015; Kreitzer and Boehmke 2016). In addition to challenging the legality of abortion, the modern conservative movement has also attempted to make an abortion harder to obtain through restricting availability and access to the practice (Ziegler 2020). Therefore, policies that share the commonality of making it harder to obtain an abortion—what scholars of the politics and policy of abortion (e.g., Kreitzer 2015) call *anti-abortion* policy—fit firmly within the conservative end of the ideological spectrum.

The authors of a recent study identified and tracked the adoption of 29 distinct anti-abortion policies across the U.S. states for a nearly forty-year period starting with the national legalization of abortion in the U.S. Supreme Court's 1973's *Roe v. Wade* decision.[1] Taking their data on state-level adoptions of anti-abortion policy, and categorizing and transforming their data to identify cases of invention and borrowing as was discussed in chapter 3 and implemented in chapters 5 and 6, we can ascertain whether increased conservatism predicts invention and whether electoral vulnerability predicts borrowing in the area of anti-abortion policy. The anti-abortion policy adoption data in Kreitzer and Boehmke (2016) come from state *legislative* decision-making. This means that we are able to provide a conservative analog to the legislative analysis conducted in chapter 5. The conservative analog offers a nice extension to the legislative chapter utilizing RPS—which, given that state legislatures have been the institutional actors most likely to adopt RPS policy, is one of the central analyses of the book. Given that Kreitzer and Boehmke identify legislative policy action and that the leading repository of abortion-related policy devotes its coverage of policy developments to tracking state anti-abortion *legislation* (Guttmacher Institute 2020), I do not include a conservative analog to the regulatory analysis in chapter 6. In the conclusion of the book, I offer

---

1. While Kreitzer and Boehmke collect data on anti-abortion policy adoption from 1973 to 2013, for analytical purposes their collected data spans from 1973 to 2012. This is because some of the key control variables used in their analysis are missing for the year 2013. Since I use all of their control variables in the analysis here, similar to Kreitzer and Boehmke, I do not include observations from the year 2013.

thoughts about how a regulatory analysis could be conducted in a conservative policy area and how the analytical framework employed in this book could be expanded across a host of policy areas.[2]

Altogether, categorizing the adoptions in the Kreitzer and Boehmke study as invention or borrowing yield hundreds of positive instances of invention and borrowing. Adding the same government ideology variable used earlier in the book to the variables used by Kreitzer and Boehmke to predict anti-abortion policy adoption reveals that government ideology influences invention with respect to anti-abortion policy. Moreover, the association between government ideology and invention is negative; given that the government ideology variable is measured in such a way that 0 denotes perfect conservatism while 100 denotes perfect liberalism, a negative relationship between government ideology and invention in anti-abortion policy suggests that state legislatures with higher levels of conservatism are more likely to invent with respect to anti-abortion policy, which gives credence to the idea that legislatures with greater conservatism are more likely to ignore the fact that a policy has never been tried and support adopting it because they believe it is worth adopting as it advances their worldview. Relatedly, I do not find a statistical association between government ideology and borrowing in anti-abortion policy, which may suggest that the very existence of these policies (in terms of their already having been adopted in another state or other states) makes them more palatable to legislatures that are ideologically moderate compared to policies that have never been tried in another state or other states.

Turning to electoral vulnerability, however, I discover that the finding from chapter 5 is in fact flipped, with electoral vulnerability influencing inventing but having no discernible effect on borrowing. This is a noteworthy result, and my best explanation as to why it could be occurring has to do with the possibility that moral policies—of which abortion policy is a prime example and perhaps *the* prime example (Mooney 1999)—are

2. Finding a conservative policy area to utilize for studying regulatory policy-making first requires us to identify an area that both meets the classification of being conservative and features a substantial amount of regulatory policy adoption. Given that the abortion area is dominated by legislative action as indicated by the work of Kreitzer and Boehmke (2016) and the Guttmacher Institute (2020), an interested researcher would need to find a different area to examine, and in the book's conclusion I outline how state-level policies allowing for hydraulic fracturing (or "fracking") might allow for such an analysis. Given that gathering the data for just the RPS policy area was a multiyear effort, replicating this book's framework in new areas would be an intensive yet fruitful extension of this research.

seen through a lens of "right versus wrong" or "life versus death" (Ryan 2017) and therefore relatively immune from concerns about track record. When an issue is perceived in the stark terms of "good versus evil," whether the nuts and bolts of a programmatic action can be perceived by constituents based on other states' experiences may matter less than the impression that lawmakers are taking a stand on the side of good and against that of evil. In this case, lawmakers may view invention (or *novel* adoption) as a way to show that they are especially committed to taking a stand on the side of good in the moral cause, and electorally vulnerable lawmakers may view such signaling as a valuable way to secure the support of constituents who care about the moral issue. The same lawmakers may believe there is a less of a premium from constituent issue supporters with respect to borrowing, which could explain the lack of a discernible relationship between electoral vulnerability and the borrowing of anti-abortion policy.

This chapter proceeds as follows. I first go over how I transform Kreitzer and Boehmke's data to perform my analyses. I then show empirical results. I follow empirical results with a discussion of why I believe results turned out the way they did. And I end with a discussion of the chapter's potential implications for the study of borrowing moving forward.

Transforming Kreitzer and Boehmke's Data

Since I utilize data from other scholars to perform the analyses in this chapter, I first discuss the nature of the Kreitzer and Boehmke data and then expound upon how I transformed this data for the purposes of examining invention and borrowing in anti-abortion policy.[3] Kreitzer and Boehmke gathered data on the state-level adoption of any of 29 anti-abortion policies and structured their data so that it could be investigated using pooled event history analysis (Boehmke 2009). Their identification of so many distinct anti-abortion policy choices lets me scrutinize when state legislatures invent and borrow within the anti-abortion policy space.

I transform Kreitzer and Boehmke's data using the same procedure and definitions discussed in chapter 3. Invention occurs when a state is the first U.S. state to adopt a particular anti-abortion policy—meaning one of

---

3. When I mention Kreitzer and Boehmke for the remainder of this chapter, I am referring to Kreitzer and Boehmke (2016).

the distinct anti-abortion policies identified by Kreitzer and Boehmke—*or* if a state adopts that policy by the next year after the first state adopted the policy. Borrowing occurs if a state adopts a policy any time after the year in which the initial adopting state adopted the policy.[4] Similar to what was discussed in chapter 3 and implemented in chapters 5 and 6 of this book and elsewhere (Parinandi 2020), the risks of inventing and borrowing a particular anti-abortion policy are disjointed to reflect the idea that inventing and borrowing have mutually exclusive definitions and that policymakers cannot simultaneously entertain the prospect of inventing and borrowing with respect to the same policy.[5] Also similar to the discussion in chapter 3 of this book and implementation in chapters 5 and 6 of this book and elsewhere (Parinandi 2020), states gain the opportunity to invent with respect to any of the anti-abortion policies in the year 1973, which is the year corresponding to when Kreitzer and Boehmke start their dataset. The year 1973 witnessed the Supreme Court's famous *Roe v. Wade* decision legalizing abortion and also witnessed a slew of state policy-making attempting to limit abortion access within the confines of the *Roe v. Wade* decision. Allowing for states to have the opportunity to invent the anti-abortion policies starting in 1973 reflects the idea that the *Roe v. Wade* case ushered in the possibility that states could devise novel ways to limit abortion access given the decision in *Roe*. Analogously, based on my conceptualization of borrowing, I wait until two years after a first state invented a policy before allowing states to borrow with respect to that same policy. The last year in which I analyze data is 2012, which is also the last year included in Kreitzer and Boehmke's models.

Categorizing and transforming the Kreitzer and Boehmke data yields two dependent variables of interest: *legislative invention* and *legislative borrowing*. There are 104 positive occurrences of the legislative inventing vari-

---

4. An example from the Kreitzer and Boehmke data is useful here. In 1996, South Carolina was the first state to adopt a policy requiring a mandatory ultrasound for a patient seeking to obtain an abortion. Any other state adopting the same policy (a mandatory ultrasound requirement) in 1996 or 1997 would have its action classified as invention (as it turns out, no other state adopted the mandatory ultrasound requirement in either 1996 or 1997, making South Carolina the only inventor). Any state adopting the same policy from 1998 onward (there are several, such as Wisconsin in 1998) would have its action classified as borrowing.

5. Building on the same example as in the previous footnote, I am merely stating that a state cannot simultaneously entertain inventing and borrowing the same policy. Applied to the "mandatory ultrasound" example, all states lose the opportunity to invent with respect to this policy by 1998 but gain the opportunity to borrow this policy in 1998.

able (with 18,782 opportunities to invent) and 568 positive occurrences of the legislative borrowing variable (with 26,831 opportunities to borrow).[6] The unit of analysis here is anti-abortion policy-state-year. As with chapter 5, my key independent variables for both dependent variables are *government ideology* and *median incumbent vote share*.[7] In the models pertaining to both dependent variables, I include *all* of the right-hand-side variables utilized in the Kreitzer and Boehmke article. Variables include measurements of "public preferences" toward abortion (including state-level conservative attitudes toward abortion [*Norrander*] as well as state-level *religious adherence* rates);[8] party-related variables including whether a state has a *unified Democratic legislature*, the amount of a state legislature consisting of *female Democrats*, and whether a state has a *Democratic governor*; and a variable related to the whether it is difficult to launch *initiatives* in a state (Kreitzer and Boehmke 2016, 134).

Other variables included in their analysis are the *median income* of a state and the *population* of a state. Kreitzer and Boehmke also include variables corresponding to the influence of time: these include a binary variable capturing whether or not a state is making a decision after the *Webster v. Reproductive Health Services* case of 1989, a linear *year* variable, and a nonlinear *year squared* variable.[9] The authors lastly include a *neighbors* vari-

---

6. If the year 2013 were included in the borrowing data, there would be 620 positive occurrences of borrowing. The number of positive occurrences of invention is unaffected by Kreitzer and Boehmke not including the year 2013 in their analysis, as there are no adoptions in 2013 that either meet the criteria of being the initial adoption of a specific anti-abortion policy in any state across the United States or being within the next calendar year after the initial adoption of a specific anti-abortion policy in any state across the United States.

7. Similar with the other empirical chapters, I substitute mean incumbent vote share for the median incumbent vote share variable and find no change in substantive results. These results are available in table A15 of the appendix. In this table, I use the same model as in table 8 but show the same selected variables for visual appeal. Using the percentage of legislative races in a state's most recent electoral year that had a victory margin of under 10% does not achieve statistical significance with respect to invention or borrowing.

8. "Norrander" refers to Barbara Norrander and Clyde Wilcox's investigation into state conservative attitudes regarding abortion. The Norrander and Wilcox (1999) piece and the attitudes it captures are a central part of Kreitzer and Boehmke's analysis and therefore are also utilized here.

9. I only include the *year* and *year squared* variables in models pertaining to borrowing. This is because the year and year squared variables are perfectly correlated in the invention data, meaning that we cannot simultaneously estimate both variables in predicting invention. In the invention models, I only include the *year* variable. In table A16 of the appendix, I substitute the *year squared* variable for the *year* variable in inventing models and find results unchanged. Here,

able capturing the amount of geographically adjacent states that adopted the same anti-abortion policy. As with earlier chapters in the book, I utilize logistic regression with standard errors clustered by state to investigate legislative inventing and borrowing.

Empirical Results

In table 8, I display empirical results pertaining to legislative inventing and borrowing. Model specifications 1 and 2 correspond to using the variables from Kreitzer and Boehmke as controls but adding government ideology and median incumbent vote share. Model specifications 3 and 4 contain the same variables as in specifications 1 and 2, but here I add additional controls employed in earlier chapters of the book. These additional controls include Berry et al.'s measure of *citizen ideology*, the fraction of anti-abortion policy adoptions that have occurred in *ideologically similar* states to a given state, the fraction of *prior invention* in anti-abortion policy that has occurred in a state (for the invention specification), and the fraction of *prior borrowing* in anti-abortion policy that has occurred in a state (for the borrowing specification). Also for the borrowing specification, I include a *featureyear* variable capturing the number of years that have elapsed since a given anti-abortion policy was first adopted across the states.[10]

A quick glance at table 8[11] reveals that the government ideology variable relates negatively and is statistically significant with respect to invention in both invention model specifications but lacks such a statistically significant

---

I use all of the variables used in invention models in table 8 but show the same selected variables for visual appeal.

10. Similar with earlier parts of the book and with Parinandi (2020), I do not include the featureyear variable with respect to invention since observations drop out of the invention dataset two years after a given anti-abortion policy was first adopted across the U.S. states. The featureyear variable is not bounded in the same way regarding borrowing, meaning that we can see how a fuller range of this variable influences borrowing.

11. As with the previous empirical chapters, I do not include all variables in table 8 for the sake of visual appeal. Specifically, in table 8, I do not show results for variables related to time trends, some socioeconomic factors, and the impact of a court case (*Webster*). Interested readers should consult table A17 of the appendix, where I display results for variables not shown here. In table A18 of the appendix, I account for whether a state allows for lawmaking via direct ballot initiative. Table A18 displays select variables for visual appeal but uses the same models as in tables 8 and A17.

TABLE 8. Ideology and Electoral Vulnerability on Anti-Abortion Legislative Invention and Borrowing (Selected Variables)

Variable	Legislative Invention (1)	Legislative Borrowing (2)	Legislative Invention (3)	Legislative Borrowing (4)
Government Ideology	-0.012*	-0.005	-0.012*	-0.003
	(0.006)	(0.004)	(0.006)	(0.006)
Median Incumbent	-0.011**	0.003	-0.012**	0.003
Legislator Vote Share	(0.005)	(0.003)	(0.006)	(0.003)
Norrander	0.443	0.449	0.501	0.477
	(0.758)	(0.318)	(0.812)	(0.331)
Religious Adherence	1.594	0.965	2.073*	1.107
	(0.978)	(0.675)	(1.080)	(0.692)
Unified Democratic	0.115	-0.132	0.089	-0.155
Legislature	(0.300)	(0.147)	(0.320)	(0.155)
Female Democrats	-1.235	-4.900***	-1.905	-4.702**
	(3.202)	(0.792)	(3.290)	(1.816)
Democratic Governor	-0.116	-0.101	-0.116	-0.144
	(0.339)	(0.146)	(0.345)	(0.196)
Initiatives	0.063	0.070***	0.085	0.072***
	(0.053)	(0.026)	(0.061)	(0.027)
Neighbors	6.632***	2.555***	6.511***	2.562***
	(0.755)	(0.216)	(0.747)	(0.216)
Citizen Ideology			-0.0006	-0.001
			(0.001)	(0.007)
Ideological Similarity			-1.834*	0.805*
			(1.046)	(0.487)
Prior Invention			-8.957	
			(5.540)	
Prior Borrowing				-2.620
				(3.060)
Observations	18,782	26,831	18,782	26,831
	(104)	(568)	(104)	(568)

*** = critical value of 0.01; ** = critical value of 0.05; * = critical value of 0.10

relationship with respect to borrowing in both borrowing model specifications. Figure 10 displays the relationship between government ideology with respect to both dependent variables. The figure utilizes model specifications 3 and 4 (which include more control variables) and sets binary control variables to their most frequently occurring values.

In figure 10, the solid lines pertain to the "main" estimated predicted probabilities of inventing and borrowing while the dashed lines correspond to lower and upper bounds from 95 percent confidence intervals. In the

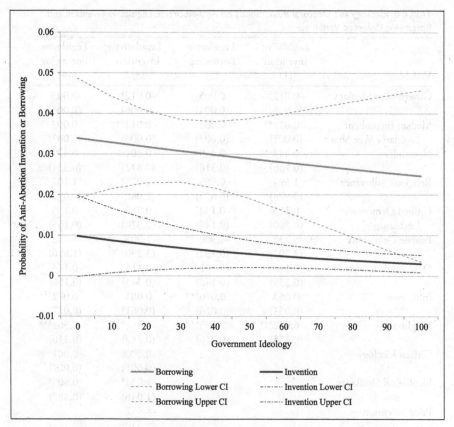

Fig. 10. Comparison of Government Ideology on Anti-Abortion Legislative Invention and Borrowing
Source: Data on abortion policy adoption comes from Kreitzer and Boehmke (2016). Data on government ideology comes from Berry et al. (1998).

figure, notice that the slopes for legislative ideology trend downward with respect to inventing *and* borrowing. This makes sense considering that increased values of the government ideology variable signify greater liberalism, that inventing and borrowing given the Kreitzer and Boehmke data signify adopting anti-abortion policy, and that we should expect increased liberalism to relate negatively with adopting anti-abortion policy regardless of whether that adoption is novel or borrowed. Also notice that the predicted probability for borrowing is higher than the predicted probability for invention. This too makes sense considering that there are many more cases of borrowing than there are of invention (568 versus 104);

when the positive cases of each event are divided by the number of opportunities for each event to occur and then multiplied by 100—568 divided by 26,831 for borrowing and 104 divided by 18,782 for invention—we get positive event probabilities of 2.1% for borrowing and 0.5% for invention. Borrowing is therefore simply more likely, and we should perhaps not be surprised by the higher predicted probability for borrowing compared to invention.

At the same time, notice that the slope of government ideology is steeper with respect to invention than it is with respect to borrowing. This may be difficult to observe in the figure due to scaling differences in the predicted probabilities of invention and borrowing, but the influence of government ideology on invention versus borrowing over the range of the government ideology variable can be calculated from estimated predicted probabilities of invention and borrowing. Over the range of the government ideology variable (as the variable goes from pure conservatism to pure liberalism), the predicted probability of invention decreases from 0.00978 to 0.00296, a decrease of 69.7%. Over the same range of the government ideology variable, the predicted probability of borrowing decreases from 0.03391 to 0.02459, a decrease of 27.4%. The decrease in predicted probability for invention is thus more than double the decrease in predicted probability for borrowing. Ultimately, I find evidence suggesting that state legislatures are more likely to invent anti-abortion policy as they become more conservative in ideological orientation. When this finding is combined with the earlier finding linking greater liberalism in state legislatures to increased invention in RPS, the possibility opens up that increased ideological extremism in *both* directions could drive policy invention. Further, the findings from table 8 and table 3 earlier in the book showing the lack of a statistically significant relationship between government ideology and borrowing (in both the anti-abortion and RPS contexts) suggests that ideological extremism has more explanatory power with respect to invention than it does with respect to borrowing.

Moving on and discussing electoral vulnerability, a glance at table 8 reveals that increased vulnerability makes invention in anti-abortion policy more likely but has no discernible effect on borrowing. Figure 11 displays the influence of electoral vulnerability (as seen through the median incumbent vote share variable) on anti-abortion invention and borrowing. Once again, solid lines pertain to "main" estimated predicted probabilities while dashed lines relate to lower and upper bounds from 95% confidence inter-

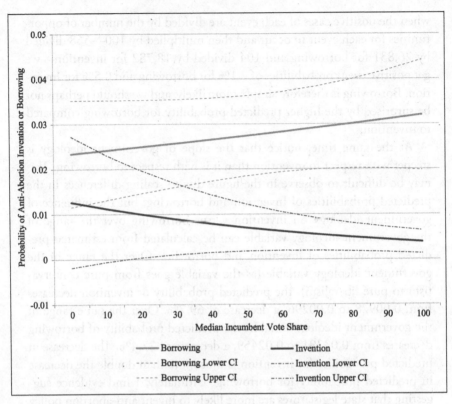

Fig. 11. Comparison of Median Incumbent Vote Share on Anti-Abortion Legislative Invention and Borrowing

Source: Data on abortion policy adoption comes from Kreitzer and Boehmke (2016). Data on electoral vulnerability comes from Klarner et al. (2013).

vals. Also, as with the earlier figure in this chapter, I again utilize model specifications 3 and 4, and I set binary control variables to their most frequently occurring values.

Figure 11 corroborates the directionality of the trends unearthed in table 8. Rising median incumbent vote share (denoting reduced electoral vulnerability) makes anti-abortion invention less likely but increases the probability of anti-abortion borrowing. The divergent directions of slope here are different than in the case of RPS legislation, when the slope of median incumbent vote share traveled in the same direction for invention and borrowing.[12] More generally, returning to the tables displaying

_____

12. It is useful to emphasize that the predicted probability figures display estimated predicted

multivariate regression results and comparing the electoral vulnerability findings from table 3 in chapter 5 to table 8 in this chapter—and specifically pointing to the observation that the median incumbent vote share variable relates significantly to borrowing but not invention for RPS while the median incumbent vote share variable relates significantly to invention but not to borrowing for anti-abortion policy—suggests that the role of electoral vulnerability in fostering invention and borrowing might differ by policy type. I turn next to explaining why results were consistent for government ideology across RPS and anti-abortion policies and why they were different for electoral vulnerability across RPS and anti-abortion policies.

Preliminary Thoughts on Empirical Results

In this section, I provide thoughts as to why empirical results appear the way that they do. The result linking greater governmental conservatism to an increased likelihood of legislative anti-abortion invention suggests that, similar to a liberal policy space (RPS), the adoption of novel policy in a conservative policy space (anti-abortion) is also spearheaded by ideologues. My explanation in the left-leaning RPS space (and in Parinandi 2020) was that ideological extremists not only have the interest needed to learn about novel policy proposals fitting their ideological worldview but also have the zeal to support adopting such proposals in spite of the proposals never having been adopted elsewhere because the extremists think the proposals will advance their view of the world (for the ideologically extreme, in short, the importance of belief can override the importance of evidence in driving support for policy adoption). A similar finding for the anti-abortion area raises the possibility that my earlier explanation is not limited to the left-leaning end of the ideological spectrum but also applies to the right-leaning end.

In the earlier analysis—see table 3—I did not find the same level of

---

probabilities for invention and borrowing for various values of a specified independent variable (government ideology in figure 10 and median incumbent vote share in figure 11) *alongside* other continuous variables (held to their means) in the invention or borrowing models and other binary variables (held to their most frequently occurring values) in the invention or borrowing models. This means that the values of the predicted probability curves take other variables into consideration even if we focus on visualizing specific explanatory variables such as government ideology or median incumbent vote share (Long and Freese 2006; Williams 2011).

statistical support for linking increased government liberalism to increased RPS borrowing that I found when linking increased government liberalism to increased RPS inventing. One possibility that I put forth earlier about the discrepancy is that the existence of evidence might increase the appeal of adoption across a wider ideological range of legislatures than would be likely to support adoption absent evidence. I gave qualitative examples of decidedly nonliberal state legislatures (e.g., Indiana) supporting RPS borrowing and offered that the increased ideological diversity of borrowers vis-à-vis inventors could partly account for a stronger statistical link between rising government liberalism and RPS invention compared to rising RPS borrowing.

Looking at anti-abortion policy and comparing the statistical association between government conservatism (as seen by lower levels of the government ideology variable) and invention versus government conservatism and borrowing in table 8, we see the same dynamic at play as in the RPS case in the sense that government ideology (except here, it is conservatism and not liberalism) has a more pronounced statistical association with invention than it does with borrowing. As was the case with RPS, here, there is anecdotal evidence suggesting that a wider ideological array of states embrace anti-abortion borrowing compared to the ideological array of states embracing anti-abortion invention. If we compare anti-abortion invention and borrowing activity among states that have government ideology scores in the highest one-third of the government ideology score (implying that these states are quite liberal), we see that 21.4% instances of borrowing occur in this grouping of states compared to 15.3% of instances of invention.[13] If we compare anti-abortion invention and borrowing activity among the most liberal states in the United States—those states with government ideology scores between 90 and 100—we see that the percentage of instances of inventing that occur among this group of very liberal states is only 0.9% while the percentage of instances of borrowing occurring among this group is 2.9%.[14] This suggests that anti-abortion

---

13. This percentage comparison takes 2013 into account for borrowing. If we drop 2013 to make the comparison correspond more cleanly to the borrowing data used in the regression analysis, the percentage of instances of borrowing occurring among states with a government ideology score greater than 66.6 increases to 22.1%.

14. If we drop 2013 in the borrowing percentage calculation, the percentage of instances of borrowing that occur among this group of very liberal states is 2.4%. It is important to compare percentages of cases and not raw numbers of cases since instances of anti-abortion borrowing are more numerous than instances of anti-abortion invention.

borrowing is more accessible to an ideologically wider group of states than is anti-abortion inventing.

It is more challenging to explain electoral vulnerability. In chapter 5, I discussed how electoral vulnerability could do a better job of explaining RPS borrowing compared to RPS invention based on the idea of observability. Borrowed policies have observable track records from other states' experimentation, and these track records can be invoked by lawmakers who can tell their constituents that they are trying to replicate policy successes seen elsewhere (Volden 2006; Makse and Volden 2011). Rising electoral vulnerability, I argued, might induce lawmakers to place a greater emphasis on borrowing during adoption based on the idea that the lawmakers might expect increased electoral vulnerability to translate into greater skepticism from voters, thereby meaning that lawmakers can use other states' experiences to try to assuage their own skeptical voters.

In the case of anti-abortion policy, however, electoral vulnerability does a better job of explaining inventing than it does of explaining borrowing. Specifically, the median incumbent vote share variable (as well as the mean incumbent vote share variable if we use that as a substitute) relates significantly and negatively with anti-abortion invention but does not relate significantly with anti-abortion borrowing. My best explanation for why electoral vulnerability increases borrowing with respect to RPS but inventing with respect to anti-abortion policy has to do with the possibility that observability might function differently based on whether a policy area is deemed to be moral or not.

Moral policies (Mooney and Lee 1999) are viewed within the nexus of "good versus evil" and tend to resonate with voters insofar as voters want lawmakers to take a stand on the side of good against evil. Along the same vein, moral issues may elicit starkly dichotomous opinions and deemphasize context in favor of black and white thinking. For instance, an opponent of abortion may look at abortion as a purely binary (right versus wrong) issue and dismiss context related to the issue. That same binary worldview may also cause an abortion opponent to downweight the importance of the track record as a skepticism-reducing tool. This is because the abortion opponent intrinsically believes that adopting policy making abortion harder to obtain (the 29 anti-abortion policies documented by Kreitzer and Boehmke all make abortion harder to obtain) is valuable and does not need to be persuaded by the experiences of other states. In other words, needing the experiences of other states to confirm one's support for a policy suggests that a person is somewhat undecided about that policy. If that person subscribes to a worldview where abortion is evil and should be made more difficult to obtain (as many adherents in the anti-abortion movement do), then that person is unlikely to find other states' experiences to be of much use in influencing their support for anti-abortion policy.[15]

At the same time, the abortion opponent may be especially receptive to the signal that lawmakers are making extraordinary commitments to advancing the cause of restricting abortion. One way lawmakers can send a signal to abortion opponents that they are making extraordinary commitments is by adopting novel anti-abortion policy. Recall from chapter 5 that I discussed how North Dakota's legislature made that state the very first in the country to ban abortion when a fetus is shown to have some type of genetic abnormality (Eligon and Eckholm 2013). Commenting about the legislation, recall that Paul Maloney of North Dakota Right to Life (an anti-abortion organization) remarked that "we have the kind of legislative body that would pass these kinds of pieces of legislation" (quoted in Eligon and Eckholm 2013: A13). The comment from Maloney potentially reflects a view that North Dakota's legislature has the courage to adopt anti-abortion policies that other states had previously not countenanced. And taken more broadly, the comment suggests that abortion opponents may look favorably upon unprecedented attempts to advance their cause.[16]

Lawmakers, for their part, generally know what their constituents want and most likely would know if anti-abortion constituents are receptive to invention as a signal of issue commitment (Fenno 1978). If lawmakers regard anti-abortion opponents to be an integral part of their voter coalition, they may be more likely to attempt to invent anti-abortion policy as a way to cultivate anti-abortion bona fides with anti-abortion-minded constituents.[17] Given that such lawmakers may view invention as a method to

15. It helps to reiterate about what evidence means here: I am talking about a cue that voters may receive about a policy from that policy having been adopted in other states. In the context of moral policy, I am not saying that voters completely dismiss evidence in making opinions about policy. However, to the extent that moral policy is considered in binary terms by the public, voters might be less swayed by evidence compared to a policy area that is less binary in its public perception.

16. This is not to say that abortion opponents dislike anti-abortion borrowing. On the contrary, borrowing in this area also advances the anti-abortion cause. However, unprecedented adoption may be especially valuable to abortion opponents as a signal of the commitment that lawmakers have for pushing the anti-abortion agenda.

17. There is some support for this statement in the empirical results from table 8. Compar-

demonstrate their bona fides to anti-abortion constituents, increased electoral vulnerability may make these lawmakers more likely to signal their commitment to anti-abortion voters through invention. And insofar as invention is a stronger way to signal commitment to anti-abortion voters than is borrowing—which is plausible if we interpret comments from the North Dakota Right to Life organization to mean that this organization is especially proud that the North Dakota legislature has the courage to adopt unprecedented and novel anti-abortion policy—then it is possible that increased electoral vulnerability could exert greater influence on anti-abortion invention compared to anti-abortion borrowing.[18]

This discussion brings us back to the issue of speculating about why electoral vulnerability induces inventing with anti-abortion policy but borrowing with RPS. If anti-abortion policy is more commonly regarded by citizens to be an exemplar of moral policy (and hence evaluated through the binary lens of right versus wrong) than is RPS policy, then it is possible that track record may play a more prominent role with respect to RPS policy adoption compared to anti-abortion policy adoption. There is reason to believe that anti-abortion policy is more commonly regarded as moral (and interpreted as right versus wrong) than is RPS. Anti-abortion policy arguably has a stronger unanimity of purpose than does RPS. While all of the policies in the Kreitzer and Boehmke study seek to explicitly restrict a woman's access to abortion services, there is much less unanimity in terms of how RPS policies advance classic environmental goals like reducing the utilization of fossil fuels and cutting carbon dioxide emissions. The word "renewable" has been defined flexibly by policymakers with states like Michigan, Ohio, Pennsylvania, and West Virginia incorporating coal-

---

ing models 3 and 4, notice that the coefficient value associated with the religious adherence variable is larger (as well as statistically significant) with respect to invention but not to borrowing. Increased religious adherence may correspond with an increased tolerance for anti-abortion policy-making among a state's residents (Kreitzer and Boehmke 2016). The larger (and statistically significant) association between religious adherence and invention (versus borrowing) suggests the possibility that lawmakers may look to invention as a way to signal their bona fides with anti-abortion voters.

18. Recall that this is not to say that these lawmakers do not value borrowing (although I do not find a statistically significant relationship in table 8). It is rather that invention may carry a greater signal of commitment among abortion opponents, leading to the possibility that vulnerable lawmakers desiring anti-abortion support may be especially likely to invent. The different directionality of the slope with respect to borrowing suggests that vulnerable lawmakers (compared to less vulnerable lawmakers) are not as singularly influenced by borrowing.

based resources within their RPS programs. Even when the way in which a state defines renewable energy is less obvious—as when South Dakota includes municipal solid waste within its RPS program—the connection between that state's RPS program and a classic environmental goal such as lowering carbon emissions may still be nebulous: for example, a common way to convert municipal solid waste into energy involves burning it, which may actually increase carbon emissions compared to using fossil fuels such as natural gas (Zero Waste Europe 2019).

I bring up the above example because it shows that RPS policy has a greater diversity of purpose than does anti-abortion policy. This is to say, RPS policy elicits a wider range of objectives about what that policy will programmatically do compared to anti-abortion policy. This wider range of objectives itself matters because it suggests that proponents of RPS policy are less binary in their thinking about RPS than are anti-abortion proponents regarding abortion. The idea here is that binary thinking about an issue—and remember that a hallmark of a moral issue is that it tends to encourage binary thinking about that issue—may lead to narrow views about the kinds of objectives that should be pursued when policy is crafted to deal with that issue. In contrast, if thinking about an issue is more diverse, there may be a concomitant diversity of objectives pursued in policy-making dealing with that issue.[19] Given that the RPS area exhibits a greater diversity of objectives than does anti-abortion policy, and given that less diversity of objectives may be associated with binary conceptualization of an issue (which again is more likely in moral policy), then the designation of an area as moral may be more appropriate with anti-abortion policy rather than with RPS. There is public opinion data that supports the idea that abortion is more widely regarded as a moral issue compared to renewable energy. Research from Hess et al. (2016) reveals that the attitudes of Americans are relatively open regarding renewable energy; at the same time, work from Bowman and Marisco (2014) argues that the attitudes of Americans concerning abortion have largely not changed since the *Roe v. Wade* decision. The stickiness of attitudes regarding abor-

---

19. Moral perception of an issue might lead to narrow views about policy objectives because the stark conceptualization of the issue as right versus wrong diminishes the possibility that objectives not directly aligned with the mission of elevating right over wrong (in the eyes of abortion opponents, this means restricting abortion access) are pursued in the course of making policy. On an issue that is seen in less moral terms, there may be less fixation on right versus wrong, thereby allowing for a greater diversity of objectives in policy-making dealing with that issue.

tion combined with the more flexible and open-ended nature of attitudes regarding renewable energy suggests that the public may be more receptive to learning about renewable energy policy-making and consequently more swayable by evidence, thereby giving added credence to the claim that observability matters more for renewable energy compared to abortion.

Highlighting how anti-abortion may be considered to be more of a moral issue area than RPS allows us to return to the discussion of track record and how it might matter differentially with regard to how electoral vulnerability influences adoption in RPS versus anti-abortion policy. In a less moral issue area such as RPS, the public may lack concrete opinions about whether policy-making is right or wrong, which opens up the possibility that the public is persuadable using evidence. Given that this is a policy area where the public is receptive to evidence, and given that increased electoral vulnerability might create a view among lawmakers that the public is skeptical, increased electoral vulnerability may increase the likelihood of borrowing, as lawmakers hope to assuage the public by claiming that they are replicating experiments tried elsewhere. In a more moral issue area such as anti-abortion, however, the public may be more likely to have ex-ante opinions of right versus wrong and be less amenable to persuasion through evidence. Given that this is a policy area where the public is less receptive to evidence, the way that lawmakers might deal with electoral vulnerability is not to invoke evidence but rather to double down on moral appeals in hopes of convincing moral-issue-inclined members of the public that the lawmakers are committed to advancing the moral cause by adopting unprecedented policy that moves the moral cause forward.[20]

There are some clarification issues I would like to address. First, the observation that lawmakers operating under increased electoral vulnerability are more likely to invent to signal commitment to anti-abortion voters does not mean that such behavior is entirely absent with respect to RPS policy. In table 3 in chapter 5, the median incumbent vote share is negatively related to RPS invention, suggesting that there is some effort to demonstrate commitment to constituents that especially desire an RPS.

---

20. An assumption here is that lawmakers do not try to jeopardize their electoral chances by making the policy adoption decisions that they do. That is, lawmakers will not advocate borrowing in RPS or inventing in anti-abortion if they think doing either will hurt their electoral chances. What might change across the two policy areas is the role that evidence potentially plays in assuaging interested members of the public, leading to a situation where evidence is emphasized in RPS and less emphasized in anti-abortion policy.

However, the significance of the median incumbent vote share variable with respect to anti-abortion invention but not RPS invention suggests that electoral vulnerability explains anti-abortion invention better than it does RPS invention. One reason why this might be the case, to use the logic I have put forth in this chapter, is that the relative unanimity of objectives surrounding anti-abortion policy makes it more likely that abortion opponents will believe that an unprecedented policy will move their cause forward (with the requisite verdict, of course, that lawmakers are displaying courage in a novel way). Less unanimity of objective in RPS suggests that lawmakers would get less of a bump from dedicated environmentalists with respect to RPS than lawmakers would receive from dedicated abortion opponents with respect to anti-abortion policy, which in turn might explain why the median incumbent vote share variable is linked to anti-abortion invention but not RPS invention.[21]

A second clarification pertains to the relationship between electoral vulnerability and anti-abortion borrowing. My explanation for why I could not find a significant link between the median incumbent vote share variable and anti-abortion borrowing hinged on the idea that electoral vulnerability increased borrowing insofar as lawmakers relied on the track record contained in borrowed policies as a form of evidence to use with constituents. If constituents are willing to overlook evidence, which is possible in a policy area such as anti-abortion that is interpreted through the lens of right and wrong (Mooney and Lee 1995; Mooney 1999), then much of the value of invoking evidence to voters diminishes for lawmakers.

One potential question regarding the above explanation pertains to how it can coexist with the finding that a wider ideological group of lawmakers are receptive to anti-abortion borrowing as opposed to anti-abortion invention. Given that the difference between invention and borrowing is the existence of a track record, the observation that borrowing is more ideologically widespread than invention suggests that some ideologically nonconservative lawmakers may be influenced by an anti-abortion policy's

---

21. An illustration might help here. In 2004, Pennsylvania created an RPS and invented by adding coal-based sources to its RPS program. If someone were a dedicated environmentalist in Pennsylvania, how would they evaluate their state's invention? It is not likely that they would celebrating the inclusion of coal. Moreover, the inclusion itself may dampen enthusiasm among dedicated environmentalists about whether RPS invention will generally advance their cause. This same dampening seems unlikely in the anti-abortion space, where there is not a single policy that makes abortion easier to obtain or more available.

track record. Is it possible that lawmakers might be receptive to evidence even when borrowing has not been found to be statistically significant in the case of electoral vulnerability?

I think the answer is yes. The observation that anti-abortion borrowing occurs across ideologically diverse legislatures means that anti-abortion policy passes various stages of the legislative process across these ideologically diverse states. What this means as we move away from purely conservative states is that nonconservative lawmakers are more likely to play gatekeeping roles (e.g., committee chairs or cochairs) in the various rounds of review that transpire in the course of a bill becoming a law. In this more ideologically diverse environment, common "best practice" policies should be more likely to survive different stages of the legislative process, suggesting that evidence might also play a macro-level role in facilitating anti-abortion borrowing. The observation that median incumbent vote share does not appear to significantly influence borrowing (based on the idea that constituents may care less about evidence in morality policy) does not preclude the possibility that the existence of a track record might matter in getting a policy with a conservative flavor (anti-abortion policy) to advance through different rounds of legislative review with different (and potentially ideologically diverse) legislators. This is to say, "common practices" (which by definition have been adopted across different states) might be fortuitously positioned to be adopted across ideologically diverse legislatures even if electoral vulnerability is not statistically linked to anti-abortion borrowing.

Conclusion

In this chapter, I moved away from the RPS policy area and analyzed a canonical conservative policy area—anti-abortion policy—to investigate how the theory explicated in chapter 5 performs when applied in the conservative direction. In doing this, I utilized legislative anti-abortion adoption data from Kreitzer and Boehmke (2016), transformed this data to comport with my operationalization of invention and borrowing, evaluated this data using pertinent variables in conjunction with Kreitzer and Boehmke's right-hand-side variables, and offered preliminary thoughts about results.

The result with respect to government ideology operates in the same way as in the RPS case except with the anticipated expectation that it is greater conservatism in legislatures that leads to more anti-abortion inventing. This result, when considered alongside the finding linking greater liberalism in legislatures to more RPS inventing, suggests that ideologues spearhead novel policy adoption in policy areas that fit within their ideological worldviews. The lack of a significant relationship between government ideology and *both* RPS borrowing and anti-abortion borrowing suggests that borrowing in these policy areas is more accessible across ideologically diverse legislatures than is inventing.

Switching to electoral vulnerability, however, we see different results across the policy areas: specifically, the median incumbent vote share variable relates significantly with RPS borrowing but not RPS inventing, and the same variable relates significantly with anti-abortion inventing but not anti-abortion borrowing. In explaining this discrepancy, I draw upon the idea that moral policies are seen by much of the public through a binary lens, which diminishes the receptiveness that the public might have in using other states' adoption cues to persuade it about anti-abortion policy. The same binary lens might explain the link between electoral vulnerability and anti-abortion inventing, as lawmakers try to signal their commitment to constituents who care about moral policy. This result suggests that observability might function differently across moral and nonmoral policy areas. Earlier in this book, I described observability as the ease with which constituents can perceive benefits associated with a policy (with the implication that it also describes the ease with which lawmakers can sell a policy to constituents), and I suggested that lawmakers turn to RPS borrowing as a way to make policy-making in this area observable to constituents. The binary nature of moral policy, however, suggests that moral policy-making can be observable to constituents absent borrowing; constituents who value action with respect to moral policy may in fact be more receptive to invention insofar as inventing is a stronger signal of commitment.

One potential avenue for future inquiry corresponds with applying this framework to other moral policy areas, including liberal manifestations of abortion policy.[22] Another extension involves decomposing this analysis across different stages of the legislative process; I have offered a macro-level

---

22. The Guttmacher Institute, perhaps the leading repository of abortion-related policy information, heavily places its emphasis on state laws that restrict abortion. One could search states' legislative archives for policies that enhance abortion access and perform the same analysis as was done in this chapter on those collected policies.

analysis here, but a micro-level legislator-centered investigation (where the individual legislator rather than the state legislature is the unit of analysis) can pinpoint how this process occurs at the individual level. An added benefit of the individual analysis is that it would allow us to ascertain how the influences of ideology and electoral vulnerability drive legislator behavior across the various stages of the legislative process (e.g., sponsorship, cosponsorship, committee deliberation, and floor voting). While I analyze invention and borrowing through adoption, adoption is preceded by other important legislative actions, and studying these earlier actions can shed light on the chronology of invention and borrowing. A third possibility motivated by the abortion case involves pushing on the concept that morality policy is interpreted through the binary lens of right and wrong. Although abortion may plausibly still be perceived in this binary manner, other policies that were traditionally considered to be moral (for example, gambling) have become widespread and may have ostensibly lost their moral connotation. It would be fascinating to evaluate whether the electoral dynamics surrounding an issue like gambling change as the issue loses its moral connotation.[23] Taken alongside the rest of the book, the findings from this chapter can help augment a future agenda on invention and borrowing. In the book's conclusion, I elaborate on that agenda in greater detail.

---

23. The process here would involve gathering all state-level gambling laws, identifying state-level gambling subpolicies, categorizing state-level gambling subpolicies as invention or borrowing, and replicating the analytical procedure utilized in this book.

CHAPTER 9

Conclusion

In recent years, the dysfunction of the federal government in terms of being able to address myriad policy challenges has brought renewed focus to the U.S. states as potential vehicles for tackling significant environmental, social, political, and economic problems. The enthusiasm showered upon the states as possible problem solvers partly emanates from a view perhaps best espoused by U.S. Supreme Court Justice Louis Brandeis, when he identified the states as incubators of novel policy. Federalism, in this view, provides a reservoir for addressing policy challenges where the states take matters into their own hands and produce inventive policies that could serve as blueprints for later policy-making. Thus, even if the federal government has been or is unable to move policy forward in a particular area, the states could pick up the slack and compensate for federal-level inability.

A manifestation of federal-level inability and state ability to take matters into their own hands has been electricity-related renewable energy policy, where the states have acted in the absence of federal policy-making and devised their own renewable portfolio policies to spur renewable energy development. Looking at state policy adoption with respect to RPS represents a valuable way to learn about when states would actually fill the void of federal inaction and promulgate novel policy in an area where the United States arguably sorely needs such policy. Moreover, focusing on how novel policy adoption potentially has different motivators across different institutional settings is valuable insofar as different institutional actors have played key roles in adopting RPS policies throughout the U.S. states. This book unpacks novel RPS adoption by institutional actor and thereby provides observers of American green energy policy with a roadmap of where they might expect novel within-U.S. renewable energy policy developments to occur. At the same time, the book advances a way in which the topic of novel state-level policy adoption identified by Brandeis can be investigated systematically, thereby allowing for a richer understanding of *when* states in the American federal system might push for inventive policy solutions in the course of taking policy matters into their own hands.

In the next few pages, I describe the book's contributions and offer potential lessons to observers of renewable energy policy, state politics, and American federalism. The lessons serve as a guidepost to inform observers, practitioners, and scholars about how institutional venue matters for the propagation of novel renewable energy policy, and the lessons may provide clues and an analytical framework for exploring the propagation of other novel policy-making across federal systems featuring significant state-level (or, in the language of comparative political science, significant subnational) policy autonomy. I follow up a discussion of the book's contributions and potential lessons with a treatment of how the book's conceptual and empirical advances can spark a much broader investigation into the mechanics of novel state-level policy-making. The sparking of this broader investigation could help shape political science and public policy research on policy adoption in the U.S. states as well as in other federal contexts. I now turn to elaborating about the book's contributions in the order in which they appear throughout the book.

Invention Can Be Identified and Operationalized

For over a half century, political science has utilized Jack Walker's definition of innovation and has left aside the issue of when a state chooses to adopt policy that is novel across the system of all states rather than just being novel to that state itself (Walker 1969; Parinandi 2020; Mooney 2020). While the use of Walker's definition has led to an amassing of knowledge into when states adopt policies that they previously did not have, it has sidestepped the exploration of Brandeis's original claim that a given state may adopt policy that is novel across the universe of states; and while scholars (Kousser 2005; Karch 2007; Berry and Berry 2018) have made note of this omission, research has not systematically interrogated state-level novel policy adoption.

One of the major contributions of this book is that I identify a way to systematically identify and analyze novel policy adoption across the states and thereby help to align research on adoption with the famous opinion that Brandeis authored nearly a century ago. My emphasis on identifying invention or novel adoption at the subpolicy or policy feature level is also helpful, as it permits the exploration of novel policy-making *within* a policy area (much policy adoption scholarship has treated all adoptions of a policy area—such as lottery systems—as if they are equivalent in terms of content); and my conceptualization of how invention and borrowing can be distinguished from each other comports with rich literature on diffusion (Volden, Ting, and Carpenter 2008), which assumes that some amount of time must pass before states can observe the novel policy actions of other states.

Taken one step further, the integration of the concepts of invention and borrowing with a prevailing way in which leading scholarship (Boehmke 2009; Boushey 2016) has modeled adoption within a policy area—pooled event history analysis—means that my framework for examining concepts of invention and borrowing is not disconnected from empirical modeling choices used in adoption scholarship writ large. This is important, as it suggests that scholars of policy adoption may be able to integrate the concepts of invention and borrowing in their own work in the future. Ultimately, this book gives form to the concept of invention and shows how it can be studied using accessible tools common to political science.

Invention Can Be Analyzed by Institutional Actor

Besides illuminating a way to identify and operationalize invention for analysis, the book also shows how invention can be investigated by institutional actor or venue. This is particularly important as the leading institutions of government vary in their responsibilities and operation and resultantly vary in when they adopt novel policy. Ignoring that different institutional actors play a role in adopting novel policy would lead to a dissatisfactory exploration into the inventive capacity of the U.S. states that not only would neglect the idea foundational to political science that institutions with different responsibilities might behave differently from one another (March and Olsen 2011) and would also neglect the fact that legislatures *and* regulatory agencies are both key foci of state-level policy-making. The institution-specific investigation of RPS invention offered in this book sheds light on ways in which institutional mission influences invention and also represents an invitation for researchers and scholars in the field to learn more about how institutional differences can impact policy adoption, an objective that I believe will only become more pressing in the future as many look to regulatory or technocratic governance to bypass legislative decision-making (Alessina and Tabellini 2008).

Ideology Explains Invention More Than Borrowing in Legislative RPS Adoption

One of the mysteries about novel policy adoption centers on the extent to which ideology influences legislatures (the chief lawmaking branch) to invent policy: Is novel policy-making the province of committed ideologues who believe in the worth of advancing policy into proverbially uncharted territory, or is there a less clear role for ideology? The analysis of RPS adoption, a left-leaning area (Potrafke 2010), provides a window into addressing this question from the liberal direction.[1] My finding linking increased liberalism to increased RPS invention suggests that at least for renewable energy policy, it is the ideologues (in this case, liberals) who push for policy to be advanced into uncharted territory and who are more likely to believe that such action is worthwhile even though analogues or templates do not exist for doing so. My finding showing the lack of a clear connection between increased liberalism and RPS borrowing suggest that an ideologically diverse grouping of state legislatures is willing to embrace a policy once it has been tested by a pioneering state.

These findings have substantial implications for how we understand novel policy adoption in renewable energy policy. Assuming that observers want more invention and pioneering policy-making in the area of renewables, then ideological extremism in the liberal direction is beneficial insofar as it leads to novel policies entering the menu of renewable portfolio policies employed across the system of states. The fact that ideology is less influential in explaining borrowing is also beneficial in that RPS policy

---

1. I would like to reiterate that even though a number of conservative-leaning states (for example, South Dakota, Utah, and Indiana) adopted RPS policies, the idea of regulating energy to incentivize renewable energy development comports with a liberal worldview.

adoption is not limited to ideologues: less liberal states are willing to adopt RPS policy as long as it has been tried elsewhere, and this augurs well for the spread or diffusion of RPS policy-making across an ideologically heterogeneous breadth of states.[2] To sum up the findings harkening back to Brandeis's terminology, in the area of RPS, "courageous" states are those characterized by ideological liberalism while other states benefit from the courage of the former group. This courage is presumably a normative good if one supports RPS policy, but it is a normative bad—note that recklessness is the antonym of courage—if one opposes such policy.

Electoral Vulnerability Explains Borrowing More Than Inventing in Legislative RPS Adoption

Another mystery pertains to how electoral vulnerability might influence a legislature's willingness to invent RPS policy. Legislative members are subject to reelection, meaning that we can see how variation in electoral vulnerability impacts RPS invention. One might think that increased electoral vulnerability motivates legislatures to attempt a "Hail Mary pass," to use a metaphor from American football, and invent in an effort to bolster their electoral fortunes. On the flip side, one might think that increased electoral vulnerability motivates legislatures to refrain from adopting novel and untested policy. I ultimately do not find a clear connection between electoral vulnerability and legislative RPS invention. However, I do find a connection between rising electoral vulnerability and legislative RPS borrowing, which I ascribe to the possibility that lawmakers feel a need to tell voters whom they believe are skeptical that they are pursuing policy efforts seen elsewhere (Makse and Volden 2011). These findings have implications for our knowledge of RPS policy adoption. If one believes that voters should not be exposed to novel policy adoption as a result of electoral considerations (touching upon the idea again that recklessness is the antonym of courage), then it is perhaps reassuring that there is no connection between electoral vulnerability and RPS invention. Along this vein, it is perhaps also reassuring that electoral considerations push lawmakers to

---

2. If the grouping of states that borrowed were identical to the grouping of states that invented, then there arguably may be no states that would benefit from free riding off of invention. Thus, the fact that a more ideologically diverse grouping of states borrows gives some credence to Brandeis's argument about the virtue of giving states policy autonomy.

adopt policies that have already been tested elsewhere. The findings are perhaps disappointing if one believes that electoral considerations should influence novel RPS adoption; however, results from the anti-abortion chapter should give us pause in terms of proclaiming that we can universally predict how electoral vulnerability influences invention compared to borrowing across all policy areas. The idea that electoral vulnerability could differentially impact legislative RPS invention and borrowing adds additional intrigue and inspiration to the book's study of RPS policy adoption by public utilities commissions. While members of state legislatures generally face electoral concerns, the universe of state public utilities commissions is divided between states where commissioners face accountability from voters through direct election and states where commissioners are not elected, thereby allowing us to see whether the absence or presence of direct election impacts RPS invention.

Public Utilities Commissions Are Mindful of Electric Utility Companies When Deciding to Invent RPS Policy

The participation of several state public utilities commissions in inventing RPS policy begs the question of when public utilities commissions are more willing to do so. One clear theme that emerges from this study is that public utilities commissions are not likely to serve as a substitute for legislative actors in advancing RPS. Not only have public utilities commissions invented much less than legislatures, but invention by public utilities commissions is heavily impacted by fears of pushback from entrenched electric utility companies. These fears not only motivate public utilities commissions to invent RPS when they perceive that they may face less pushback from entrenched electric utility companies (which I show occurs under deregulation), but to the extent that public utilities commissioners act more like legislators and less like regulators when they are elected instead of appointed (remember that direct election relates positively with both RPS invention and borrowing), legislative institutions will probably continue to assume the mantle regarding the promulgation of RPS policy. Given that deregulation has only occurred in less than half of the states and given that deregulation has other issues—for example, a new debate is brewing as to whether the scope of deregulation in Texas is responsible for the massive electricity outages that residents of the state experienced in February 2021 (Blunt and Gold 2021)—it is perhaps unrealistic to advocate for deregulation as a way to spur invention. Ultimately, while important, the regulatory pathway is secondary to the legislative one in producing RPS invention.

Anti-Abortion Invention Is Also Driven by Ideologues, and It May Be Spurred by Electoral Vulnerability

The link between ideological extremism and legislative invention is not just limited to novel policy adoption in RPS. To inquire about whether policy in an overtly conservative direction follows similar contours and to rule out the possibility that invention itself is purely a liberal phenomenon—it may be the case that invention may have liberal origins due to liberals believing in the role of government to solve problems through policy formulation—I investigate invention in the realm of anti-abortion policy. The anti-abortion area is desirable to study since it is legislatively driven; data on adoption has been gathered at the subpolicy or policy feature level by the authors of another paper (Kreitzer and Boehmke 2016), meaning that I do not need to go through the process of gathering data at this level of granularity; and the area has featured minimal federal intervention in the states short of explicitly prohibiting the states from banning abortion outright (Kreitzer and Boehmke 2016; Ziegler 2020). The anti-abortion area thus presents a nice corollary to legislative RPS invention, which also had adoption data gathered at a subpolicy or policy feature level of granularity and featured minimal federal intervention.

Study of legislative anti-abortion policy invention reveals that ideologues also drive conservative policy invention. This is important in that it suggests that liberals and conservatives, to the extent that they like their own policy initiatives and dislike those of the other side, may want to keep power for themselves and block the other side from gaining it so that they can maximize their own novel policy production but limit that of the other side. Interestingly, though, even on the conservative side, an ideologically more heterogeneous group of legislatures appears to borrow compared to the group inventing, suggesting again that ideologically driven inventions can become acceptable to a broader audience of legislatures. Turning to electoral vulnerability, a fascinating finding is that vulnerability increases the likelihood of anti-abortion inventing: I ascribe this to the possibility that electoral vulnerability may work differently with respect to moral policy (of which anti-abortion is arguably a better exemplar than RPS), and an implication of this is that future work should perhaps systematically address how electoral vulnerability influences invention across moral and potentially less moral policies (I discuss this issue further in the second major section of the conclusion). This anti-abortion chapter ultimately serves as a bridge between the RPS-centric emphasis of this book and the birth of a broader research agenda that could utilize the framework I have created here to more generally investigate state-level invention. Additionally, the finding gleaned from this chapter showing that ideologues also partake in conservative invention could serve as a catalyst to embark on the arduous processes of generalizing this framework across a broad swath of areas as well as incorporating moderate policy areas to study (I discuss how these endeavors could be tackled later in this chapter).

Final Thoughts

In this book, I try to advance the fields of state politics and public policy by moving the conversation on policy adoption from an arguably five-decade focus on diffusion and toward the topic identified by Brandeis about when a state would choose to invent and adopt novel policy. The area that I explore in the bulk of this book, RPS, pertains to one of the great energy and environmental policy challenges of our time. Moreover, the fact that the federal government has largely passed the buck on this area to the individual states suggests that tracing state-level novel policy adoption is particularly important, since the federal government has not shown itself to be a reliable substitute venue for RPS invention. By highlighting when RPS invention occurs and structuring my investigation to focus on the state-level institutions (here, legislatures and public utilities commissions) most responsible for RPS policy adoption, I provide students, scholars, and practitioners with a guide to where they can expect advances in American renewable energy policy to arise. The addition of an analysis on anti-abortion policy invention in chapter 8 not only opens up the possibility that some of the theoretical drivers explored with respect to RPS have resonance in other policy areas, but this addition also serves as the salvo for a broader and potentially valuable foray into the dynamics of state invention more generally. In the next section, I identify a host of questions (as well as potential strategies for addressing those questions) that could comprise the foundation for an entire research agenda on state policy invention, the fruition of which would enrich our knowledge about the problem solving capacity of American federalism.

Toward Building a Broader Research Agenda around State Policy Invention

Insofar as policymakers, scholars, and the public will continue to look to the individual states to serve as substitutes for federal-level dysfunction, it is crucial for us to learn more about the broad inventive capacity of the American states. Given the widespread feeling that federal dysfunction shows no sign of abating any time soon, the time to shed more light on Brandeis's prophetic opinion is now.[3] In the pages that follow, I elaborate on how spillover projects that either use or are based on the framework developed here can deepen our knowledge of state policy invention and act as a springboard for future practitioners and scholars of American politics, public policy, and state politics and policy to conceptualize and weigh novel state-based policy solutions. The same spillover projects could also ultimately help usher in a new generation of state policy-making related research.

(I) Extending My Framework across Diverse Policy Areas

In the book, I studied RPS policy adoption for a number of solid reasons: it deals with an important issue where federal action has largely been lacking; it features state-level policy adoption, allowing for the analysis of invention put forth in this book; and it features variation in invention by institution, allowing for the analysis of legislative and regulatory invention. The gathering, coding, and processing of the RPS data was a painstaking endeavor

---

3. In an interview of former U.S. House Speaker John Boehner in *Politico*, journalist Tim Alberta describes a "stark divide" in Washington "between longtime pols like Boehner and Biden who yearn for a more amicable time, and newcomers who view the bitter acrimony of the Bush and Obama years as normal" (Alberta 2017). Given that younger members of the federal government have been acculturated in more acrimonious times, federal-level dysfunction may not end in the near future.

and took close to half a decade to accomplish. I was able to integrate the anti-abortion data from Kreitzer and Boehmke (2016) only because this data was already in subpolicy form, had already been identified as being legislative in nature (allowing me to use this data to analyze legislative invention), and was seen as emblematic of the states devising their own solutions given a lack of federal clarity (allowing me to continue along the path of analyzing how the states invent when they take policy-making into their hands).[4]

One may wish to extend the framework devised here across a greater diversity of policy areas, and such an extension is a worthwhile effort. A group of prominent diffusion scholars recently compiled a massive dataset called the "State Policy Innovation and Diffusion," or "SPID" dataset (Boehmke et al. 2018). SPID encompasses adoption data on 728 policies adopted by the states over more than a century of time. Applying my framework to SPID would help to establish general patterns (across a tremendous diversity of areas) of invention. However, there are several processing steps that need to be accomplished before such an analysis can occur. Adoption data in SPID that is gathered at the policy level would have to be gathered at the policy feature or subpolicy level so that we could identify invention and borrowing within each of the policies comprising the SPID dataset. Then, in order to evaluate legislative or regulatory invention using this massive dataset, lawmaking documents for each instance of adoption for the 728 policies would have to be gathered so we can identify what institution is behind a given adoption. Information about which institutions are responsible for the adoptions in SPID are not currently available, would be labor intensive to acquire, and would represent a major breakthrough that would facilitate the use of my framework with the SPID data. If one wants to extend the number of areas but preserve the focus on state invention given a lack of federal intervention, one would need to find and take out policies from SPID that featured federal intervention. Finally, after these steps have been completed, instances of invention and borrowing have been identified and coded as such, and pooled event history data structures have been created for legislative and regulatory invention, the invention framework I advance here can be used in conjunction with

---

4. While the U.S. Supreme Court outlawed the unconditional denial of abortion in *Roe v. Wade*, it gave the states tremendous latitude to set their own access policies, thereby letting the states take policy-making matters into their own hands. As of 2022, the Supreme Court, of course, has given the states the ability to ban abortion as they see fit.

SPID.[5] Extending the framework developed here through using SPID represents a potentially large advance for the field of state politics and is a natural follow-up to this project.

(II) Extending the Analysis to Incorporate Changes in Federal-Level Intervention

A major motivator for this project and, frankly, for the use of RPS as an area of study, is that state governments can take matters into their own hands given federal inaction or dysfunction and adopt novel solutions to pressing challenges. RPS is arguably not the only area where the federal government has left it to the states to devise their own solutions to challenges. Historically, one could look at state policy experimentation in the 1950s and 1960s prior to the passage of the federal Clean Air Act or the creation of the Environmental Protection Agency (this state experimentation served as a major inspiration for federal clean air policy-making). In the present, one could look at the spate of state policy experimentation with respect to recreational marijuana legalization, which has arguably featured a lack of federal intervention insofar as the federal government has chosen not to enforce its laws against recreational marijuana use in states that have undergone legalization. State-level experimentation with stay-at-home or lockdown policy-making in the early stages of the COVID-19 pandemic also potentially fits the bill, as the federal government neglected to coordinate a policy response across the states (Kettl 2020). Finally, persistent federal dysfunction (Binder 2015) may make the occurrence of letting states handle their own policy-making more likely. Thus, the topic of investigating state policy-making when the federal government does not intervene is not limited to RPS but extends to other pressing areas where the states represent the forefront of policy advancement within the American federal system.[6]

But what happens to the state-level capacity to invent when the federal

---

5. Analogous steps obviously apply for using SPID to analyze legislative and regulatory borrowing.

6. Indeed, upon locating and gathering policy feature level adoption data in these areas as well as identifying which institutions are responsible for those adoptions, researchers can explore state-level invention and borrowing in these other important areas.

government actually intervenes in state-level policy-making? An important view of federalism in the middle of the twentieth century was the idea that the federal government and states would work together in a cooperative fashion to address significant problems (Grodzins 1960; Peterson 1995). While the vision of federal-state cooperation receded at first due to the rise of a pro-decentralization "New Federalism" governing philosophy in the 1980s (Peterson 1995) and has suffered more recently due to federal dysfunction (for example, Appelbaum 2015), the dream of the federal and state governments working together remains alluring and may gain steam in the near future. In this vein, understanding how federal involvement may influence state-level invention is key to preparing for a possible world where the federal government plays a larger role in coordinating policy-making with state governments.

The framework developed in this book can be utilized to advance our knowledge of how federal intervention potentially impacts state-level invention. One way to work toward this goal would be to transform the SPID data as outlined earlier, identify variables that could map onto federal intervention for policy areas that are characterized as having federal intervention (for example, using state-level air pollution policy as a guide, one could capture and incorporate the number of mandates issued by the federal Environmental Protection Agency governing toxic gases), and include variables capturing such federal intervention in the analysis of state policy-making. Although the Obama-era Clean Power Plan was devised after the conclusion of the time period of this study, and although the Clean Power Plan was not enacted, if it were enacted, researchers could take its stipulations and add them to future studies of state-level electricity policy adoption to decipher how the design of federal intervention influences the inventive promise of the states as proffered by Brandeis. To use a different example, one could apply my framework to exploring state-level invention and borrowing in welfare policy before and after the 1996 federal law (Personal Responsibility and Work Opportunity Reconciliation Act) transforming welfare to see how the federal law potentially changed state-level invention and borrowing behavior (Volden 2002a; Volden 2002b). In sum, investigating how federal intervention might influence state invention and borrowing may grow in importance if a philosophy of cooperative federalism reemerges between the federal government and the states.

(III) Tracing How State Inventions Influence Federal Policy Adoption

The extension just discussed dealt with using the framework that I have devised to investigate state invention in policy areas where the federal government actively intervenes in state policy-making. However, my project can also stimulate research into how inventions by state governments influence later federal-level policy-making. Work by Bulman-Pozen (2014) and Orren and Skowronek (2017) suggests that state-level inventions inform federal policy-making, and findings from this project can be harnessed to further explore this phenomenon.[7] Federal-level attempts to meaningfully intervene in setting renewable energy development imperatives in state-specific electricity sectors, whether in the form of the Clean Power Plan or some version of the Green New Deal, have failed to be successfully adopted. Should they ultimately be adopted in some form—which is possible given Democratic control of Congress and the arrival of the Biden administration—we would have a golden opportunity to study how state inventions impact later federal policy-making. If some version of the Clean Power Plan or Green New Deal were to be adopted, we could identify feature-level components of this policy-making, trace whether any of these feature-level components were previously invented by state governments as part of their RPS policy-making, and then evaluate which states are the ones that are most likely to be followed by the federal government. This extension both complements the work of Bulman-Pozen and Orren and Skowronek and addresses the timely and important issue of how state-level experimentation can eventually shape national policy.

---

7. Bulman-Pozen (2014) argues that the federal-state distinction is largely becoming synonymous with a Democratic-Republican divide predicated upon which party is in control of the states versus the federal government, which implies that the products of state invention could be taken up by federal-level co-ideologues of the inventing state governments to form the basis of those federal officials' policy proposals. Orren and Skowronek's (2017) article also emphasizes that state invention functions as an important way through which the states try to guide federal policymakers should the federal government try to enact policy in the same policy area as the states.

(IV) Extending the Analysis to Study Ideologically "Moderate" Policy Areas

The study of left-leaning policy (RPS) and, to a lesser extent, right-leaning policy (anti-abortion) has been useful insofar as it shows that ideological extremism can drive inventing in ideologically congruous policy areas among legislatures. If one agrees with these inventions and wants them to occur and be introduced to the corpus of state policy experimentation, then the finding perhaps tempers some of the negative reputation that ideological extremism has received in contemporary American politics. However, observers might wonder what ideologically "moderate" invention looks like and whether there are areas or issues where ideologically moderate legislatures take the lead in adopting novel policy. The framework that I have advanced in this book can be extended to incorporate potentially moderate policy areas. The strategy that I would advocate for pursuing this extension would be to transform the SPID data along the lines indicated in the first extension (identify subpolicies for each of policies in that dataset; find out which institution adopted which subpolicy so that we can appropriately analyze invention by institutional actor; and code instances of invention along with transforming data to allow for pooled event history analysis). After this has occurred, researchers could then select policies that appear to be ideologically moderate in nature and perform analyses similar to those executed in this book to interrogate moderate invention. One considerable challenge that researchers might face in doing this would be designating which policy areas fall under an ideologically moderate distinction. The politicization of nearly all policy-making—perhaps typified by the fact that something as seemingly agreeable as how to handle the COVID-19 pandemic has become the subject of sharp ideological disagreement (Calvillo et al. 2020)—suggests that it might be difficult to find a policy area that is truly moderate. Unpacking the challenge of identifying moderate policy-making will be a prerequisite to extending the analysis executed in this book to a moderate area. One potential way that scholars may be able to better identify moderate areas would be to survey state lawmakers and state residents, asking each to rate each policy area from the SPID data in terms of ideological position. Areas where the ratings of lawmakers and residents match or are fairly similar would then be given a specific ideological designation, with the concomitant effect being that areas designated as moderate could then be used to populate the analysis of ideologically moderate policy-making.

Moderate legislatures should be more likely to invent in moderate policy areas. However, the unidimensional (left-to-right) way in which ideology is typically measured suggests that there might be no statistical association between the ideological orientation of a legislature and moderate policy invention. At the same time, borrowing has been shown to be amenable to ideologically broad sets of lawmakers in left-leaning (RPS) policy and right-leaning (anti-abortion) policy, suggesting that it also might be attractive (as well as nonsignificant statistically due to the unidimensional nature of ideology measures) to ideologically diverse actors in moderate policy. An extension in the moderate direction should consider examining this possibility.

(V) Extending the Analysis to Study Regulatory Invention in a Conservative Area

One of the strengths of this study is that it not only analyzes legislative invention but also tackles regulatory invention. However, whereas I included a conservative extension for the legislative analysis (anti-abortion policy adoption, which has largely been legislative in nature), I did not include a conservative extension for the regulatory analysis. One possible way to add this extension would be to identify a right-leaning area where regulators have had an opportunity to adopt policy, identify and collect subpolicies (along with dates and institutional actors responsible) that have been adopted in that area, transform the subpolicy adoption data to allow for the investigation of invention and borrowing, and then extract regulatory instances of invention and borrowing (along with corresponding instances of nonadoption) to facilitate analysis. A promising candidate for this extension might be policy related to allowing for hydraulic fracturing (or "fracking") operations in a given state. Fracking involves using large amounts of water to free up energy resources located primarily in shale deposits, and the practice of fracking has exploded in the American energy sector over the past decade (Allison and Parinandi 2020). States' public utilities commissions can use their authority as overseers of their respective electricity markets to facilitate utilization of fracking-derived energy. Given that research has shown that ideological conservatives are more supportive of fracking than are others to the left on the ideological spectrum (Howell et al. 2019), it is possible that incorporating public utilities commission action on facilitating fracking operations might allow for the framework developed in this book to be deployed toward the objective of investigating regulatory invention in a conservative area.

To my knowledge, there is not a preexisting database that houses a fairly comprehensive history of fracking policy across the states, so this may need to be assembled by researchers. Once such a database has been assembled and possible instances of regulatory invention have been structured in a testable format, however, I have some thoughts about how regulatory invention might look in a conservative policy area. RPSs have generally attempted to get electric utility companies to transition away from fossil fuels in electricity generation and have been opposed by electric utility companies insofar as these companies do not want to transition to new energy sources; a consequence of this opposition is that public utilities commissions try to invent RPS policy when companies are less likely to mount challenges, which I argue obtains under deregulation. Fracking explicitly utilizes fossil fuel sources and may be supported by electric utility companies, potentially meaning that public utilities commissions do not have to invent fracking policy strategically in the hope of minimizing pushback from electric utility companies.

(VI) Extending the Study to Investigate a Wider Selection of Moral and Less Moral Policy Areas

One of the interesting findings from analyzing anti-abortion policy is the possibility that the role of evidence or track record is potentially deemphasized in policy areas considered to be moral, as people interpret moral issues through a lens of right versus wrong. One way to examine whether this possibility is widespread would be to evaluate invention across a broad swath of policy areas. This endeavor is possible using the SPID database assuming that researchers have already transformed this data in the way that I suggested in the first extension. Researchers could use a decision rule to identify policies from the SPID database that meet the designation of being moral in nature and then conduct analysis similar to that done on anti-abortion policy on that wider swath of moral policies. A simple decision rule would be to use policies outlined in Mooney (1999) as moral; doing this, however, would throw out much of the diversity of policy-making areas afforded by the SPID data. Therefore, a better decision rule may be to survey respondents on whether each of the policy areas in the SPID data meets the description of "moral" policy and then use survey results to identify moral policy areas in that data. After the moral policy areas have all been analyzed, the policy areas *not* designated as moral can then be analyzed to test whether the role of evidence is similar across the universe of policy areas that are less commonly viewed through a moral lens.

(VII) Exploring Invention and Borrowing in Regulatory Compliance

The book's investigation of regulatory invention and borrowing in RPS adoption is significant because regulatory agencies play a crucial role in policy adoption. However, regulatory agencies also execute policy, and a major component in executing policy is to ensure that regulated parties are complying with that policy. In the RPS space, compliance revolves around making sure that electric utility companies supply electricity according to the stipulations of their states' respective RPS policies. Public utilities commissions can use various strategies to communicate with, cajole, and, if necessary, enforce compliance among electric utility companies, and some of these compliance tactics might be novel while others could be borrowed. Understanding why a public utilities commission might inaugurate a novel compliance-inducing tactic or borrow an existing one from other states would be helpful in deciphering how RPS regimes are being upheld throughout the states, and my framework can be utilized to explore this topic. Researchers would need to identify various compliance tactics, classify the tactics as invention or borrowing, and then employ the pooled event history technique to investigate why states' public utilities commissions pursued the compliance-inducing tactics that they did. This is another area where, to my knowledge, there is not a centralized source compiling state RPS compliance strategies. Nonetheless, one could perhaps capture these from a close reading of state RPS compliance documents and annual reports and use the content therein to examine compliance. While I have no ex-ante opinion about how variation in regulatory design influences compliance, it is possible that public utilities commissions in states with deregulated electricity sectors are more likely to pursue novel compliance-inducing tactics for the same reason put forth as to why these same commissions are more likely to invent novel RPS policy.

(VIII) Exploring Invention and Borrowing in Policy Termination and Abandonment

Much of the intellectual inspiration for this book has come from a desire to speak to decades of political science scholarship (e.g., Walker 1969; Berry and Berry 1990) that deals with adoption. However, there is no reason why the exploration of invention and borrowing cannot pertain to aspects of policy-making besides adoption. Recent work by Volden (2015) has interrogated the phenomenon of states choosing to terminate or abandon policies they had adopted previously. The issue of policy termination is noteworthy in the context of Brandeis's advice about states making novel decisions and thereby creating the opportunity for lessons to emanate to other states: to put it bluntly, a pioneering state can act in a novel manner in choosing to terminate or abandon a policy and can influence potential borrowers to do the same further down the road. Researchers could analyze states that have adopted a corpus of policies (potentially using the SPID data as base data), trace if and when states abandon policies within the corpus, code instances of policy abandonment as invention or borrowing, and use the pooled event history framework—where states that adopted a policy have the opportunity to abandon it and can either abandon it through invention or borrowing—to investigate the determinants of states behaving as inventors or borrowers in terms of abandoning policy.

In addition to applying my definitions of invention and borrowing to policy abandonment, researchers could think creatively about how other kinds of policy-making actions can represent invention and borrowing. For example, choosing *not* to adopt a policy could be categorized as invention or borrowing, and scholars may wish to know whether some famous nonadopters (such as Mississippi with respect to having a state lottery) chose to be novel in making their decision and why this might have been the case. In any event, stretching the analysis of invention and borrowing beyond adoption would increase our understanding of a fuller range of ways in which states might be acting in line with Brandeis's observation.

(IX) Capturing the Preferences of State Regulatory Agencies

The regulatory analysis in chapter 6 focused on identifying institutional facets that influence invention and borrowing in RPS adoption. Although I included state government ideology as a control variable, this measure is based heavily on legislative ideology and does not satisfactorily capture the preferences of regulators themselves. The broader point is that we should invest in devising a compelling measure of regulatory preferences so that the desires of regulators themselves can more readily be modeled and integrated into studies of regulatory policy-making. Given that measures of state government ideology are typically weighted toward legislative behavior, that regulators often do not have partisan affiliations, and that regulatory contracts or missions may make explicitly partisan behavior difficult to observe (Fortunato and Parinandi 2021), creating a new measure of regulatory preferences would go a long way toward advancing studies of regulatory behavior.

One way to potentially create such a measure for state public utilities commissions would be to first assume that any regulatory decision that advances electric utility company interests be considered conservative in nature while any decision that goes against those interests be considered liberal in nature (Parinandi and Hitt 2018). Using that assumption as a guidepost, researchers could trace how a commissioner on a given state's public utilities commission for a given year voted on decisions; then the researchers could create a measure capturing the percentage of times the commissioner voted to advance electric utility company interests and use this measure as a proxy for the commissioner's preferences. The commissioner's yearly preference rating could be combined with the ratings of other commissioners in the same regulatory body (perhaps through taking the median of all of the commissioners' ratings) to yield a rating of the preferences of a state's entire public utilities commission. Creating and operationalizing this rating scheme would take considerable work: for starters, decisions would have to be made about what constitutes pro-electric-utility-company policy-making in a variety of contexts (such as rate-setting, permitting, and other public utilities commission-driven policy-making); then individual-level public utilities commissioner actions pertaining to those contexts would need to be gathered across the 50 states to allow for individual-level ratings to be created and to allow for those individual-level ratings to be combined to generate commission-level ratings. The creation of these ratings would greatly augment the study of public utilities commission decision-making in a host of areas and is a worthwhile extension to this project. Furthermore, the establishment of a public-utilities-commission-based preference rating system could inform the development of preference rating systems for other regulatory agencies. One, for example, could imagine a similar logic being utilized to generate state-level insurance commission preferences, and the creation of such preference ratings for a litany of state-level regulatory agencies could dramatically facilitate exploration of a number of topics related to state-level regulatory policy-making.

(X) Focusing on Individual-Level Lawmaking

While this book advances the study of state politics by operationalizing and analyzing the concepts of invention and borrowing, I do not deviate from the dominant paradigm within the state politics and policy adoption fields of investigating adoption from the vantage point of collective decision-making (Graham et al. 2013; Gilardi and Wasserfallen 2019). The focus on collective decision-making is understandable since adoption is a collective endeavor; however, a wealth of knowledge could be gained if researchers analyzed invention and borrowing from the individual legislator level. Focusing on individual legislators allows us to see how individual covariates such as a legislator's education or occupation influence that legislator's propensity to back inventive policy-making. One also need not focus only on the adoption stage; an individual legislator-level analysis could leverage within-legislature variation in terms of who supports advancing inventive policy in sponsorship, cosponsorship, committee voting, and adoption to get a richer and more detailed picture of the drivers of invention across the legislative process. Elsewhere (Parinandi, Langehennig, and Trautmann 2020), I have shown that individual-level covariates differentially influence the uptake of energy policy across different—cosponsorship versus adoption—stages of the legislative process. It is possible that the same dynamic might be at play with respect to explaining the advancement of inventive policy; that is, the same individual-level covariate (e.g., educational status) could differentially account for invention across different stages of the lawmaking process. Exploring this possibility would provide invaluable service in terms of helping us decipher how the willingness to tackle problems in novel ways (the promise of state autonomy, as out-lined by Brandeis) snakes across various state-level legislative processes. Like many of the other extensions, this enterprise can be accomplished using the SPID data, provided that researchers identify legislative actions, gather data on individual-level components of those legislative actions, and gather data across the different stages of those legislative actions.

(XI) Utilizing a Political Rather Than Technocratic Definition of Track Record

Another possible spinoff from this project involves emphasizing a political rather than technocratic conceptualization of track record. In the book, I follow in the vein of Brandeis and much of the policy diffusion literature in looking at borrowing as an action that produces tangible policy benefits to the borrower. However, it is possible to reimagine the concept of bor-rowing as being an action that produces primarily political rather than policy-specific benefits. Picture, for example, that policymakers in state Y see that policymakers in state X adopted a policy solely to improve their fortunes with a particular interest group; policymakers in state Y would also like to improve their fortunes with the same interest group, see that their peers in state X have done this, and therefore follow suit. This process at the extreme could potentially occur without consideration given to the policy benefits of borrowing. If we were to reconceptualize borrowing in this manner, it could reveal new insights into the nature of policy experi-mentation and diffusion generally.

(XII) Analyzing Deregulation in a Different Policy Area

This book's foray into the relationship between market regulation and invention and borrowing focuses on the electricity sector. Although deregulation in the electricity sector represents one of the most important instances of deregulation within the United States, this begs the question of whether deregulation in other areas comports with the dynamics laid out in this book. As a possible extension to the book, one could look at the nature of policy adoptions that occurred prior to and after deregulation of the airline industry in the United States and then investigate whether the nature of regulatory invention differed based on the advent of deregulation. One possible drawback with this approach is that it applies to federal rather than state-level policy-making; however, the issue area should still allow for a test of the theory explicated using electricity deregulation and RPS on a different application of deregulation.

(XIII) Examining Citizen Ideology in Greater Detail

In the book, I devote a great deal of attention to analyzing the role that government ideology has with respect to influencing invention and borrowing. I do this for a couple of reasons. First, government officials are the ones adopting policy, meaning that focusing on government ideology establishes a clear link between the belief systems of those government officials and the policy design choices that they make. Second, much of the policy experimentation and diffusion literature grapples with the topic of how government ideology impacts policy-making, thereby better integrating this book with preexisting experimentation and diffusion literature. Nonetheless, the issue of how citizen ideology influences invention and borrowing is worth examining, and one possibility could include interviewing and surveying citizens about how their beliefs influence exact opinions about how policy should be crafted.

(XIV) Final Thoughts

The book represents a foray into trying to understand how prominent institutional actors within the U.S. states have taken the initiative to develop novel policy solutions to problems in areas where the federal government has been unable to decisively act. While I focus on an area that is of paramount importance as some governments in the United States attempt to adjust to a changing climate and devise ways to secure elusive energy independence (Lipscy and Hughes 2013), both the general topic that I investigate and the framework that I employ to investigate it are arguably expandable to other policy areas, and I have given scholars a way forward to build upon the work developed here and to conduct broader inquiries into how novel policy-making functions at the state level.

Broader inquiries may presumably be necessary so long as the federal government continues to exhibit dysfunction and inadequacy: I have detailed when and under what conditions invention has occurred with respect to state renewable portfolio adoption, and the results of this exploration can be used by interested observers to pinpoint where we should be focusing our attention if we want to detect instances of novel renewable-energy-related policy-making.[8] Furthermore, the institution-specific focus may help observers decide that some paths may or may not be worth pursuing: the potential that public utilities commissions, for example, are so concerned with pushback from electric utility companies may give pause to those who think that public utilities commissions are the natural outlet from which renewable energy policy should be promulgated. Studies of a similar nature may be necessary to help guide observers in areas of state policy-making ranging from immigration to firearm safety to autonomous vehicles. These studies provide clues as to how the federal system can address a host of unanswered challenges but also move the study of adoption toward a recognition that there are different kinds of adoption that are worth exploring in their own right. In this book, I have developed the language as well as the conceptual and empirical tools to make that recognition clear, and I have outlined a suite of ideas that could advance our knowledge about the inventive capacity of the states and interrogate Brandeis's insight into the foreseeable future.

---

8. Individuals who want to advocate for the dissemination of novel RPS policy across other states can use results here to guide their search for novel RPS adoption.

Appendix

TABLE AI. List of RPS Features Analyzed in Book

Sources Defined as "Renewable"

Feature	Year First Adopted	Feature Number[a]
Advanced Nuclear/Nuclear	2008	1
Biomass/Densified Fuel Pellets/Synthetic Gas	1994	9
Biomass Thermal	2011	11
CHP/Cogeneration	1997	13
Co-Firing	2007	17
Coal Bed Methane	2009	19
Clean Coal/Coal Technology/Carbon Capture and Storage/Gasification/Coal Gasification	2004	21
Coal Mine Methane	2004	23
Compressed Air Energy Storage	2010	29
Solar Light Pipes/Daylighting	2006	31
Electricity from Waste Heat/Waste Heat/Recycled Energy	2007	35
Energy Demand Reduction	2011	37
Energy Storage	2002	43
Fuel Cells/Hydrogen	1997	47
Fuel Cells Using Renewable Fuels/Renewable Fuels/Biodiesel/Ethanol/Methanol	1997	49
Geothermal Direct-Use	2006	55
Geothermal Electric	1997	57
Geothermal Heat Pumps	1999	59
Hydroelectric/Small Hydroelectric/Pumped Storage Hydroelectric	1983	61
Landfill Gas/Anaerobic Digestion/Biogas	1997	67
Low Emission Renewables	1998	69
Microturbines	2008	73
Municipal Solid Waste/Energy from Waste/Energy Recovery Processes	1997	75
Natural Gas	2009	77
Ocean Thermal	1997	81
Other Distributed Generation Technologies	2004	83
Photovoltaics/Solar AC/Solar HVAC/Solar Space Cooling/Solar Pool Heating	1996	85
Pyrolysis	2010	89
Seawater AC	2004	95
Solar Thermal Electric	1983	101
Solar Thermal Process Heat/Solar Space Heat	1996	111
Solar Water Heat	1999	113
Tidal Energy	1997	117
Waste Coal	2004	121
Tire-Derived Fuel/Waste Tires	2003	125
Wave Energy	1997	127
Wind	1983	129
Zero-Emission Technology with Substantial Long-Term Production Potential	2002	131

RPS Target Rates/Thresholds

Feature	Year First Adopted	Feature Number[a]
0.5% of Retail Electricity (Required)	1996	133
1.1% of Retail Electricity (Required)	2000	135
15% of Retail Electricity (Required)	2001	137
20% of Retail Electricity (Required)	2002	139
33% of Retail Electricity (Required)	2011	141
10% of Retail Electricity (Required)	2002	143
30% of Retail Electricity (Required)	1997	145
13% of Retail Electricity (Required)	1998	147
27% of Retail Electricity (Required)	2007	149
25% of Retail Electricity (Required)	2007	151
9% of Retail Electricity (Voluntary)	2001	153
40% of Retail Electricity (Required)	2006	155
15% of Retail Electricity (Voluntary)	2001	157
10% of Retail Electricity (Voluntary)	2001	159
105 Megawatts of Capacity (Required)	1992	161
20% of Generating Capacity (Required)	2009	163
7.5% of Retail Electricity (Required)	2004	165
9.5% of Retail Electricity (Required)	2007	167
22.1% of Retail Electricity (Required)	2010	169
500 Megawatts of Capacity (Required)	2008	171
600 Megawatts of Capacity (Required)	2008	173
950 Megawatts of Capacity (Required)	1994	175
11% of Retail Electricity (Voluntary)	2007	177
1% of Retail Electricity (Required)	1997	179
23.8% of Retail Electricity (Required)	2007	181
24% of Retail Electricity (Required)	2004	183
1% of Retail Electricity (Voluntary)	2004	185
12.5% of Retail Electricity (Required)	2007	187
5% of Retail Electricity (Required)	2007	189
15% of Generating Capacity (Voluntary)	2010	191
18% of Retail Electricity (Required)	2004	193
16% of Retail Electricity (Required)	2004	195
2880 Megawatts of Capacity	1999	197
5880 Megawatts of Capacity	2005	199
10% of Retail Electricity Based on 2005 Load (Required)	2005	201
12% of Retail Electricity Based on 2007 Load (Required)	2007	203
15% of Retail Electricity Based on 2007 Load (Required)	2007	205
5 Megawatts of Capacity	1998	207
2.2% of Retail Electricity (Required)	1999	209
4% of Retail Electricity (Required)	1999	249
1,260 Megawatts of Capacity (Required)	2003	323

RPS Carve-Outs

Feature	Year First Adopted	Feature Number[a]
Photovoltaics	2004	213
Wind	1994	215
Solar/Solar-Electric	1997	217
Biomass	1994	219
Hydroelectric	2007	221
Offshore Wind	2010	225
Distributed Generation/Customer-Sited	2004	227
Swine Waste	2007	229
Poultry Waste	2007	231

RPS Credit Trading

Feature	Year First Adopted	Feature Number[a]
Credit Trading Permitted	1997	233

Combinations of Features in RPS Programs

Feature	Year First Adopted	Feature Number[a]
Combining policy features 61, 109, 129, and 161 within an RPS program.	1992	235
Combining policy features 9, 129, 175, 215, and 219 within an RPS program.	1994	237
Combining policy features 85, 109, 111, and 133 within an RPS program.	1996	239
Combining policy features 9, 13, 47, 57, 61, 75, 117, 129, 145, and 233 within an RPS program.	1997	241
Combining policy features 9, 57, 85, 129, 179, 217, and 233 within an RPS program.	1997	243
Combining policy features 9, 49, 57, 61, 67, 75, 81, 85, 109, 117, 127, 129, and 137 within an RPS program.	2002	245
Combining policy features 9, 13, 47, 49, 61, 67, 69, 81, 109, 117, 127, 129, and 147 within an RPS program.	1998	247
Combining policy features 9, 49, 57, 61, 67, 85, 109, 117, 127, 129, 233, and 249 within an RPS program.	1999	251
Combining policy features 9, 57, 59, 61, 67, 117, 127, 129, 197, and 233 within an RPS program.	1999	253
Combining policy features 9, 57, 61, 67, 85, 109, 117, 127, 129, 210, and 233 within an RPS program.	1999	255
Combining policy features 9, 57, 59, 61, 67, 109, 113, 117, 127, 129, 197, and 233 within an RPS program.	1999	257

Combinations of Features in RPS Programs

Feature	Year First Adopted	Feature Number[a]
Combining policy features 9, 67, 85, 109, 111, 113, 129, and 135 within an RPS program.	2000	259
Combining policy features 9, 47, 49, 57, 59, 61, 67, 75, 81, 85, 109, 111, 113, 127, 129, and 153 within an RPS program.	2001	261
Combining policy features 9, 61, 109, 129, 159, 175, 215, and 219 within an RPS program.	2001	263
Combining policy features 9, 61, 85, 109, 129, and 157 within an RPS program.	2001	265
Combining policy features 9, 57, 75, 85, 109, 111, 129, 137, 217, and 233 within an RPS program.	2001	267
Combining policy features 9, 57, 67, 75, 85, 109, 111, 113, 129, 137, 217, and 233 within an RPS program.	2002	269
Combining policy features 9, 43, 49, 57, 61, 67, 75, 81, 85, 109, 117, 127, 129, and 139 within an RPS program.	2002	271
Combining policy features 9, 49, 57, 61, 67, 109, 129, 131, 143, and 233 within an RPS program.	2002	273
Combining policy features 9, 57, 67, 75, 85, 109, 111, 113, 125, 129, 137, 217, and 233 within an RPS program.	2003	275
Combining policy features 9, 47, 61, 67, 75, 109, 129, 159, 215, 219, and 323 within an RPS program.	2003	277
Combining policy features 9, 13, 47, 49, 61, 67, 69, 81, 85, 109, 117, 127, 129, 143, and 233 within an RPS program.	2003	279
Combining policy features 9, 57, 61, 67, 75, 85, 109, 111, 113, 125, 129, 137, 217, and 233 within an RPS program.	2003	281
Combining policy features 9, 49, 57, 61, 67, 75, 81, 109, 117, 127, 129, 165, and 233 within an RPS program.	2004	283
Combining policy features 9, 13, 47, 49, 57, 59, 61, 67, 75, 81, 85, 95, 109, 111, 113, 127, 129, and 139 within an RPS program.	2004	287
Combining policy features 9, 49, 61, 67, 81, 109, 129, and 195 within an RPS program.	2004	289
Combining policy features 9, 13, 47, 49, 61, 67, 81, 85, 117, 127, 129, 183, 185, and 227 within an RPS program.	2004	291

Combinations of Features in RPS Programs

Feature	Year First Adopted	Feature Number[a]
Combining policy features 9, 13, 47, 49, 57, 61, 67, 75, 117, 129, 145, and 233 within an RPS program.	2004	293
Combining policy features 9, 21, 23, 47, 49, 57, 61, 67, 75, 83, 85, 109, 111, 113, 121, 129, 193, 213, and 233 within an RPS program.	2004	295
Combining policy features 9, 49, 57, 61, 67, 109, 129, 143, and 233 within an RPS program.	2004	297
Combining policy features 61, 67, 201, and 233 within an RPS program.	2005	299
Combining policy features 9, 57, 61, 67, 75, 85, 109, 111, 113, 125, 129, 139, 217, and 233 within an RPS program.	2005	301
Combining policy features 9, 47, 49, 57, 61, 67, 81, 109, 117, 127, 129, 143, and 233 within an RPS program.	2005	303
Combining policy features 9, 57, 59, 61, 67, 109, 113, 117, 127, 129, 199, and 233 within an RPS program.	2005	305
Combining policy features 9, 49, 57, 61, 67, 85, 109, 111, 117, 127, 129, 143, and 233 within an RPS program.	2006	307
Combining policy features 9, 13, 47, 49, 57, 61, 67, 75, 117, 129, 155, and 233 within an RPS program.	2006	311
Combining policy features 9, 13, 47, 49, 61, 67, 69, 75, 81, 85, 109, 117, 127, 129, 143, and 233 within an RPS program.	2006	313
Combining policy features 9, 43, 49, 57, 61, 67, 75, 81, 85, 109, 117, 127, 129, 139, and 233 within an RPS program.	2006	315
Combining policy features 9, 49, 57, 61, 67, 109, 129, 201, and 233 within an RPS program.	2006	317
Combining policy features 9, 49, 57, 61, 81, 109, 117, 127, 129, 137, and 233 within an RPS program.	2006	319
Combining policy features 9, 13, 31, 49, 55, 57, 59, 61, 67, 85, 109, 111, 113, 129, 137, 227, and 233 within an RPS program.	2006	321
Combining policy features 9, 17, 47, 61, 67, 75, 109, 129, 145, 151, 215, 219, and 233 within an RPS program.	2007	325

Combinations of Features in RPS Programs

Feature	Year First Adopted	Feature Number[a]
Combining policy features 9, 49, 57, 61, 67, 109, 129, 131, 139, 143, and 233 within an RPS program.	2007	327
Combining policy features 9, 35, 47, 57, 61, 67, 109, 129, 159, and 233 within an RPS program.	2007	329
Combining policy features 9, 35, 49, 57, 61, 67, 109, 129, 139, 143, and 233 within an RPS program.	2007	331
Combining policy features 9, 49, 57, 61, 67, 75, 81, 109, 117, 127, 129, 167, 217, and 233 within an RPS program.	2007	333
Combining policy features 9, 57, 61, 67, 75, 109, 117, 127, 129, 203, and 205 within an RPS program.	2007	335
Combining policy features 9, 49, 57, 61, 67, 109, 129, 137, and 233 within an RPS program.	2007	337
Combining policy features 9, 47, 49, 59, 61, 67, 81, 111, 113, 117, 127, 129, 181, 217, 219, 221, and 233 within an RPS program.	2007	339
Combining policy features 9, 55, 57, 61, 67, 75, 85, 109, 111, 113, 125, 129, 139, 217, and 233 within an RPS program.	2007	341
Combining policy features 9, 49, 61, 67, 75, 85, 109, 129, and 177 within an RPS program.	2007	343
Combining policy features 9, 47, 57, 61, 67, 75, 81, 85, 109, 117, 127, 129, 143, 151, 189, and 233 within an RPS program.	2007	345
Combining policy features 9, 13, 47, 49, 61, 67, 69, 75, 81, 85, 109, 117, 127, 129, 149, and 233 within an RPS program.	2007	347
Combining policy features 9, 47, 49, 57, 61, 67, 81, 85, 109, 117, 127, 129, 139, 213, and 233 within an RPS program.	2007	349
Combining policy features 9, 49, 61, 67, 81, 109, 129, 195, and 233 within an RPS program.	2007	351
Combining policy features 9, 49, 61, 67, 85, 109, 129, 151, 215, and 233 within an RPS program.	2007	353
Combining policy features 9, 13, 47, 57, 61, 67, 109, 111, 113, 127, 129, 143, 187, 217, 229, 231, and 233 within an RPS program.	2007	355
Combining policy features 9, 49, 57, 61, 67, 109, 129, 131, 139, 143, 215, 217, 227, and 233 within an RPS program.	2007	357

Combinations of Features in RPS Programs

Feature	Year First Adopted	Feature Number[a]
Combining policy features 9, 49, 57, 61, 67, 85, 109, 117, 127, 129, 217, 233, and 249 within an RPS program.	359	2007
Combining policy features 61, 109, 129, 161, and 233 within an RPS program.	361	2007
Combining policy features 9, 49, 57, 61, 67, 81, 109, 117, 127, 129, 137, and 233 within an RPS program.	363	2007
Combining policy features 9, 35, 47, 57, 61, 67, 75, 109, 129, 159, and 233 within an RPS program.	2008	365
Combining policy features 9, 13, 47, 57, 61, 67, 85, 109, 111, 113, 127, 129, 143, 187, 217, 229, 231, and 233 within an RPS program.	2008	367
Combining policy features 9, 13, 47, 57, 61, 67, 75, 81, 85, 109, 117, 127, 129, 139, and 233 within an RPS program.	2008	369
Combining policy features 9, 49, 57, 61, 67, 75, 81, 109, 117, 127, 129, 139, 217, and 233 within an RPS program.	2008	371
Combining policy features 9, 13, 47, 49, 57, 61, 67, 75, 85, 109, 117, 129, 155, and 233 within an RPS program.	2008	373
Combining policy features 1, 9, 13, 21, 35, 43, 47, 49, 57, 61, 67, 73, 75, 85, 109, 129, 151, 217, and 233 within an RPS program.	2008	375
Combining policy features 9, 49, 57, 61, 67, 75, 81, 85, 109, 117, 127, 129, 137, and 233 within an RPS program.	2008	379
Combining policy features 9, 13, 21, 57, 61, 67, 75, 109, 117, 127, 129, 171, 173, and 233 within an RPS program.	2008	381
Combining policy features 9, 49, 61, 67, 75, 85, 109, 129, 137, 217, and 233 within an RPS program.	2008	383
Combining policy features 9, 13, 21, 57, 61, 67, 75, 109, 117, 127, 129, 143, 171, 173, and 233 within an RPS program.	2008	385
Combining policy features 9, 13, 47, 49, 57, 59, 61, 67, 75, 81, 85, 95, 109, 111, 113, 127, 129, and 155 within an RPS program.	2009	387
Combining policy features 49, 61, 67, 85, 109, 111, 129, 163, and 233 within an RPS program.	2009	389

Combinations of Features in RPS Programs

Feature	Year First Adopted	Feature Number[a]
Combining policy features 9, 55, 57, 61, 67, 75, 85, 109, 111, 113, 125, 129, 151, 217, and 233 within an RPS program.	2009	391
Combining policy features 9, 49, 61, 67, 85, 109, 129, 151, 213, 215, and 233 within an RPS program.	2009	395
Combining policy features 9, 49, 57, 61, 67, 75, 81, 85, 109, 117, 127, 129, 169, and 233 within an RPS program.	2010	397
Combining policy features 9, 19, 21, 35, 47, 49, 57, 61, 67, 77, 85, 109, 121, 125, 129, 151, and 233 within an RPS program.	2009	399
Combining policy features 9, 47, 57, 61, 67, 75, 81, 85, 109, 117, 127, 129, 143, 151, 189, 213, and 233 within an RPS program.	2009	401
Combining policy features 9, 49, 57, 61, 67, 75, 85, 109, 117, 127, 129, 217, 233, and 249 within an RPS program.	2010	405
Combining policy features 9, 13, 23, 29, 47, 57, 61, 67, 75, 81, 85, 109, 117, 127, 129, 139, and 233 within an RPS program.	2010	407
Combining policy features 9, 35, 49, 57, 61, 67, 85, 109, 129, 143, 145, 227, and 233 within an RPS program.	2010	409
Combining policy features 9, 13, 47, 49, 61, 67, 81, 85, 113, 117, 127, 129, 183, 185, and 227 within an RPS program.	2010	411
Combining policy features 9, 13, 47, 49, 57, 61, 67, 75, 83, 85, 109, 117, 129, 155, and 233 within an RPS program.	2010	413
Combining policy features 9, 31, 49, 57, 61, 67, 85, 89, 109, 111, 113, 117, 127, 129, 143, and 233 within an RPS program.	2010	415
Combining policy features 9, 57, 61, 67, 75, 83, 85, 109, 129, and 191 within an RPS program.	2010	417
Combining policy features 1, 9, 13, 21, 23, 35, 43, 47, 49, 57, 61, 67, 73, 75, 85, 109, 129, 151, 217, and 233 within an RPS program.	2010	421
Combining policy features 9, 49, 57, 61, 67, 75, 85, 109, 117, 127, 129, 217, 225, 233, and 249 within an RPS program.	2010	423
Combining policy features 9, 47, 49, 57, 61, 67, 81, 85, 109, 117, 127, 129, 151, 213, and 233 within an RPS program.	2010	425

Combinations of Features in RPS Programs

Feature	Year First Adopted	Feature Number[a]
Combining policy features 9, 43, 49, 57, 61, 67, 75, 81, 85, 109, 117, 127, 129, 141, and 233 within an RPS program.	2011	427
Combining policy features 9, 49, 57, 61, 67, 75, 81, 85, 109, 113, 117, 127, 129, 139, 217, and 233 within an RPS program.	2011	429
Combining policy features 9, 13, 37, 47, 57, 61, 67, 85, 109, 111, 113, 127, 129, 143, 187, 217, 229, 231, and 233 within an RPS program.	2011	431
Combining policy features 1, 9, 19, 21, 47, 49, 55, 57, 59, 61, 67, 75, 85, 109, 113, 129, 159, and 233 within an RPS program.	2011	433
Combining policy features 9, 49, 61, 67, 85, 109, 129, 151, 213, 215, 227, and 233 within an RPS program.	2011	439
Combining policy features 9, 11, 31, 49, 57, 59, 61, 67, 85, 89, 109, 111, 113, 117, 127, 129, 143, and 233 within an RPS program.	2011	441

[a] "Feature Number" refers to individual policy components (or groups of components) that could comprise RPS programs. There are gaps in the numbers for two reasons: first, even numbers refer to non-adoption of the corresponding odd-numbered policy feature with the prior feature number; and second, I utilized a process for identifying and eliminating feature names that are synonyms of features included in the dataset, creating the gaps in "feature number."

TABLE A2. List of Original Documents for RPS Policymaking

(italicized documents contain policy adoptions)

State	Document Name	Year
Arizona	*ACC Decision 59943*	1996
Arizona	*ACC Decision 62506*	2000
Arizona	ACC Decision 63334	2001
Arizona	ACC Decision 63486	2001
Arizona	*ACC Decision 69127*	2006
Arizona	*ACC Decision 72500*	2011
California	*SB 1078*	2002
California	*SB 1038*	2002
California	AB 57	2002
California	SB 67	2003
California	Docket 03-RES-1078	2003
California	Decision 03-06-071	2003
California	Rulemaking 04-04-026	2004
California	Decision 04-06-014	2004
California	Decision 04-06-015	2004
California	Decision 04-06-013	2004
California	Decision 04-07-029	2004
California	Ruling for Phase 2 of RPS Program	2004
California	Ruling Releasing Renewable Avoided Cost Calculation	2005
California	Decision 05-05-011	2005
California	Decision 05-07-039	2005
California	Decision 05-10-014	2005
California	05-11-025	2005
California	05-12-042	2005
California	*SB 107*	2006
California	AB 32	2006
California	Resolution E-3980	2006
California	Decision 05-06-039	2006
California	Decision 06-10-019	2006
California	Decision 06-10-050	2006
California	SB 1036	2007
California	AB 809	2007
California	Decision 07-05-028	2007
California	Decision 07-07-027	2007
California	Decision 07-09-024	2007
California	Executive Order S-21-09	2009
California	AB 2514	2010
California	Decision 10-03-021	2010
California	*SBX 1-2*	2011
California	Decision 129354	2011
Colorado	*Ballot Initiative 37*	2004
Colorado	SB 05-143	2005
Colorado	Docket 05R-112E	2005

TABLE A2—*Continued*

State	Document Name	Year
Colorado	*HB 1281*	2007
Colorado	*HB 1001*	2010
Connecticut	*H 5005*	1998
Connecticut	Docket 98-06-15	1998
Connecticut	H 6621	1999
Connecticut	*SSB 733*	2003
Connecticut	H 6428	2003
Connecticut	Docket 03-10-19	2004
Connecticut	Docket 04-02-07	2004
Connecticut	H 7501	2005
Connecticut	Docket 05-04-16	2005
Connecticut	Docket 04-01-13	2005
Connecticut	S 212	2006
Connecticut	Docket 05-07-19	2006
Connecticut	Docket 04-01-12RE01	2006
Connecticut	H 8006	2007
Connecticut	*H 7432*	2007
Connecticut	Docket 07-06-07	2007
Connecticut	Docket 03-12-10RE01	2007
Connecticut	Docket 05-04-16RE01	2007
Connecticut	Docket 07-08-11	2008
Connecticut	SB 1243	2011
Delaware	*SB 74*	2005
Delaware	Docket 56, Order 6793	2005
Delaware	Docket 56, Order 6885	2006
Delaware	Docket 56, Order 6931	2006
Delaware	Title 7, DNREC 106	2006
Delaware	*SB 19/House Amendment 1*	2007
Delaware	Docket 56, Order 7276	2007
Delaware	SB 328	2008
Delaware	Order 7377	2008
Delaware	Order 7494	2008
Delaware	SB 173	2009
Delaware	Order 7699	2009
Delaware	*SS1 for SB 119*	2010
Delaware	SB 124	2011
Delaware	CDR 26-3000-3008	2005-2011
Hawaii	*SLH 2001, Act 272/HB 173*	2001
Hawaii	*SB 2474*	2004
Hawaii	*SB 3185*	2006
Hawaii	Order 23191	2007
Hawaii	Memorandum of Understanding	2008
Hawaii	*HB 1464*	2009
Illinois	*Public Act 92-0012*	2001

TABLE A2—*Continued*

State	Document Name	Year
Illinois	*Public Act 095-0481*	2007
Illinois	Public Act 095-1027	2009
Illinois	*Public Utilities Act*	2009
Illinois	Public Act 96-0033	2009
Illinois	Public Act 96-0159	2009
Illinois	ICC Order 09-0342	2009
Illinois	ICC Docket 08-0519 Final Order	2009
Illinois	ICC Docket 09-0373	2009
Illinois	83 Illinois Administrative Code, Part 455	2010
Illinois	*HB 1458*	2011
Illinois	HB 1865	2011
Illinois	*SB 1652*	2011
Indiana	*SB 251*	2011
Iowa	*Iowa Code 476.41*	1983
Iowa	Chapter 1252, Sections 31-33	1990
Iowa	Chapter 1017	1992
Iowa	Chapter 1163, Section 97	1992
Iowa	*Chapter 1166, Section 1*	1992
Iowa	Chapter 1196, Section 11	1996
Iowa	Chapter 4, Sections 11 and 36	2001
Iowa	Chapter 1109, Section 4	2002
Iowa	Chapter 29, Sections 2-6	2003
Iowa	*Utilities Board Order, Docket AEP-07-1*	2007
Iowa	Chapter 1032, Section 106	2008
Iowa	Chapter 1126, Section 31	2008
State	Document Name	Year
Iowa	Chapter 1128, Sections 14-15	2008
Iowa	Chapter 1133, Sections 6 and 9	2008
Iowa	Chapter 1191, Section 129	2008
Iowa	Chapter 148, Sections 1-2	2009
Iowa	Chapter 1061, Section 180	2010
Iowa	IAC 199-15.11	2010
Iowa	Chapter 25, Section 125	2011
Iowa	Chapter 77, Section 1	2011
Kansas	*Renewable Energy Standards Act*	2009
Kansas	KAR 82-16	2010
Maine	*LD 1804 / Public Law 316*	1997
Maine	Docket 97-584	1998
Maine	Docket 2002-494, Chapter 311	2003
Maine	*Docket 2004-505*	2004
Maine	LD 2041	2006
Maine	Public Law 403	2007
Maine	Docket 2007-391	2007
Maine	*LD 2283*	2008

TABLE A2—*Continued*

State	Document Name	Year
Maine	*LD 1810*	2010
Maine	Public Act 413	2011
Maryland	*HB 1308 / SB 869*	2004
Maryland	PSC Comar 20-61	2005
Maryland	*HB 1016 / SB 595*	2007
Maryland	*HB 375 / SB 209*	2008
Maryland	HB 368 / SB 268	2008
Maryland	HB 1166 / SB 348	2008
Maryland	HB 471 / SB 277	2010
Maryland	HB 1121 / SB 690	2011
Maryland	*HB 933 / SB 717*	2011
Massachusetts	*Chapter 164 Acts of 1997*	1997
Massachusetts	*225 CMR 14.00*	2002
Massachusetts	Policy Statement on the RPS Eligibility of Retooled Biomass Plants	2005
Massachusetts	*Green Communities Act / SB 2768*	2008
Massachusetts	225 CMR 15.00	2009
Massachusetts	220 CMR 17.00 Emergency	2010
Massachusetts	*225 CMR 14.00*	2010
Michigan	*Public Act 295*	2008
Michigan	*PSC Order U-15800*	2008
Michigan	PSC Order U-15900	2010
Minnesota	*SF 1706*	1994
Minnesota	Docket RP-98-32	1999
Minnesota	*SF 0772*	2001
Minnesota	*HF 9*	2003
Minnesota	Docket CI-03-869	2004
Minnesota	*SF 4*	2007
Minnesota	Docket CI-04-1616 (1)	2007
Minnesota	Docket CI-04-1616 (2)	2007
Minnesota	SF 2996	2008
Minnesota	CI-04-1616	2008
Minnesota	SF 1197	2011
Missouri	*SB 54*	2007
Missouri	SB 1181	2008
Missouri	*Proposition C*	2008
Missouri	4 CSR 240-20.100	2010
Missouri	SB 795	2011
Montana	*SB 415*	2005
Montana	*HB 681*	2007
Nevada	*AB 366 / Restructuring Legislation*	1997
Nevada	*SB 372*	2001
Nevada	*NAC 704.8831-704.8893*	2002
Nevada	*AB 296*	2003

TABLE A2—*Continued*

State	Document Name	Year
Nevada	*AB 429*	2003
Nevada	NAC 704.8901-704.8939	2004
Nevada	*AB 3*	2005
Nevada	Docket 05-7050	2006
Nevada	*AB 1*	2007
Nevada	*SB 358*	2009
Nevada	AB 150	2011
New Hampshire	*HB 873*	2007
New Hampshire	HB 1268	2008
New Hampshire	*PUC Chapter 2500*	2008
New Jersey	*Electric Discount and Energy Competition Act*	1999
New Jersey	*NJAC 14:8*	2004 (could only locate more recent version)
New Jersey	*BPU Solar Transition Order*	2007
New Jersey	SB 2936	2008
New Jersey	*AB 3520*	2010
New Jersey	SB 2036	2010
New Mexico	*PRC Case Number 3619*	2002
New Mexico	SB 43	2004
New Mexico	17.9.572 NMAC	2004
New Mexico	*SB 418*	2007
New Mexico	*17.9.572 NMAC*	2007
New Mexico	SB 549	2011
New York	*Case 03-E-0188 9/24/2004*	2004
New York	Case 03-E-0188 12/16/2004	2004
New York	Case 03-E-0188 4/14/2005	2005
New York	Case 03-E-0188 10/31/2005	2005
New York	Case 03-E-0188 11/2/2005	2005
New York	Case 03-E-0188 1/26/2006	2006
New York	Case 03-E-0188 6/28/2006 (1)	2006
New York	Case 03-E-0188 6/28/2006 (2)	2006
New York	Case 03-E-0188 6/28/2006 (3)	2006
New York	Case 03-E-0188	2009
New York	Case 03-E-0188 1/8/2010	2010
New York	Case 03-E-0188 2/16/2010	2010
New York	Case 03-E-0188 4/2/2010 (1)	2010
New York	*Case 03-E-0188 4/2/2010 (2)*	2010
New York	Case 03-E-0188 12/3/2010	2010
North Carolina	*SB 3*	2007
North Carolina	*04 NCAC 11 R08-64*	2008
North Carolina	SB 90	2009
North Carolina	SB 886	2010

TABLE A2—*Continued*

State	Document Name	Year
North Carolina	NCUC Order, Docket E-100 Subsection 113	2010
North Carolina	*SB 75*	2011
North Dakota	*Administrative Code 69-09-08*	2006
North Dakota	*HB 1506*	2007
North Dakota	PUC Order, Case PU-07-318	2008
Ohio	*SB 221*	2008
Ohio	ORC 4928.64	2008
Ohio	*OAC 4901: 1-40*	2009
Ohio	*SB 232*	2010
Oklahoma	*HB 3028*	2010
Oregon	*SB 838*	2007
Oregon	OAR 330-160-0015 to 330-160-0050	2008
Oregon	*HB 3039*	2009
Oregon	HB 3674	2010
Oregon	PUC Order 10-200	2010
Pennsylvania	*SB 1030*	2004
Pennsylvania	AEPS Implementation Order 1	2005
Pennsylvania	AEPS Implementation Order 2	2005
Pennsylvania	Docket M-00051865	2005
Pennsylvania	Docket M-00051865 (1)	2006
Pennsylvania	Docket M-00051865 (2)	2006
Pennsylvania	Docket L-00050174	2006
Pennsylvania	Docket L-00050175	2006
Pennsylvania	HB 1203	2007
Pennsylvania	HB 2200	2008
Pennsylvania	Docket L-00060180	2008
Pennsylvania	*Docket M-00051865*	2009
Pennsylvania	Docket M-2009-2093383	2009
Rhode Island	*HB 7375*	2004
Rhode Island	Docket 3659	2005
Rhode Island	*CRIR 90-060-015*	2007
South Dakota	*HB 1123*	2008
South Dakota	Docket RM11-011 Final Rules	2011
Texas	*SB 7*	1999
Texas	*PUCT Substantive Rule 25.173*	1999
Texas	PUCT Project 26848	2003
Texas	PUCT Project 28407	2004
Texas	*SB 20*	2005
Texas	HB 1090	2007
Texas	PUCT Project 33492	2007
Utah	*SB 202*	2008
Utah	SB 99	2009
Utah	*HB 192*	2010
Utah	HB 228	2010

TABLE A2—*Continued*

State	Document Name	Year
Utah	*SB 104*	2010
Vermont	*30 VSA 8001*	2005
Vermont	*CVR 30 000 054.4.300*	2006
Vermont	*SB 209*	2008
Vermont	Act 159	2010
Vermont	Act 47	2011
Virginia	*Code 56-585.2*	2007
Virginia	HB 1994	2009
Washington	*Initiative 937*	2006
Washington	Energy Independence Act	2006
Washington	*WAC 480-109*	2007
Washington	WAC 194-37	2007
West Virginia	*Code 24-2F-1 / HB 103*	2009
West Virginia	SB 350	2010
West Virginia	Case 11-0249-E-P	2011
Wisconsin	*Act 204*	1998
Wisconsin	*Act 9*	1999
Wisconsin	*Act 141*	2006
Wisconsin	*SB 273*	2010
Wisconsin	*SB 81*	2011
Wisconsin	*CR-10-147*	2011

TABLE A3. List of Documents Used to Identify Synonyms

(*Note:* This table is used to determine whether two different feature names describe the same feature. This is important so that features listed in DSIRE are not mistakenly classified as invention or borrowing. I consult the sources in the table to decide whether a feature listed in DSIRE is the same as another feature. If two features are the same, the names of the two features are merged and the earlier feature's year of first adoption is used to designate invention.)

Sources Defined as "Renewable"

Advanced nuclear is a process where new reactors and reactors that use nonwater coolants and are efficient are used to generate electricity (DOE 1). **Advanced nuclear** and **nuclear** are synonyms.

Anaerobic digestion is a process where anaerobic bacteria break down organic materials into biogas/landfill gas that can then be used for electricity (DOE 2). **Anaerobic digestion, biogas,** and **landfill gas** (the end product of the anaerobic digestion process) are synonyms.

Biodiesel is a source and specifically a type of renewable fuel that is manufactured from vegetable oils, animal fats, and recycled restaurant grease (DOE 3/NREL 1). **Biodiesel, renewable fuels,** and **fuel cells using renewable fuels** are synonyms.

Biomass is a source and refers to using plants, plant-based materials to generate electricity (NREL 2/Biomass Energy Centre UK). **Densified fuel pellets** (a fuel source created from plant matter) and **synthetic gas** (another fuel source that can be created from plant matter) are synonyms.

Biomass thermal is a process whereby biomass energy is utilized to produce heat rather than electricity or fuel for transportation—two other common uses of biomass energy (Biomass Thermal Energy Council). No synonyms found.

Combined Heat and Power (CHP)/Cogeneration is a process whereby efficiency is maximized by using the same system to produce electricity and heat rather than using two different systems (DOE 4). No synonyms found.

Clean coal describes several processes whereby coal is "cleanly" (e.g., resulting in fewer carbon emissions) utilized to generate electricity (DOE 5). Clean coal may be synonymous with **coal gasification, coal technology, coal-fired with carbon capture and sequestration, fuel produced by a coal gasification or liquefaction facility, gasification, and integrated gasification combined cycle technologies,** and **synthetic gas.**

Co-Firing is a process whereby different energy sources (e.g., biomass and coal) are combined to generate electricity (Pennsylvania State University Extension). No synonyms found.

Coal bed methane is a source where the methane gas from coal beds is utilized for energy (DOE 6). Unlike **coal mine methane,** coal bed methane is not extracted during mining and exists naturally in coal beds (EPA 1). No synonyms found.

Coal gasification is a process where coal is turned into a gasoline for electricity (DOE 5). **Coal gasification** is a major **clean coal** process.

Coal mine methane is a source where methane gas escaping from coal mines is utilized for energy (EPA 1). No synonyms found.

Coal technology is a generic term synonymous with **clean coal/coal gasification** (see **clean coal/coal gas**).

Coal-fired with carbon capture/sequestration is when carbon released from the burning of coal is buried under the ground (EPA 2). Subsumed by **clean coal/coal gasification** (see **clean coal/coal gasification**).

Compressed air energy storage is a process where air is compressed, pressurized, and kept underground and then heated to generate electricity (Energy Storage Association). No synonyms found.

Daylighting is a process where windows are used to light buildings and reduce energy use (DOE 7). Although daylighting is different from **solar light pipes**, the latter has been called "solar light pipe daylighting," meaning the two concepts may be synonyms.

Densified fuel pellets are a source and type of **biomass** where plants are compressed and used for energy (Washington State University Extension Energy Program). Subsumed by **biomass** (see **biomass**).

Electricity from waste heat is a process where heat from industrial uses is utilized (through steam and a turbine) to generate electricity (Heat Is Power). **Recycled energy** and **waste heat** may be synonyms.

Energy demand reduction is a process where incentives reduce demand for electricity (EIA 1). No synonyms found.

Energy from waste is a process whereby nonrecyclable wastes are converted into heat or electricity, or both (EPA 2). **Energy from waste** and **energy recovery processes** may be synonyms with **municipal solid waste**.

Energy recovery processes describe a process where waste is converted into energy. This term is subsumed by **municipal solid waste** (see **municipal solid waste**).

Energy storage is an intermediate source that depends on the use of sophisticated batteries to preserve energy until the energy is needed for use (NREL 3). No synonyms found.

Ethanol is a corn-based source (DOE 8). **Ethanol** may be synonymous with **renewable fuels** and **fuel cells using renewable fuels**.

Fuel cells are devices that create energy through mixing **hydrogen** and oxygen (producing electricity and water as waste) (California Energy Commission 1). **Fuel cells** may be synonymous with **hydrogen**.

Fuel cells using renewable fuels describe fuel cell devices utilizing **renewable fuels** for the hydrogen stock to power the cell (California Energy Commission 1). **Fuel cells using renewable fuels** are synonyms with **ethanol** and **renewable fuels**.

Fuel produced by a coal gasification or liquefaction facility is subsumed by clean coal/coal gasification (see **clean coal** or **coal gasification**).

Gasification is subsumed by **clean coal/coal gasification** (see **clean coal** or **coal gasification**).

Geothermal direct-use is a process and source where hot water is piped to the surface and the heat from the water is used for heat (Geothermal Energy Association). No synonyms found.

Geothermal electric is a process and source where steam from the Earth is used to drive a turbine and generate electricity (NREL 4). No synonyms found.

Geothermal heat pumps refer to a process and source where air is pumped through a coiled underground loop to generate hot and cool air for heating and cooling (Geothermal Energy Association). No synonyms found.

Hydroelectric refers to a process and source where water drives a turbine and generates electricity (DOE 9). **Small hydroelectric** (a restriction on the hydroelectric facility size) and **pumped storage hydroelectric projects** may be synonyms.

Hydrogen refers to a source that is utilized in a **fuel cell** to produce electricity. **Hydrogen** is subsumed by **fuel cells** (see **fuel cells**).

Integrated gasification combined cycle technologies are subsumed by **clean coal/coal gasification** (see **clean coal** or **coal gasification**).

Landfill gas is a source and refers to the energy created through **anaerobic decomposition** (DOE 10). **Landfill gas** may be synonymous with **anaerobic decomposition** and **biogas**.

Low emission renewables refer to processes that generate electricity with the reduced production of carbon dioxide (Connecticut Light and Power presentation). No synonyms found.

Microturbines are a process based on jet engine technology that utilizes efficient turbines to generate electricity (EPA 3). No synonyms found.

Municipal solid waste is a source and refers to burning waste to create steam and then electricity (EIA 2). **Municipal solid waste** may be synonymous with **energy from waste** and **energy recovery processes**.

Natural gas is a source and refers to the extraction and use of hydrocarbon gases found underground to generate electricity (DOE 12). No synonyms found.

Nuclear is a source and process and refers to using nuclear fission to generate electricity. **Nuclear** may be synonymous with **advanced nuclear**.

Ocean thermal is a source and process and refers to methods where thermal differences between layers of the ocean are used to drive a turbine and make electricity (DOE 13). No synonyms found.

Other distributed generation technologies refer to a suite of local methods that can be utilized to generate electricity near the source of consumption (EPA 4). No synonyms found.

Photovoltaics refer to a source and process and describe capturing the electricity generated when sunlight shines on silicon cells (NREL 5). Many **solar AC** and **solar HVAC** systems are powered through **photovoltaics** and it is possible that **solar pool heating** systems are powered through **photovoltaics**, meaning that **photovoltaics** may actually capture use of **solar AC**, **solar HVAC**, and **solar pool heating**.

Pumped storage hydroelectric projects refer to a source and process and describe how water in a reservoir can be released to drive a turbine and generate electricity and then settle in a lower reservoir before being pumped back to the elevated storage reservoir during periods of low electricity demand (Duke Energy). **Pumped storage hydroelectric projects** may be synonymous with **small hydroelectric** and **hydroelectric**.

Pyrolysis is a process by which organic material (this could be biomass but also could be plastic) is heated in the absence of oxygen. Heating in the absence of oxygen prevents burning and allows for combustible provisions of the heated organic material to be used as fuel (USDA and Pyrocrat Systems). No synonyms found.

Recycled energy is a process and refers to capturing residual heat from industrial processes and using that residual heat to generate electricity (Recycled Energy Development). **Recycled energy** may be synonymous with **electricity from waste heat** and **waste heat**.

Renewable fuels are a source and describe fuel made from sources such as **ethanol, biodiesel**, and **methanol** (DOE 14). **Renewable fuels** may be synonymous with **biodiesel, ethanol, methanol,** and **fuel cells using renewable fuels.**

Seawater AC is a source and process and refers to using cooler water in the ocean for indoor air conditioning (New York Times). No synonyms found.

Small hydroelectric refers to small-scale, local use of **hydroelectric** energy (NREL). **Small hydroelectric** may be subsumed by **hydroelectric** (see **hydroelectric**).

Solar AC refers to a process by which energy from sunlight is utilized (in a number of different process-specific ways) via absorption and desiccant systems with a refrigerant to cool air (NREL 7). According to NREL, these are costly and quite rare. **Solar AC** may be synonymous with **solar HVAC** and **solar space cooling** and to the degree that **solar AC** is powered by **photovoltaics** (the system advertised by the Lennox Corporation during a search), **solar AC** may be synonymous with **photovoltaics.**

Solar HVAC refers to a processes where energy from sunlight is utilized (typically via photovoltaic cells) to provide heating, cooling, and ventilation in an integrated system (Lennox Corporation). **Solar HVAC** may be synonymous with **solar AC** and **solar space cooling.** Moreover, to the degree that both predominantly utilize **photovoltaics** to drive their systems, **solar HVAC** and **solar AC** may be synonymous with **photovoltaics.**

Solar light pipes are a process and refer to the use of piping and concentrators to carry sunlight from windows and skylights to darker parts of large buildings—this is in contrast to **daylighting**, which uses skylights to light buildings (Florida Solar Energy Center). Although the two concepts are different, **solar light pipes** have been referred to as "solar light pipe daylighting," meaning that the two concepts may be synonymous.

Solar pool heating refers to a process whereby water from a swimming pool is circulated via a pump to solar collectors—where the pool water meets heat collected from sunlight—and heated through interaction with sunlight (DOE 15). There is no indication that the pool pump is powered through **photovoltaics**, but it is possible since a pool heating and pump vendor (Greenlogic Energy) offers this, meaning that **solar pool heating** may be synonymous with **photovoltaics.**

Solar space heat refers to a process whereby heat from the sun is absorbed into a collector and then distributed throughout a building with the use of a ventilation system (NREL 7). **Solar space heat** may be synonymous with **solar thermal process heat**, which describes a similar process.

Solar space cooling refers to utilizing sunlight (typically from a **photovoltaic** system) to cool a property (Arizona Corporation Commission Decision 69127). **Solar space cooling** may be synonymous with **solar AC, solar HVAC,** and to the degree that it is powered by solar panels, **photovoltaics.**

Solar thermal electric refers to a process whereby heat from the sun is collected and utilized to heat liquid and create steam and generate electricity through the driving of a turbine (California Energy Commission 2). No synonyms found.

Solar thermal process heat refers to a process whereby sunlight is utilized to heat large buildings, either through collection and ventilation (similar to **solar space heat**) or through the use of a boiler (EPA 5). **Solar thermal process heat** may therefore be synonymous with **solar space heat.**

Solar water heat refers to a process whereby sunlight is utilized and channeled to heat water for use (NREL 7). No synonyms found.

Synthetic gas can be produced from **biomass** (University of Minnesota) and therefore may also be subsumed by **biomass.**

Tidal energy is a source and process and refers to the use of barrier dams, fences, and turbines to trap energy—caused by the Moon's gravity—and generate electricity (DOE 16). No synonyms found.

Tire-derived fuel is a source and refers to the burning of tires to generate fuel. **Tire-derived fuel** may be synonymous with **waste tires** (Waste 360), which describes the same exact source.

Waste coal is a source and refers to the burning of the discards from coal mining in order to generate electricity (Energy Justice Network). No synonyms found.

Waste heat is subsumed by **electricity from waste heat** (see **electricity from waste heat**).

Waste tires describe the same essential concept as **tire-derived fuel** and may be synonymous with **tire-derived fuel.**

Wave energy is a source and process and refers to creating energy from utilizing the bobbing or oscillating motion of the kinetic energy of waves (DOE 17). No synonyms found.

Wind is a source and process and refers to creating energy from the movement of wind pushing a turbine (DOE 18). No synonyms found.

Final Target RPS Rates/Thresholds
No synonyms found.

RPS Carve-outs

Biomass refers to using plants, plant-based materials, and residues from plants/plant-based materials to generate electricity (NREL 2/Biomass Energy Centre UK). A biomass carve-out/technology minimum requires that some amount of electricity be generated from "biomass" but does not specify that certain types of **biomass** must be used rather than others. No synonyms found.

Customer-sited is another phrase used to describe **distributed generation** (Public Service Commission of Wisconsin). A **customer-sited** carve-out/technology minimum may be synonymous with a **distributed generation** carve-out/technology minimum.

Distributed generation refers to a whole suite of local methods that can be utilized to generate electricity near the source of consumption (EPA 4). A **distributed generation** carve-out/technology minimum may be synonymous with a **customer-sited** carve-out/technology minimum.

Hydroelectric refers to when electricity is generated from running water pushing a turbine (DOE 9). A **hydroelectric** carve-out/technology minimum specifies that some amount of electricity must be generated from **hydroelectric** sources/processes. No synonyms found.

Offshore wind refers to wind installations offshore rather than on land (DOE 19). A wind carve-out/technology minimum is not synonymous since the **wind** carve-out/technology minimum does not specify that some amount of electricity should be derived from onshore versus offshore installations, while an **offshore wind** carve-out/technology minimum makes this explicit. No synonyms found.

Photovoltaics refers to using silicon panels and sunlight to generate electricity (NREL 5). Although **photovoltaic** technology is a subset of **solar/solar-electric** energy generation, a **photovoltaic** carve-out/technology minimum is not the same as a **solar/solar-electric** technology minimum since the **photovoltaic** carve-out/technology minimum requires the use of silicon cells while a **solar/solar-electric** carve-out/technology minimum could allow for use of other **solar** technologies, such as **solar thermal**. No synonyms found.

Poultry waste refers to using waste from poultry (similar to the **swine waste** case above) to generate electricity (Baltimore Sun). A **poultry waste** carve-out/technology minimum specifies that some amount of energy must be derived from **poultry waste**. No synonyms found.

Solar refers to creating energy from the power of sunlight (NREL 8). This electricity could be derived from the use of **photovoltaic** technology or **solar thermal** processes. A **solar** carve-out/technology minimum (which requires some amount of electricity to be derived from a solar source regardless of whether **photovoltaics** or **solar thermal** processes are utilized to generate that electricity) may be synonymous with a solar-electric carve-out/technology minimum, which roughly emphasizes the same concept.

Solar-electric refers to creating electricity from the power of sunlight (NREL 8). A **solar-electric** carve-out/technology minimum specifies that some amount of electricity be derived from **solar-electric** sources/processes (which are typically **photovoltaic** or **solar thermal**) and may be synonymous with a **solar** carve-out/technology minimum.

Swine waste refers to using hog waste (typically via **anaerobic decomposition** into **biogas** to generate electricity (North Carolina Bioenergy Council). A **swine waste** carve-out/technology minimum specifies that some amount of energy must be derived from **swine waste**. No synonyms found.

Wind refers to creating energy from the movement of wind pushing a turbine (DOE 18). One may believe that a wind carve-out/technology minimum is synonymous with an offshore wind carve-out/technology minimum, but this is not the case since a wind carve-out/technology minimum does not specify that some amount of wind generation must be from onshore or offshore installations while an offshore wind carve-out/technology minimum explicitly specifies that electricity generation must be from offshore wind installations. No synonyms found.

Links to Sources Discussed in Table A3

Baltimore Sun: "New Plan Seeks to Turn Chicken Manure to Energy," by Timothy Wheeler (March 22, 2015):
http://www.baltimoresun.com/features/green/blog/bs-md-poultry-litter-plant-20150320-story.html

Biomass Energy Centre UK: Biomass description page:
http://www.biomassenergycentre.org.uk/portal/
page?_pageid=76,15049&_dad=portal&_schema=PORTAL

Biomass Thermal Energy Council: Biomass Energy Thermal FAQs page:
https://www.biomassthermal.org/resource/faq.asp

California Energy Commission 1: Consumer Energy Center-Fuel Cells for Electricity page:
http://www.consumerenergycenter.org/renewables/fuelcells/

California Energy Commission 2: Consumer Energy Center-Solar Thermal Electricity
  page:
  http://www.consumerenergycenter.org/renewables/solarthermal/
Connecticut Light and Power: "The LREC/ZREC Program: An Opportunity to Develop
  Behind-the-Meter Renewable Generation in Connecticut" presentation:
  http://www.ctpower.org/wp-content/uploads/2012/06/NU-and-UI-Presentation-
  June-13-2012.pdf
DOE 1: U.S. Department of Energy's Advanced Nuclear Reactors page:
  http://www.energy.gov/ne/advanced-modeling-simulation/advanced-nuclear-reactors
DOE 2: U.S. Department of Energy's Anaerobic Digestion Basics page:
  http://energy.gov/eere/energybasics/articles/anaerobic-digestion-basics
DOE 3: U.S. Department of Energy's Alternative Fuels Data Center Biodiesel page:
  http://www.afdc.energy.gov/fuels/biodiesel.html
DOE 4: U.S. Department of Energy's Combined Heat and Power Basics page:
  http://energy.gov/eere/amo/combined-heat-and-power-basics
DOE 5: U.S. Department of Energy's Clean Coal Research page:
  http://energy.gov/fe/science-innovation/clean-coal-research
DOE 6: U.S. Department of Energy's Coal Bed Methane primer:
  http://energy.gov/fe/downloads/coalbed-methane
DOE 7: U.S. Department of Energy's Daylighting page:
  http://energy.gov/energysaver/daylighting
DOE 8: U.S. Department of Energy's Alternative Fuels Data Center Ethanol page:
  http://www.afdc.energy.gov/fuels/ethanol.html
DOE 9: U.S. Department of Energy's Hydropower Basics page:
http://energy.gov/eere/water/hydropower-basics
DOE 10: U.S. Department of Energy's Alternative Fuels Data Center Renewable Natural
  Gas (Biomethane) page:
  http://www.afdc.energy.gov/fuels/natural_gas_renewable.html
DOE 11: U.S. Department of Energy's Alternative Fuels Data Center's Methanol page:
  http://www.afdc.energy.gov/fuels/emerging_methanol.html
DOE 12: U.S. Department of Energy's Alternative Fuels Data Center Natural Gas
  webpage:
  http://www.afdc.energy.gov/fuels/natural_gas.html
DOE 13: U.S. Department of Energy's Ocean Thermal Energy Conversion Basics page:
  http://energy.gov/eere/energybasics/articles/ocean-thermal-energy-conversion-basics
DOE 14: U.S. Department of Energy's Alternative Fuels Data Center page:
  http://www.afdc.energy.gov/
DOE 15: U.S. Department of Energy's Swimming Pool Heating page:
  http://energy.gov/energysaver/swimming-pool-heating
DOE 16: U.S. Department of Energy's Tidal Energy Basics page:
  http://energy.gov/eere/energybasics/articles/tidal-energy-basics
DOE 17: U.S. Department of Energy's Wave Energy Basics page:
  http://energy.gov/eere/energybasics/articles/wave-energy-basics
DOE 18: U.S. Department of Energy's Wind Energy page:
  http://energy.gov/science-innovation/energy-sources/renewable-energy/wind
DOE 20: U.S. Department of Energy's Offshore Wind Research and Development page:
  http://energy.gov/eere/wind/offshore-wind-research-and-development

Duke Energy: Duke Energy's "How Do Pumped-Storage Hydro Plants Work?" page:
https://www.duke-energy.com/about-energy/generating-electricity/pumped-storage-how.asp

EIA 1: U.S. Energy Information Administration's Electricity Utility Demand-side Management Archive page:
http://www.eia.gov/electricity/data/eia861/dsm/

EIA 2: U.S. Energy Information Administration's Waste-to-Energy (Municipal Solid Waste) page:
http://www.eia.gov/Energyexplained/?page=biomass_waste_to_energy

Energy Justice Network: Energy Justice Network's Waste Coal page:
http://www.energyjustice.net/coal/wastecoal

Energy Storage Association: Compressed Air Energy Storage page:
http://energystorage.org/compressed-air-energy-storage-caes

EPA 1: U.S. Environmental Protection Agency's Coalbed Methane Outreach Program Frequent Questions:
https://www3.epa.gov/cmop/faq.html

EPA 2: U.S. Environmental Protection Agency's Carbon Dioxide Capture and Sequestration page:
https://www3.epa.gov/climatechange/ccs/

EPA 2: U.S. Environmental Protection Agency's Energy Recovery from Waste page:
https://www3.epa.gov/epawaste/nonhaz/municipal/wte/

EPA 3: U.S. Environmental Protection Agency's Renewable Energy Fact Sheet on Microturbines:
https://owpubauthor.epa.gov/scitech/wastetech/upload/Microturbines.pdf

EPA 4: U.S. Environmental Protection Agency's Distributed Generation page:
https://www.epa.gov/energy/distributed-generation

EPA 5: U.S. Environmental Protection Agency's Renewable Industrial Process Heat page:
https://www.epa.gov/rhc/renewable-industrial-process-heat

Florida Solar Energy Center: Florida Solar Energy Center's Solar Piped Daylighting page:
http://www.fsec.ucf.edu/en/consumer/buildings/basics/windows/solar_lighting/piped.htm

Geothermal Energy Association: "Geothermal Basics Question and Answer" (September 2012) report:
http://geo-energy.org/reports/Gea-GeothermalBasicsQandA-Sept2012_final.pdf

Greenlogic Energy: Greenlogic's Pool Heating page:
http://www.greenlogic.com/Pool-Heating/

Heat Is Power: About Waste Heat page:
http://www.heatispower.org/waste-heat-to-power/

Lennox Corporation: Catalog of Solar AC/HVAC equipment:
http://www.lennox.com/products/systems/sunsource

New York Times: "Using Seawater for Air Conditioning" by Kate Galbraith (April 30, 2009):
http://green.blogs.nytimes.com/2009/04/30/using-seawater-for-air-conditioning/?_r=1

North Carolina Bioenergy Council: "Hog Wild about Biogas" page:
https://research.cnr.ncsu.edu/sites/ncbioenergycouncil/2015/08/20/289/

NREL 8: National Renewable Energy Laboratory's Solar Energy Basics page:
http://www.nrel.gov/learning/re_solar.html

NREL 1: National Renewable Energy Laboratory's Biofuels Basics page:
  http://www.nrel.gov/learning/re_biofuels.html
NREL 2: National Renewable Energy Laboratory's Biomass Energy Basics page:
  http://www.nrel.gov/learning/re_biomass.html
NREL 3: National Renewable Energy Laboratory's "The Role of Energy Storage with
  Renewable Electricity Generation" report:
  http://www.nrel.gov/docs/fy10osti/47187.pdf
NREL 4: National Renewable Energy Laboratory's Geothermal Energy Production Basics
  page:
  http://www.nrel.gov/learning/re_geo_elec_production.html
NREL 5: National Renewable Energy Laboratory's Solar Photovoltaic Technology Basics
  page:
  http://www.nrel.gov/learning/re_photovoltaics.html
NREL 6: National Renewable Energy Laboratory's "Small Hydropower Systems" report:
  http://www.nrel.gov/docs/fy01osti/29065.pdf
NREL 7: National Renewable Energy Laboratory's Solar Process Heat Basics page:
  http://www.nrel.gov/learning/re_solar_process.html
Pennsylvania State University Extension: Co-firing biomass with coal report:
  http://extension.psu.edu/publications/ub044/view
Public Service Commission of Wisconsin: Customer-Sited Electric Generating Facilities
  page:
  http://psc.wi.gov/renewables/customerSited.htm
Pyrocat Systems: "What Is Pyrolysis" page:
  http://www.pyrolysisplant.com/what-is-pyrolysis/
Recycled Energy Development: Recycled Energy Development's "Answers to Your
  Energy Recycling Questions" page:
  http://www.recycled-energy.com/main/energy-recycling-questions
University of Minnesota: "Syngas Production Using a Biomass Generation Process":
  http://license.umn.edu/technologies/
  z07080_syngas-production-using-a-biomass-gasification-process
USDA: U.S. Department of Agriculture's "What Is Pyrolysis" page:
  http://www.ars.usda.gov/Main/docs.htm?docid=19898
Washington State University Energy Extension Program: "Developing a Wood Pellet/
  Densified Biomass Industry in Washington State: Opportunities and Challenges"
  report:
  http://www.energy.wsu.edu/Documents/Densified%20Biomass%20Report.pdf
Waste 360: Waste 360's Scrap Tires page:
  http://waste360.com/Landfill_Management/scrap_tires_tdf_

TABLE A4. Full Results for Models Shown in Table 3 of Chapter 5

Variable	Inventing (1)	Borrowing (2)
Government Ideology	0.014**	0.011
	(0.007)	(0.010)
Median Incumbent Vote Share	–0.007	–0.022***
	(0.005)	(0.007)
Real Energy Price	–0.082	–0.037
	(0.051)	(0.062)
Citizen Ideology	0.019	0.029**
	(0.014)	(0.013)
Leg. Professionalism	–0.566	0.385
	(1.254)	(1.673)
State Per Capita Income	0.010	–0.015
	(0.015)	(0.012)
Urban Percentage	0.008	0.034**
	(0.015)	(0.014)
Change in Unemployment	–0.190	0.003
	(0.155)	(0.165)
Fossil Fuel Production	–0.002	0.001
	(0.003)	(0.004)
Deregulated	–0.087	0.659*
	(0.352)	(0.399)
Unified Democratic Government	–0.487	0.016
	(0.389)	(0.514)
Party Decline	0.183	0.313
	(0.391)	(0.495)
Geographic Neighbor	1.929***	1.541
	(0.739)	(1.109)
Ideological Neighbor	–0.475	–1.413
	(1.040)	(1.124)
Prior Inventing	1.171	
	(2.513)	
Prior Borrowing		–62.854***
		(16.635)
Year	0.241***	0.066
	(0.045)	(0.042)
Featureyear		0.160***
		(0.007)
Wald X^2	168.71***	827.84***
Observations	182,984	47,433
	(169)	(357)

*** = critical value of 0.01; ** = critical value of 0.05; * = critical value of 0.10

TABLE A5. Results Including Direct Ballot Initiative for Models in Table 3 of Chapter 5

Variable	Inventing (1)	Borrowing (2)
Government Ideology	0.014**	0.011
	(0.006)	(0.010)
Median Incumbent Vote Share	–0.008	–0.021***
	(0.006)	(0.007)
Direct Ballot Initiative	–0.419	0.066
	(0.361)	(0.363)
Real Energy Price	–0.085*	–0.036
	(0.052)	(0.067)
Citizen Ideology	0.018	0.030**
	(0.015)	(0.012)
Leg. Professionalism	–0.549	0.385
	(1.364)	(1.667)
State Per Capita Income	0.007	–0.015
	(0.017)	(0.013)
Urban Percentage	0.010	0.033**
	(0.016)	(0.014)
Change in Unemployment	–0.191	0.005
	(0.155)	(0.170)
Fossil Fuel Production	–0.002	0.001
	(0.003)	(0.005)
Deregulated	–0.104	0.662
	(0.345)	(0.405)
Unified Democratic Government	–0.482	0.010
	(0.389)	(0.519)
Party Decline	0.209	0.312
	(0.401)	(0.495)
Geographic Neighbor	2.031***	1.489
	(0.733)	(1.142)
Ideological Neighbor	–0.526	–1.402
	(1.023)	(1.129)
Prior Inventing	1.018	
	(2.564)	
Prior Borrowing		–63.098***
		(17.268)
Year	0.244***	0.065
	(0.047)	(0.042)
Featureyear		0.160***
		(0.007)
Wald X²	183.90***	849.66***
Observations	182,984 (169)	47,433 (357)

*** = critical value of 0.01; ** = critical value of 0.05; * = critical value of 0.10

TABLE A6. Results Using Mean Incumbent Vote Share for Electoral Vulnerability in Models Shown in Table 3 of Chapter 5

Variable	Inventing (1)	Borrowing (2)
Government Ideology	0.015**	0.012
	(0.007)	(0.010)
Mean Incumbent Vote Share	−0.009	−0.032***
	(0.007)	(0.007)
Real Energy Price	−0.083*	−0.049
	(0.050)	(0.059)
Citizen Ideology	0.019	0.031**
	(0.014)	(0.013)
Leg. Professionalism	−0.496	0.672
	(1.263)	(1.673)
State Per Capita Income	0.010	−0.017
	(0.016)	(0.013)
Urban Percentage	0.008	0.038***
	(0.016)	(0.014)
Change in Unemployment	−0.191	−0.005
	(0.155)	(0.164)
Fossil Fuel Production	−0.002	0.001
	(0.003)	(0.004)
Deregulated	−0.106	0.572
	(0.355)	(0.393)
Unified Democratic Government	−0.508	−0.041
	(0.387)	(0.509)
Party Decline	0.192	0.318
	(0.394)	(0.505)
Geographic Neighbor	1.938***	1.563
	(0.740)	(1.138)
Ideological Neighbor	−0.457	−1.320
	(1.036)	(1.094)
Prior Inventing	1.221	
	(2.521)	
Prior Borrowing		−63.762***
		(16.802)
Year	0.242***	0.076*
	(0.045)	(0.045)
Featureyear		0.160***
		(0.007)
Wald X^2	160.74***	850.16***
Observations	182,984 (169)	47,433 (357)

*** = critical value of 0.01; ** = critical value of 0.05; * = critical value of 0.10

TABLE A7. Results Including Legislative Term Limits for Models in Table 3 of Chapter 5

Variable	Inventing (1)	Borrowing (2)
Government Ideology	0.017**	0.011
	(0.008)	(0.010)
Median Incumbent Vote Share	−0.005	−0.022***
	(0.005)	(0.007)
Legislative Term Limits	0.699	−0.240
	(0.444)	(0.423)
Real Energy Price	−0.088	−0.032
	(0.058)	(0.061)
Citizen Ideology	0.023	0.028**
	(0.014)	(0.013)
Leg. Professionalism	−1.117	0.750
	(1.355)	(1.980)
State Per Capita Income	0.018	−0.018
	(0.016)	(0.014)
Urban Percentage	0.008	0.034**
	(0.013)	(0.014)
Change in Unemployment	−0.213	0.012
	(0.156)	(0.016)
Fossil Fuel Production	−0.002	0.001
	(0.003)	(0.004)
Deregulated	−0.220	0.704*
	(0.405)	(0.389)
Unified Democratic Government	−0.539	0.0002
	(0.424)	(0.508)
Party Decline	0.171	0.343
	(0.396)	(0.496)
Geographic Neighbor	2.091**	1.388
	(0.809)	(1.155)
Ideological Neighbor	−0.340	−1.427
	(0.994)	(1.120)
Prior Inventing	0.859	
	(3.768)	
Prior Borrowing		−63.123***
		(16.720)
Year	0.245***	0.063
	(0.053)	(0.040)
Featureyear		0.160***
		(0.007)
Wald X^2	179.14***	832.21***
Observations	182,984 (169)	47,433 (357)

*** = critical value of 0.01; ** = critical value of 0.05; * = critical value of 0.10

TABLE A8. Results Dropping Combinations for Models Shown in Table 3 of Chapter 5

Variable	Inventing (1)	Borrowing (2)
Government Ideology	0.019**	0.011
	(0.008)	(0.010)
Median Incumbent Vote Share	–0.0004	–0.022***
	(0.010)	(0.007)
Real Energy Price	–0.112	–0.032
	(0.086)	(0.062)
Citizen Ideology	0.020	0.029**
	(0.020)	(0.013)
Leg. Professionalism	–0.208	0.431
	(1.585)	(1.720)
State Per Capita Income	0.030	–0.015
	(0.029)	(0.012)
Urban Percentage	–0.004	0.035**
	(0.021)	(0.014)
Change in Unemployment	–0.328	0.003
	(0.263)	(0.167)
Fossil Fuel Production	–0.004	0.001
	(0.004)	(0.004)
Deregulated	0.033	0.697*
	(0.545)	(0.390)
Unified Democratic Government	–0.843*	0.038
	(0.508)	(0.516)
Party Decline	0.031	0.290
	(0.518)	(0.497)
Geographic Neighbor	1.586*	0.872
	(0.841)	(1.386)
Ideological Neighbor	–0.315	–1.355
	(0.976)	(1.193)
Prior Inventing	–3.553	
	(8.238)	
Prior Borrowing		–60.317***
		(16.513)
Year	0.221***	0.089**
	(0.070)	(0.041)
Featureyear		0.134***
		(0.007)
Wald X^2	274.54***	601.19***
Observations	90,924 (96)	30,926 (357)

*** = critical value of 0.01; ** = critical value of 0.05; * = critical value of 0.10

TABLE A9. Results Dropping Rates/Thresholds for Models Shown in Table 3 of Chapter 5

Variable	Inventing (1)	Borrowing (2)
Government Ideology	0.015**	0.011
	(0.006)	(0.010)
Median Incumbent Vote Share	−0.006	−0.022***
	(0.010)	(0.007)
Real Energy Price	−0.089	−0.043
	(0.073)	(0.063)
Citizen Ideology	0.020	0.029**
	(0.021)	(0.013)
Leg. Professionalism	−0.741	0.725
	(1.555)	(1.748)
State Per Capita Income	0.022	−0.010
	(0.027)	(0.013)
Urban Percentage	0.002	0.031**
	(0.024)	(0.015)
Change in Unemployment	−0.217	0.003
	(0.204)	(0.173)
Fossil Fuel Production	−0.003	0.001
	(0.004)	(0.005)
Deregulated	−0.296	0.774*
	(0.489)	(0.400)
Unified Democratic Government	−0.606	0.059
	(0.405)	(0.522)
Party Decline	−0.106	0.333
	(0.481)	(0.535)
Geographic Neighbor	1.820**	0.959
	(0.804)	(1.370)
Ideological Neighbor	−0.337	−1.457
	(0.874)	(1.217)
Prior Inventing	−5.920	
	(7.985)	
Prior Borrowing		−80.972***
		(17.210)
Year	0.239***	0.113**
	(0.059)	(0.044)
Featureyear		0.125***
		(0.006)
Wald X^2	94.59***	809.88***
Observations	129,203 (124)	34,479 (335)

*** = critical value of 0.01; ** = critical value of 0.05; * = critical value of 0.10

TABLE A10. Full Results for Models Shown in Table 6 of Chapter 6

Variable	Inventing (1)	Borrowing (2)
Deregulation	1.021**	0.318
	(0.487)	(0.835)
Elected	1.618**	2.246***
	(0.674)	(0.670)
Price of Energy	−0.109	−0.283*
	(0.124)	(0.154)
Daily Solar Radiation Level	1.101***	1.909***
	(0.311)	(0.354)
State Per Capita Income	−0.008	−0.009
	(0.029)	(0.029)
Fossil Fuel Sources	−0.018**	−0.027**
	(0.007)	(0.010)
Citizen Ideology	0.068***	0.145***
	(0.023)	(0.041)
Unified Democratic Government	0.695	−1.178
	(0.589)	(0.891)
Government Ideology	−0.024**	0.003
	(0.011)	(0.016)
Legislative Term Limits	−0.794	−0.757
	(0.717)	(0.685)
Legislative Median Incumbent Vote Share	−0.002	−0.0008
	(0.010)	(0.010)
Urban Percentage	0.020	−0.005
	(0.029)	(0.025)
Change in Unemployment	−0.296	−0.612**
	(0.195)	(0.261)
Legislative Professionalism	2.911	6.873***
	(2.119)	(2.541)
Geographic Neighbor	−0.007	2.031
	(1.588)	(1.343)
Ideological Neighbor	0.412	0.833
	(1.250)	(1.443)
Prior Inventing	−3.033	
	(8.382)	
Prior Borrowing		−20.816
		(15.664)
Year	0.263**	0.147
	(0.117)	(0.140)
Featureyear		0.150***
		(0.015)
Wald X^2	614.41***	910.17***
Observations	182,851 (36)	47,130 (54)

*** = critical value of 0.01; ** = critical value of 0.05; * = critical value of 0.10

TABLE AII. Results Including Direct Ballot Initiative for Models in Table 6 of Chapter 6

Variable	Inventing (1)	Borrowing (2)
Deregulation	1.014**	0.209
	(0.479)	(0.746)
Direct Ballot Initiative	-0.669	-1.766*
	(0.714)	(0.959)
Elected	1.817**	3.037***
	(0.732)	(0.929)
Price of Energy	-0.109	-0.294*
	(0.132)	(0.162)
Daily Solar Radiation Level	1.079***	1.723***
	(0.288)	(0.291)
State Per Capita Income	-0.010	-0.002
	(0.030)	(0.024)
Fossil Fuel Sources	-0.017**	-0.022***
	(0.007)	(0.008)
Citizen Ideology	0.068***	0.148***
	(0.024)	(0.044)
Unified Democratic Government	0.687	-1.036
	(0.573)	(0.690)
Government Ideology	-0.024**	0.001
	(0.010)	(0.014)
Legislative Term Limits	-0.490	0.131
	(0.649)	(0.633)
Legislative Median Incumbent	-0.007	-0.016
Vote Share	(0.013)	(0.012)
Urban Percentage	0.021	0.002
	(0.027)	(0.022)
Change in Unemployment	-0.289	-0.606**
	(0.190)	(0.264)
Legislative Professionalism	3.291	7.354***
	(2.073)	(2.053)
Geographic Neighbor	0.161	2.226*
	(1.598)	(1.287)
Ideological Neighbor	0.408	0.732
	(1.240)	(1.409)
Prior Inventing	-3.358	
	(8.285)	
Prior Borrowing		-18.662
		(14.147)
Year	0.264**	0.145
	(0.125)	(0.140)
Featureyear		0.150***
		(0.015)
Wald X^2	539.58***	1,289.15***
Observations	182,851 (36)	47,130 (54)

*** = critical value of 0.01; ** = critical value of 0.05; * = critical value of 0.10

TABLE A12. Results Using Mean Incumbent Vote Share for Electoral Vulnerability in Models Shown in Table 6 of Chapter 6

Variable	Inventing (1)	Borrowing (2)
Deregulation	1.025**	0.246
	(0.495)	(0.861)
Legislative Mean Incumbent	0.003	0.010
Vote Share	(0.014)	(0.020)
Elected	1.641**	2.354***
	(0.713)	(0.753)
Price of Energy	−0.112	−0.297*
	(0.130)	(0.167)
Daily Solar Radiation Level	1.123***	1.956***
	(0.317)	(0.373)
State Per Capita Income	−0.005	−0.007
	(0.030)	(0.029)
Fossil Fuel Sources	−0.018**	−0.027***
	(0.007)	(0.010)
Citizen Ideology	0.070***	0.154***
	(0.024)	(0.048)
Unified Democratic Government	0.716	−1.243
	(0.606)	(0.918)
Government Ideology	−0.025**	0.002
	(0.011)	(0.015)
Legislative Term Limits	−0.680	−0.510
	(0.719)	(0.740)
Urban	0.020	−0.009
Percentage	(0.031)	(0.023)
Change in Unemployment	−0.306	−0.648**
	(0.199)	(0.279)
Legislative Professionalism	2.727	6.994***
	(2.193)	(2.652)
Geographic Neighbor	0.056	2.094
	(1.579)	(1.324)
Ideological Neighbor	0.467	0.918
	(1.249)	(1.482)
Prior Inventing	−3.334	
	(8.366)	
Prior Borrowing		−21.005
		(15.351)
Year	0.264**	0.157
	(0.122)	(0.151)
Featureyear		0.150***
		(0.015)
Wald X^2	562.64***	915.45***
Observations	182,851 (36)	47,130 (54)

*** = critical value of 0.01; ** = critical value of 0.05; * = critical value of 0.10

TABLE A13. Results Dropping Combinations for Models Shown in Table 6 of Chapter 6

Variable	Inventing (1)	Borrowing (2)
Deregulation	0.305	0.337
	(0.742)	(0.844)
Elected	4.593	2.211***
	(3.115)	(0.658)
Price of Energy	−0.219	−0.273*
	(0.137)	(0.152)
Daily Solar Radiation Level	1.065**	1.862***
	(0.453)	(0.349)
State Per Capita Income	0.057	−0.009
	(0.097)	(0.029)
Fossil Fuel Sources	−0.007	−0.026**
	(0.012)	(0.010)
Citizen Ideology	0.082*	0.144***
	(0.043)	(0.041)
Unified Democratic Government	−0.260	−1.151
	(1.394)	(0.915)
Government Ideology	−0.043***	0.003
	(0.015)	(0.016)
Legislative Term Limits	−1.381	−0.764
	(0.977)	(0.682)
Legislative Median Incumbent Vote Share	0.019	−0.0008
	(0.030)	(0.010)
Urban Percentage	0.198	−0.003
	(0.147)	(0.025)
Change in Unemployment	−0.437*	−0.596**
	(0.250)	(0.261)
Legislative Professionalism	1.684	6.924***
	(4.402)	(2.527)
Geographic Neighbor	1.888	1.929
	(1.882)	(1.326)
Ideological Neighbor	−0.022	0.855
	(1.519)	(1.449)
Prior Inventing	−17.354	
	(16.417)	
Prior Borrowing		−19.727
		(15.612)
Year	0.284***	0.167
	(0.075)	(0.139)
Featureyear		0.130***
		(0.016)
Wald X^2	1,487.91***	657.37***
Observations	90,844 (16)	30,623 (54)

*** = critical value of 0.01; ** = critical value of 0.05; * = critical value of 0.10

TABLE AI4. Results Dropping Rates/Thresholds for Models Shown in Table 6 of Chapter 6

Variable	Inventing (1)	Borrowing (2)
Deregulation	0.678	0.415
	(0.594)	(0.894)
Elected	1.331*	2.109***
	(0.695)	(0.658)
Price of Energy	–0.115	–0.285*
	(0.113)	(0.145)
Daily Solar Radiation Level	0.977***	2.156***
	(0.259)	(0.377)
State Per Capita Income	–0.025	0.003
	(0.024)	(0.025)
Fossil Fuel Sources	–0.013**	–0.028***
	(0.006)	(0.010)
Citizen Ideology	0.056**	0.146***
	(0.025)	(0.040)
Unified Democratic Government	0.484	–1.055
	(0.784)	(0.903)
Government Ideology	–0.019	–0.0007
	(0.012)	(0.017)
Legislative Term Limits	–0.799	–1.098
	(0.744)	(0.748)
Legislative Median Incumbent	–0.006	–0.001
Vote Share	(0.009)	(0.009)
Urban	0.037	–0.018
Percentage	(0.033)	(0.024)
Change in Unemployment	–0.344	–0.640**
	(0.230)	(0.265)
Legislative Professionalism	2.086	6.797***
	(2.215)	(2.322)
Geographic Neighbor	–0.149	2.089
	(1.576)	(1.325)
Ideological Neighbor	–0.698	0.570
	(1.083)	(1.503)
Prior Inventing	0.070	
	(5.589)	
Prior Borrowing		–18.631
		(13.685)
Year	0.252***	0.180
	(0.092)	(0.128)
Featureyear		0.094***
		(0.009)
Wald X^2	646.63***	1,641.06***
Observations	129,105 (26)	34,197 (53)

*** = critical value of 0.01; ** = critical value of 0.05; * = critical value of 0.10

TABLE A15. Results Using Mean Incumbent Vote Share for Electoral Vulnerability in Models Shown in Table 8 of Chapter 8 (Selected Variables)

Variable	Legislative Invention (1)	Legislative Borrowing (2)	Legislative Invention (3)	Legislative Borrowing (4)
Government Ideology	-0.013*	-0.004	-0.012*	-0.003
	(0.006)	(0.004)	(0.007)	(0.004)
Mean Incumbent Legislator	-0.016**	0.007	-0.018**	0.007
Vote Share	(0.008)	(0.004)	(0.009)	(0.004)
Norrander	0.367	0.465	0.414	0.495
	(0.795)	(0.307)	(0.856)	(0.321)
Religious Adherence	1.577	0.954	2.076*	1.098
	(1.002)	(0.665)	(1.107)	(0.689)
Unified Democratic	0.133	-0.148	0.108	-0.165
Legislature	(0.299)	(0.147)	(0.328)	(0.148)
Female Democrats	-1.547	-4.815***	-2.281	-4.634**
	(3.195)	(1.805)	(3.275)	(1.843)
Democratic Governor	-0.101	-0.113	-0.106	-0.138
	(0.303)	(0.145)	(0.364)	(0.152)
Initiatives	0.061	0.070***	0.084	0.073***
	(0.054)	(0.025)	(0.063)	(0.026)
Neighbors	6.612***	2.558***	6.489***	2.564***
	(0.758)	(0.216)	(0.748)	(0.215)
Citizen Ideology			-0.001	-0.0009
			(0.006)	(0.002)
Ideological Similarity			-1.850*	0.780
			(1.035)	(0.485)
Prior Invention			-9.262	
			(5.655)	
Prior Borrowing				-2.739
				(3.048)
Observations	18,782	26,831	18,782	26,831
	(104)	(568)	(104)	(568)

*** = critical value of 0.01; ** = critical value of 0.05; * = critical value of 0.10

TABLE A16. Results Substituting Year Squared Variable for Year Variable in Invention Models Shown in Table 8 of Chapter 8 (Selected Variables)

Variable	Legislative Invention	Legislative Invention
Government Ideology	-0.012*	-0.012*
	(0.006)	(0.006)
Median Incumbent Legislator	-0.011**	-0.012**
Vote Share	(0.005)	(0.006)
Norrander	0.424	0.482
	(0.761)	(0.815)
Religious Adherence	1.606	2.087*
	(0.981)	(1.083)
Unified Democratic Legislature	0.115	0.089
	(0.300)	(0.320)
Female Democrats	-1.262	-1.935
	(3.203)	(3.291)
Democratic Governor	-0.114	-0.114
	(0.339)	(0.345)
Initiatives	0.063	0.085
	(0.053)	(0.061)
Neighbors	6.624***	6.502***
	(0.756)	(0.748)
Year Squared	0.00001	0.00002
	$(9.9*10^{-6})$	$(9.33*10^{-6})$
Citizen Ideology		-0.0007
		(0.001)
Ideological Similarity		-1.842*
		(1.047)
Prior Invention		-8.968
		(5.545)
Prior Borrowing		
Observations	18,782	18,782
	(104)	(104)

*** = critical value of 0.01; ** = critical value of 0.05; * = critical value of 0.10

TABLE A17. Full Results for Models Shown in Table 8 of Chapter 8

Variable	Legislative Invention (1)	Legislative Borrowing (2)	Legislative Invention (3)	Legislative Borrowing (4)
Government Ideology	−0.012*	−0.005	−0.012*	−0.003
	(0.006)	(0.004)	(0.006)	(0.006)
Median Incumbent Legislator	−0.011**	0.003	−0.012**	0.003
Vote Share	(0.005)	(0.003)	(0.006)	(0.003)
Norrander	0.443	0.449	0.501	0.477
	(0.758)	(0.318)	(0.812)	(0.331)
Religious Adherence	1.594	0.965	2.073*	1.107
	(0.978)	(0.675)	(1.080)	(0.692)
Unified Democratic	0.115	−0.132	0.089	−0.155
Legislature	(0.300)	(0.147)	(0.320)	(0.155)
Female Democrats	−1.235	−4.900***	−1.905	−4.702**
	(3.202)	(0.792)	(3.290)	(1.816)
Democratic Governor	−0.116	−0.101	−0.116	−0.144
	(0.339)	(0.146)	(0.345)	(0.196)
Initiatives	0.063	0.070***	0.085	0.072***
	(0.053)	(0.026)	(0.061)	(0.027)
Neighbors	6.632***	2.555***	6.511***	2.562***
	(0.755)	(0.216)	(0.747)	(0.216)
State Median Income	−0.447	−0.030	−0.478	−0.017
	(0.313)	(0.077)	(0.323)	(0.079)
State Population Size	0.069	0.097	0.111	0.092
	(0.259)	(0.104)	(0.283)	(0.106)
Webster	0.055	0.521**	−0.150	0.520**
	(0.273)	(0.204)	(0.270)	(0.206)
Citizen Ideology			−0.0006	−0.001
			(0.001)	(0.007)
Ideological Similarity			−1.834*	0.805*
			(1.046)	(0.487)
Prior Invention			−8.957	
			(5.540)	
Prior Borrowing				−2.620
				(3.060)
Year	0.064*	−0.097***	0.083**	−0.093***
	(0.036)	(0.018)	(0.037)	(0.025)
Year Squared		0.001***		0.001***
		(0.000)		(0.000)
Observations	18,782	26,831	18,782	26,831
	(104)	(568)	(104)	(568)

*** = critical value of 0.01; ** = critical value of 0.05; * = critical value of 0.10

TABLE A18. Results Including Direct Ballot Initiative for Models in Table 8 of Chapter 8 (Selected Variables)

Variable	Legislative Invention (1)	Legislative Borrowing (2)	Legislative Invention (3)	Legislative Borrowing (4)
Government Ideology	-0.013**	-0.004	-0.012*	-0.003
	(0.006)	(0.004)	(0.006)	(0.006)
Median Incumbent Legislator	-0.011**	0.003	-0.012*	0.003
Vote Share	(0.005)	(0.003)	(0.006)	(0.003)
Direct Ballot Initiative	-0.075	0.006	-0.188	-0.014
	(0.456)	(0.218)	(0.519)	(0.233)
Norrander	0.417	0.451	0.427	0.474
	(0.811)	(0.230)	(0.900)	(0.332)
Religious Adherence	1.645	0.960	2.212*	1.117
	(1.085)	(0.674)	(1.203)	(0.695)
Unified Democratic	0.115	-0.132	0.092	-0.156
Legislature	(0.300)	(0.147)	(0.323)	(0.155)
Female Democrats	-1.245	-4.901***	-1.942	-4.700***
	(3.214)	(1.789)	(3.312)	(1.811)
Democratic Governor	-0.108	-0.102	-0.099	-0.144
	(0.333)	(0.148)	(0.345)	(0.196)
Initiatives	0.075	0.069*	0.115	0.075*
	(0.087)	(0.041)	(0.103)	(0.044)
Neighbors	6.628***	2.555***	6.502***	2.563***
	(0.757)	(0.216)	(0.752)	(0.217)
Citizen Ideology			-0.0009	-0.002
			(0.004)	(0.008)
Ideological Similarity			-1.864*	0.805*
			(1.056)	(0.486)
Prior Invention			-9.088*	
			(5.075)	
Prior Borrowing				-2.636
				(3.121)
Observations	18,782	26,831	18,782	26,831
	(104)	(568)	(104)	(568)

References

Adger, W. Neil, Catherine Butler, and Kate Walker-Springett. 2017. "Moral Reasoning to Adaptation in Climate Change." *Environmental Politics* 26 (3): 371–90.

Adler, Scott. 2002. *Why Congressional Reforms Fail: Reelection and the House Committee System*. Chicago: University of Chicago Press.

Äklin, Michael, and Johannes Urpelainen. 2018. *Renewables: The Politics of a Global Energy Transition*. Cambridge, MA: MIT Press.

Alberta, Tim. 2017. "John Boehner Unchained." *Politico*, November/December. https://www.politico.com/magazine/story/2017/10/29/john-boehner-trump-house-republican-party-retirement-profile-feature-215741/

Aldrich, John. 2011. *Why Parties? A Second Look*. Chicago: University of Chicago Press.

Alessina, Alberto, and Guido Tabellini. 2008. "Bureaucrats or Politicians? Part II: Multiple Policy Tasks." *Journal of Public Economics* 92 (3–4): 426–47.

Allison, Juliann, and Srinivas Parinandi. 2020. "The Energy Politics of the United States." In *The Oxford Handbook of Energy Politics*, edited by Kathleen Hancock and Juliann Allison. New York: Oxford University Press.

Alt, James, and Robert Lowry. 1994. "Divided Government, Fiscal Institutions, and Budget Deficits: Evidence from the States." *American Political Science Review* 88 (4): 811–28.

Ameren. 2007. "Ameren Says Illinois Legislation Is Unconstitutional and Not in Best Interest of Illinois: Immediate Relief to Electric Customers at Risk." News release, April 20. https://ameren.mediaroom.com/news-releases?item=333

American Bar Association. 2018. "A Desperation of Powers?" January 1. https://www.americanbar.org/groups/public_education/publications/insights-on-law-and-society/volume-18/insights-issue-1-vol-1/a-deseparation-of-powers-/#:~:text=The%20federal%20bureaucracy%20is%20hardly%20mentioned%20in%20the%20United%20States%20Constitution.&text=Since%20this%20time%2C%20the%20federal,and%20roughly%203%2C000%2C000%20civil%20servants

American Energy Alliance. 2011. "Energy Townhall." https://www.americanenergyalliance.org/2011/05/in-the-pipeline-51711/

Appelbaum, Yoni. 2015. "America's Fragile Constitution." *The Atlantic*, October.

Arel-Bundock, Vincent, and Srinivas Parinandi. 2018. "Conditional Tax Competition in the American States." *Journal of Public Policy* 38 (2): 191–220.

Arizona Corporation Commission. Decision 59943 (1996). Available at: https://www .azcc.gov/

Arizona Corporation Commission. Decision 62506 (2000). Available at: https://www .azcc.gov/

Arizona Corporation Commission. Decision 69127 (2006). Available at: https://www .azcc.gov/

Arizona Corporation Commission. 2020. "ACC Mission and Background." https:// www.azcc.gov/divisions

Arizona Corporation Commission. 2022a. "Meet the Commissioners." Retrieved 3 February 2022, https://www.azcc.gov/jim-oconnor/biography

Arizona Corporation Commission. 2022b. "About the Commission." Retrieved 7 February 2022, https://azcc.gov/azinvestor/about-the-commission

Arnold, Douglas. 1990. *The Logic of Congressional Action*. New Haven: Yale University Press.

Ashworth, Scott. 2012. "Electoral Accountability: Recent Theoretical and Empirical Work." *Annual Review of Political Science* 15: 183–201.

Baker, Scott, and Alex Raskolnikov. 2017. "Harmful, Harmless, and Beneficial Uncertainty in Law." *Journal of Legal Studies* 46 (2): 281–307.

Ballotpedia. 2021. "Public Service Commissioner." https://ballotpedia.org/Public_ Service_Commissioner_(state_executive_office

Bartels, Larry. 2018. "Partisanship in the Trump Era." *Journal of Politics* 80 (4): 1483– 94.

Baybeck, Brady, William D. Berry, and David A. Siegel. 2011. "A Strategic Theory of Policy Diffusion via Intergovernmental Competition." *Journal of Politics* 73 (1): 232–47.

Bayer, Patrick, and Michael Äklin. 2020. "The European Union Emissions Trading System Reduced CO2 Emissions despite Low Prices." *Proceedings of the National Academy of Sciences* 117 (16): 8804–12.

Beck, Nathaniel, Kristian Gleditsch, and Kyle Beardsley. 2006. "Space Is More Than Geography: Using Spatial Econometrics in the Study of Political Economy." *International Studies Quarterly* 50 (1): 27–44.

Bednar, Jenna. 2008. *The Robust Federation: Principles of Design*. New York: Cambridge University Press.

Berry, Frances Stokes, and William D. Berry. 1990. "State Lottery Adoptions as Policy Innovations: An Event History Analysis." *American Political Science Review* 84 (2): 395–415.

Berry, Frances Stokes, and William D. Berry. 2018. "Innovation and Diffusion Models in Policy Research." In *Theories of the Policy Process*, 4th ed., edited by Christopher Weible and Paul Sabatier. New York: Routledge.

Berry, William, Richard Fording, Evan Ringquist, Russell Hanson, and Carl Klarner. 2010. "Measuring Citizen and Government Ideology in the U.S. States: A Reappraisal." *State Politics and Policy Quarterly* 10 (2): 117–35.

Berry, William, Evan Ringquist, Richard Fording, and Russell Hanson. 1998. "Measuring Citizen and Government Ideology in the American States, 1960–93." *American Journal of Political Science* 42 (1): 327–48.

Besley, Timothy, and Anne Case. 2003. "Political Institutions and Policy Choices: Evidence from the United States." *Journal of Economic Literature* 41 (1): 7–73.

Besley, Timothy, and Stephen Coate. 2003. "Elected versus Appointed Regulators: Theory and Evidence." *Journal of the European Economic Association* 1 (5): 1176–1206.

Binder, Sarah. 1999. "The Dynamics of Legislative Gridlock, 1947–96." *American Political Science Review* 93 (3): 519–33.

Binder, Sarah. 2003. *Stalemate: Causes and Consequences of Legislative Gridlock*. Washington, DC: Brookings Institution Press.

Binder, Sarah. 2014. "Polarized We Govern?" Center for Effective Public Management. Washington, DC: Brookings Institution Press.

Binder, Sarah. 2015. "The Dysfunctional Congress." *Annual Review of Political Science* 18: 85-101.

Blunt, Katherine, and Russell Gold. 2021. "The Texas Freeze: Why the Power Grid Failed." *Wall Street Journal*, February 19.

Boehmke, Frederick. 2009. "Approaches to Modeling the Adoption and Modification of Policies with Multiple Components." *State Politics and Policy Quarterly* 9 (2): 229–52.

Boehmke, Frederick, Mark Brockway, Bruce Desmarais, Jeffrey Harden, Scott LaCombe, Fridolin Linder, and Hanna Wallach. 2018. "State Policy Innovation and Diffusion (SPID) Database v1.0." https://doi.org/10.7910/DVN/CVYSR7, Harvard Database, V4, UNF:6:thxLqNh8In+OoHGUN4vVew== [fileUNF].

Boehmke, Frederick, and Paul Skinner. 2012. "State Policy Innovativeness Revisited." *State Politics and Policy Quarterly* 12 (3): 303–29.

Bordewich, Fergus. 2013. *America's Great Debate: Henry Clay, Stephen A. Douglas, and the Compromise That Preserved the Union*. New York: Simon and Schuster.

Borenstein, Severin, and James Bushnell. 2015. "The US Electricity Industry after 20 Years of Restructuring." *Annual Review of Economics* 7: 437–63.

Borgia, Kevin. 2012. "Guest Column: Renewable Energy Policy Made Illinois a Leader." *Rockford Register Star*, September 9. https://www.rrstar.com/x1526498631/Guest-Column-Renewable-energy-policy-made-Illinois-a-leader

Boushey, Graeme. 2010. *Policy Diffusion Dynamics in America*. New York: Cambridge University Press.

Boushey, Graeme. 2016. "Targeted for Diffusion? How the Use and Acceptance of Stereotypes Shape the Diffusion of Criminal Justice Policy Innovations in the American States." *American Political Science Review* 110 (1): 198–214.

Boushey, Graeme, and Robert McGrath. 2017. "Experts, Amateurs, and Bureaucratic Influence in the American States." *Journal of Public Administration Research and Theory* 27 (1): 85–103.

Bowman, Karlyn, and Jennifer Marisco. 2014. "Opinions about Abortion Haven't Changed since *Roe v. Wade*." *The Atlantic*, January 22.

Box-Steffensmeier, Janet, and Bradford Jones. 1997. "Time Is of the Essence: Event

History Models in Political Science." *American Journal of Political Science* 41 (4): 1414–61.

Box-Steffensmeier, Janet, and Bradford Jones. 2004. *Event History Modeling: A Guide for Social Scientists.* New York: Cambridge University Press.

Boyes, William, and John McDowell. 1989. "The Selection of Public Utility Commissioners: A Re-examination of the Importance of Institutional Setting." *Public Choice* 61 (1): 1–13.

Braithwaite, John. 2008. "The Regulatory State?" In *The Oxford Handbook of Political Institutions,* edited by Sarah Binder, R. A. W. Rhodes, and Bert Rockman. New York: Oxford University Press.

Brandeis, Louis. 1932. Opinion quoted in *New State Ice Company versus Liebmann,* 285 U.S. 262.

British Columbia (Province of). 2020. "Motor Fuel Tax and Carbon Tax." https://www2.gov.bc.ca/gov/content/taxes/sales-taxes/motor-fuel-carbon-tax

Brown, Kate, and David Hess. 2016. "Pathways to Policy: Partisanship and Bipartisanship in Renewable Energy Legislation." *Environmental Politics* 25 (6): 971–90.

Bucchianieri, Peter, Craig Volden, and Alan Wiseman. 2020. "Legislative Effectiveness in the American States." Paper submitted for the 2020 American Political Science Association Conference.

Bulman-Pozen, Jessica. 2014. "Partisan Federalism." *Harvard Law Review* 127: 1077–1146.

Butler, Daniel, Craig Volden, Adam Dynes, and Boris Shor. 2017. "Ideology, Learning, and Policy Diffusion: Experimental Evidence." *American Journal of Political Science* 61 (1): 37–49.

Butler, Lindsey, Madeleine Scammel, and Eugene Benson. 2016. "The Flint, Michigan, Water Crisis: A Case Study in Regulatory Failure and Environmental Injustice." *Environmental Justice* 9 (4): 93–97.

Byrnett, Danielle, and Daniel Shea. 2019. "Engagement between Public Utility Commissions and State Legislatures." *National Council on Electricity Policy Mini-Guide.* Washington, DC: National Council on Electricity Policy.

Cai, Hongbin, and Daniel Treisman. 2009. "Political Decentralization and Policy Experimentation." *Quarterly Journal of Political Science* 4 (1): 35–58.

California Legislature. Legislative Research webpage (2018). http://www.legislature.ca.gov/research.html

California Legislature. Senate Bill X1–2 (2011). Retrieved 12 October 2018 and accessed via the California legislative information website, http://leginfo.legislature.ca.gov/faces/billSearchClient.xhtml

Calvillo, Dustin, Bryan Ross, Ryan Garcia, Thomas Smelter, and Abraham Rutchick. 2020. "Political Ideology Predicts Perceptions of the Threat of COVID-19 (and Susceptibility to Fake News about It)." *Social Psychological and Personality Science* 11 (8): 1119–28.

Carley, Sanya, and Chris Miller. 2012. "Regulatory Stringency and Policy Drivers: A Reassessment of Renewable Portfolio Standards." *Policy Studies Journal* 40 (4): 730–56.

Carley, Sanya, Sean Nicholson-Crotty, and Chris Miller. 2017. "Adoption, Reinvention, and Amendment of Renewable Portfolio Standards in the American States." *Journal of Public Policy* 37 (4): 431–58.

Carrigan, Christopher, and Cary Coglianese. 2011. "The Politics of Regulation: From New Institutionalism to New Governance." *Annual Review of Political Science* 14: 107–29.

Cha, Ariana. 2018. "Babies with Down Syndrome Are Put on Center Stage in the U.S. Abortion Fight." *Washington Post*, March 5.

Chhibber, Pradeep, and Ken Kollman. 2004. *The Formation of National Party Systems: Federalism and Party Competition in Canada, Great Britain, India, and the United States*. Princeton: Princeton University Press.

Clark, Jill. 1985. "Policy Diffusion and Program Scope: Research Directions." *Publius* 15: 61-70.

Cleary, Kathryne, and Karen Palmer. 2020. "Renewables 101: Integrating Renewable Energy Resources into the Grid." Resources for the Future, April 15. https://www.rff.org/publications/explainers/renewables-101-integrating-renewables/

Colorado Department of Regulatory Agencies. 2020. "About Electric." Retrieved 6 October 2020, accessed at https://puc.colorado.gov/aboutelectric

Connecticut General Assembly. House Bill 5005 (1998). Retrieved 10 October 2018, accessed at https://www.cga.ct.gov/asp/cgabillstatus/cgabillstatus.asp?selBillType=Bill&which_year=1998&bill_num=5005

Consolidated Edison Company of New York. 2006. 2006 Annual Report. https://www.annualreports.com/HostedData/AnnualReportArchive/c/NYSE_ED_2006.pdf

Consolidated Edison Company of New York. 2020a. "2020 Distributed Generation Winter Workshop." https://www.coned.com/-/media/files/coned/documents/save-energy-money/using-private-generation/applying-for-interconnection/2020-winter-workshop.pdf?la=en

Consolidated Edison Company of New York. 2020b. "Our Clean Energy Commitment." https://www.coned.com/en/our-energy-future/our-energy-vision/our-energy-future-commitment#:~:text=100%25%20Clean%20Electricity%20by%202040&text=We're%20the%20seventh%20largest,renewable%20projects%20across%20the%20country

Constans, Helen. 1958. "Max Weber's Two Conceptions of Bureaucracy." *American Journal of Sociology* 63 (4): 400–409.

Consumer Reports. 2018. "2018 Energy Utilities Survey Report." https://advocacy.consumerreports.org/wp-content/uploads/2018/10/CR-2018-Energy-Utilities-Survey-Report-1.pdf

Converse, Philip. 1964. "The Nature of Belief Systems in Mass Publics." *Critical Review* 18 (1–3): 1–74.

Council of State Governments. Multiple years. *Book of the States*. Lexington, KY: CSG Press.

Cox, Gary, and Mathew McCubbins. 2005. *Setting the Agenda: Responsible Party Government in the U.S. House of Representatives*. New York: Cambridge University Press.

Crop Prophet. 2021. "U.S. Corn Production by State: The Top 11." https://www.

cropprophet.com/us-corn-production-by-state/#RankingsOfStateCornProductio nOverTime

Dal Bo, Ernesto. 2006. "Regulatory Capture: A Review." *Oxford Review of Economic Policy* 22 (2): 203–25.

Delmas, Magali, Michael Russo, and Maria Montes-Sancho. 2007. "Deregulation and Environmental Differentiation in the Electric Utility Industry." *Strategic Management Journal* 28: 189–209.

Desmarais, Bruce, Jeffrey Harden, and Frederick Boehmke. 2015. "Persistent Policy Pathways: Inferring Diffusion Networks in the American States." *American Political Science Review* 109 (2): 392–406.

Domonske, Camila. 2017. "North Carolina Repeals Portions of Controversial 'Bathroom Bill.'" *The Two-Way* (National Public Radio), March 30.

Duda, Jeremy. 2018. "Corp Comm May Take Another Look at Deregulation." *Arizona Capitol Times*, August 14.

Eick, John. 2015. "West Virginia Becomes First State to Repeal RPS." American Legislative Exchange Council "Regulatory Reform" newsletter, February 4.

ElectricChoice. 2018. Website detailing states with deregulated electricity markets. https://www.electricchoice.com/map-deregulated-energy-markets/

Eligon, John, and Eric Eckholm. 2013. "New Laws Ban Most Abortions in North Dakota." *New York Times*, March 26.

Elkins, Stanley, and Eric McKitrick. 1995. *The Age of Federalism: The Early American Republic, 1788–1800.* New York: Oxford University Press.

Epstein, David, and Sharyn O'Halloran. 1999. *Delegating Powers: A Transaction Cost Politics Approach to Policy Making under Separate Powers.* New York: Cambridge University Press.

Fenno, Richard. 1978. *Home Style: House Members in Their Districts.* Boston: Little, Brown.

Filipink, Eric. 2009. "Serving the 'Public Interest'—Traditional versus Expansive Utility Regulation." National Regulatory Research Institute Working Paper (NRRI Report 10-02).

First, Harry. 2002. "Regulated Deregulation: The New York Experience in Electric Utility Deregulation." *Loyola University Chicago Law Journal* 33 (4): 911–32.

Fleetwood, Janet. 2017. "Public Health, Ethics, and Autonomous Vehicles." *American Journal of Public Health* 107 (4): 532–37.

Flynn, D. J., and Laurel Harbridge. 2016. "How Partisan Conflict in Congress Affects Public Opinion: Strategies, Outcomes, and Issue Differences." *American Politics Research* 44 (5): 875–902.

Fortunato, David, and Srinivas Parinandi. 2021. "Social Welfare Returns to Legislative Capacity: Evidence from the Opioid Epidemic." Working paper.

Fowler, James. 2006. "Legislative Cosponsorship Networks in the U.S. House and Senate." *Social Networks* 28 (4): 454–65.

Gailmard, Sean. 2002. "Expertise, Subversion, and Bureaucratic Discretion." *Journal of Law, Economics, and Organization* 18 (2): 536–55.

Gailmard, Sean, and John Patty. 2007. "Slackers and Zealots: Civil Service, Policy Discretion, and Bureaucratic Expertise." *American Journal of Political Science* 51 (4): 873–89.

Gailmard, Sean, and John Patty. 2013. *Learning While Governing: Expertise and Accountability in the Executive Branch.* Chicago: University of Chicago Press.

Gale, William. 2017. "The Kansas Tax Cut Experiment." *Unpacked,* July 11. Washington, DC: Brookings Institution.

Gallup. 2020. "Trust in Government." https://news.gallup.com/poll/5392/trust-government.aspx

Gard, Beverly, Brandt Hershman, and Jim Merritt. 2011. "This Bill—SB 251—Offers the Right Energy Policy for State." *Indianapolis Star,* March 1. http://www.indianadg.net/sens-gard-hershman-and-merritt-this-bill-sb-251-offers-the-right-energy-policy-for-state/?fbclid=IwAR0GHkiOEfGeTtA27G0i-FoyfI3LpT4N-f2AmXVNaF9CWawZ7Liog7YVXPHY

Gerken, Heather. 2017. "We're about to See States' Rights Used Defensively against Trump." *Vox,* January 20.

Gilardi, Fabrizio. 2010. "Who Learns from What in Policy Diffusion Processes?" *American Journal of Political Science* 54 (3): 650–66.

Gilardi, Fabrizio. 2016. "Four Ways We Can Improve Policy Diffusion Research." *State Politics and Policy Quarterly* 16 (1): 8–21.

Gilardi, Fabrizio, and Fabio Wasserfallen. 2019. "The Politics of Policy Diffusion." *European Journal of Political Research* 58 (4): 1245–56.

Glaeser, Edward, and Andrei Shleifer. 2003. "The Rise of the Regulatory State." *Journal of Economic Literature* 41 (2): 401–25.

Glick, Henry, and Scott Hays. 1991. "Innovation and Reinvention in State Policymaking: Theory and the Evolution of Living Will Laws." *Journal of Politics* 53 (3): 835–50.

Gormley, William. 1983. *The Politics of Public Utility Regulation.* Pittsburgh: University of Pittsburgh Press.

Gormley, William, and Steven Balla. 2018. *Bureaucracy and Democracy: Accountability and Performance.* 4th ed. Thousand Oaks, CA: CQ Press.

Graham, Erin, Charles Shipan, and Craig Volden. 2013. "The Diffusion of Policy Diffusion Research in Political Science." *British Journal of Political Science* 43 (3): 673–701.

Gray, Virginia. 1973. "Innovation in the States: A Diffusion Study." *American Political Science Review* 67 (4): 1174–85.

Greenstone, Michael, and Ishan Nath. 2019. "Do Renewable Portfolio Standards Deliver?" Energy Policy Institute at the University of Chicago Working Paper 2019–62.

Greenwood, Tom. 2015. "Metro Detroit Roads Ranked 4th Worst in U.S." *Detroit News,* July 23.

Greve, Michael. 2001. "Laboratories of Democracy: Anatomy of a Metaphor." American Enterprise Institute, March 31.

Grodzins, Morton. 1960. "The Federal System." In *Goals for Americans.* Englewood Cliffs, NJ: Prentice-Hall.

Gromet, Dena, Howard Kunreuther, and Richard Larrick. 2013. "Political Ideology Affects Energy-Efficiency Attitudes and Choices." *Proceedings of the National Academy of Sciences of the United States of America.* https://doi.org/10.1073/pnas.1218453110

Gross, Liza. 2018. "Confronting Climate Change in the Age of Denial." *PLoS Biology* 16 (10): e3000033.

Grossback, Lawrence, Sean Nicholson-Crotty, and David Peterson. 2004. "Ideology and Learning in Policy Diffusion." *American Politics Research* 32 (5): 521–45.

Gruenspecht, Howard. 2019. "The U.S. Coal Sector: Recent and Continuing Challenges." Cross-Brookings Initiative on Energy and Climate Report. Washington, DC: Brookings Institution.

Gualmini, Elisabetta. 2008. "Restructuring Weberian Bureaucracy: Comparing Managerial Reforms in Europe and the United States." *Public Administration* 86 (1): 75–94.

Guthrie, Graeme. 2006. "Regulating Infrastructure: The Impact on Risk and Investment." *Journal of Economic Literature* 44: 925–72.

Guttmacher Institute. 2020. "State Legislation Tracker." Retrieved 11 November 2020, from https://www.guttmacher.org/state-policy

Harkness, Peter. 2018. "Federalism Is Broken: Can It Be Fixed?" *Governing*, July.

Hays, Scott. 1996. "Influences on Reinvention during the Diffusion of Innovations." *Political Research Quarterly* 49 (3): 631–50.

Heeter, Jenny, and Lori Bird. 2012. "Including Alternative Resources in State Renewable Portfolio Standards: Current Design and Implementation Experience." National Renewable Energy Laboratory Paper SA09.3110.

Hess, David, Quan Mai, and Kate Pride Brown. 2016. "Red States, Green Laws: Ideology and Renewable Energy Legislation in the United States." *Energy Research and Social Science* 11: 19–28.

Hickel, Jason. 2020. "Quantifying National Responsibility for Climate Breakdown: An Equality-Based Attribution Approach for Carbon Dioxide Emissions in Excess of the Planetary Boundary." *Lancet Planetary Health* 4 (9): E399-E404.

Hinz, Greg. 2004. "Donald Harmon, 37." *Crain's Chicago Business*. https://www.chicagobusiness.com/awards/donald-harmon

Holland, Stephen, Jonathan Hughes, and Christopher Knittel. 2009. "Greenhouse Gas Reductions under Low Carbon Fuel Standards." *American Economic Journal: Economic Policy* 1: 106–46.

Hoosier Environmental Council. 2021a. https://www.hecweb.org/

Hoosier Environmental Council. 2021b. "Sustainable Energy." https://www.hecweb.org/issues/sustainable-economy/

Hosmer, David, and Stanley Lemeshow. 2000. *Applied Logistic Regression*. Hoboken, NJ: John Wiley and Sons.

Howell, Emily, Christopher Wirz, Dominique Brossard, Dietram Scheufele, and Michael Xenos. 2019. "Seeing through Risk-Colored Glasses: Risk and Benefit Perceptions, Knowledge, and the Politics of Fracking in the United States." *Energy Research and Social Science* 55: 168–178.

Huber, John D., and Charles Shipan. 2002. *Deliberate Discretion? The Institutional Foundations of Bureaucratic Autonomy*. New York: Cambridge University Press.

Hughes, Llewelyn, and Phillip Lipscy. 2013. "The Politics of Energy." *Annual Review of Political Science* 16: 449–69.

Hurlburt, David. 2008. "A Look behind the Texas Renewable Portfolio Standard: A Case Study." *Natural Resources Journal* 48 (1): 129–61.

Illinois Environmental Council. 2020a. "Who We Are." https://ilenviro.org/about/

Illinois Environmental Council. 2020b. "Energy." https://ilenviro.org/energy/

Illinois General Assembly. Senate Bill 1592 (2007). https://www.ilga.gov/legislation/publicacts/fulltext.asp?Name=095-0481

Illinois Senate Democratic Caucus. 2021. "Awards and Honors." http://www.donharmon.org/about-senator-harmon/about-senator-harmon-2

Indiana General Assembly. Senate Bill 251 (2011). http://www.in.gov/legislative/2414.htm

Iowa Legislature. Alternative Energy Law (1983). Retrieved October 10, 2018 from a scan of 1983 Iowa Session Laws.

Jackson, Jesse, Jr. 2004. "Reagan: A Legacy of States' Rights." *The Nation*, June 17.

Joint Utilities 2004. "Brief Opposing Exceptions." Filed July 8. http://documents.dps.ny.gov/public/MatterManagement/CaseMaster.aspx?MatterSeq=17612

Ka, Sangjoon, and Paul Teske. 2002. "Ideology and Professionalism: Electricity Regulation and Deregulation over Time in the American States." *American Politics Research* 30 (3): 323–43.

Karch, Andrew. 2007. *Democratic Laboratories: Policy Diffusion among the American States*. Ann Arbor: University of Michigan Press.

Kettl, Donald. 2008. "Public Bureaucracies." In *The Oxford Handbook of Political Institutions*, edited by Sarah Binder, R. A. W. Rhodes, and Bert Rockman. New York: Oxford University Press.

Kettl, Donald. 2020. "States Divided: The Implications of American Federalism for COVID-19." *Public Administration Review* 80 (4): 595–602.

Kim, Eun Sung, Joonseok Yang, and Johannes Urpelainen. 2016. "Does Power Sector Deregulation Promote or Discourage Renewable Energy Policy? Evidence from the States, 1991–2012." *Review of Policy Research* 33 (1): 22–50.

Klarner, Carl, William Berry, Thomas Carsey, Malcolm Jewell, Richard Niemi, Lynda Powell, and James Snyder. 2013. "State Legislative Elections Returns Data, 1967–2010." Available at https://hdl.handle.net/1902.1/20401

Knittel, Christopher. 2006. "The Adoption of State Electricity Regulation: The Role of Interest Groups." *Journal of Industrial Economics* 54 (2): 201–22.

Kogan, Vladimir, Stephane Lavertu, and Zachary Peskowitz. 2016. "Performance Federalism and Local Federalism: Theory and Evidence from School Tax Referenda." *American Journal of Political Science* 60 (2): 418–35.

Koubi, Vally. 2019. "Climate Change and Conflict." *Annual Review of Political Science* 22: 343-60.

Kousser, Thad. 2005. *Term Limits and the Dismantling of Legislative Professionalism*. New York: Cambridge University Press.

Krehbiel, Keith. 1998. *Pivotal Politics: A Theory of U.S. Lawmaking*. Chicago: University of Chicago Press.

Kreitzer, Rebecca. 2015. "Politics and Morality in State Abortion Policy." *State Politics and Policy Quarterly* 15 (1): 41–66.

Kreitzer, Rebecca, and Frederick Boehmke. 2016. "Modeling Heterogeneity in Pooled Event History Analysis." *State Politics and Policy Quarterly* 16 (1): 121–41.

Kwoka, John. 2002. "Governance Alternatives and Pricing in the U.S. Electric Power Industry." *Journal of Law, Economics, and Organization* 18 (1): 278–94.

Kwoka, John, Michael Pollitt, and Sanem Sergici. 2010. "Divestiture Policy and Operating Efficiency in U.S. Electric Power Distribution." *Journal of Regulatory Economics* 38: 86–109.

Laffont, Jean-Jacques, and Jean Tirole. 1991. "The Politics of Government Decision-Making: A Theory of Regulatory Capture." *Quarterly Journal of Economics* 106 (4): 1089–1127.

Lagerberg, Francesca. 2015. "BEPS: Businesses Call for Clarity." Retrieved July 24, 2020, https://www.grantthornton.global/en/insights/articles/tax-planning-2015/

Lawson, Corrina. 2012. "Niagara Falls, Power and Tesla." *Wired*, August 31. https://www.wired.com/2012/08/niagara-falls-power-and-tesla/

Leech, Beth. 2010. "Lobbying and Influence." In *The Oxford Handbook of American Political Parties and Interest Groups*, edited by Sandy Maisel, Jeffrey Berry, and George C. Edwards III. New York: Oxford University Press.

LegiScan. 2022. "Indiana Senate Bill 251." https://legiscan.com/IN/votes/SB0251/2011

Legislative Assembly of North Dakota. House Bill 1506 (2007). https://www.legis.nd.gov/

Leiserowitz, Anthony, Edward Maibach, Seth Rosenthal, John Kotcher, Matthew Ballew, Matthew Goldberg, and Abel Gustafson. 2018. *Climate Change in the American Mind: December 2018*. Yale University and George Mason University. New Haven: Yale Program on Climate Change Communication.

Lewis, David. 2012. "The Personnel Process in the Modern Presidency." *Presidential Studies Quarterly* 42 (3): 577–96.

Lipscy, Phillip, and Llewellyn Hughes. 2013. "The Politics of Energy." *Annual Review of Political Science* 16: 449–69.

Long, J. Scott, and Jeremy Freese. 2006. *Regression Models for Categorical Dependent Variables Using Stata*. College Station, TX: Stata Press.

Luber, Mindy. 2013. "Protecting Renewable Portfolio Standards from Cynical Attacks." *CleanEnergy.Org* blog, March 22.

Lupia, Arthur. 1994. "Shortcuts versus Encyclopedias: Information and Voting Behavior in California Insurance Reform Elections." *American Political Science Review* 88 (1): 63–76.

Makse, Todd, and Craig Volden. 2011. "The Role of Policy Attributes in the Diffusion of Innovations." *Journal of Politics* 73 (1): 108–24.

Marbury versus Madison, 5 U.S. (1 Cranch) 137 (1803).

March, James, and Johan Olsen. 2011. "Elaborating the 'New Institutionalism.'" In *The Oxford Handbook of Political Science*, edited by Robert Goodin. New York: Oxford University Press.

Marron, Donald, and Adele Morris. 2016. "How to Use Carbon Tax Revenues." Tax Policy Center at Brookings Institution. https://www.brookings.edu/wp-content/uploads/2016/07/howtousecarbontaxrevenuemarronmorris.pdf

Maryland General Assembly. House Bill 375 (2008). http://mgaleg.maryland.gov/

Maryland General Assembly. House Bill 1308 (2004). http://mgaleg.maryland.gov/

Massachusetts General Court. Chapter 164 of Acts of 1997. https://malegislature.gov/Laws/SessionLaws/Acts/1997/Chapter164

Matejka, Mike. 1999. "The Historical Development of Industry and Manufacturing in Illinois." https://www.lib.niu.edu/1999/iht639941.html

Maxmen, Amy, and Jeff Tollefson. 2020. "Two Decades of Pandemic War Games Failed to Account for Donald Trump." *Nature* 584: 26–29.

Mayhew, David. 1974. *Congress: The Electoral Connection*. New Haven: Yale University Press.

McCann, Pamela, Charles Shipan, and Craig Volden. 2015. "Top-Down Federalism: State Policy Responses to National Government Discussions." *Publius: The Journal of Federalism* 45 (4): 495–525.

McCarty, Nolan. 2019. *Polarization: What Everyone Needs to Know*. New York: Oxford University Press.

McCubbins, Mathew, Roger Noll, and Barry Weingast. 1987. "Administrative Procedures as Instruments of Political Control." *Journal of Law, Economics, and Organization* 3: 243-77.

McCubbins, Mathew, and Thomas Schwartz. 1984. "Congressional Oversight Overlooked: Police Patrols versus Fire Alarms." *American Journal of Political Science* 28 (1): 165-79.

McGreevey, Patrick. 2011. "Governor Brown Signs Law Requiring 33% of Energy Be Renewable by 2020." *Los Angeles Times*, April 13.

Meier, Kenneth, Mallory Compton, John Polga-Hecimovich, Miyeon Song, and Cameron Wimpy. 2019. "Bureaucracy and the Failure of Politics: Challenges to Democratic Governance." *Administration and Society* 51 (10): 1576–1605.

Meyer, Robinson. 2019. "A Very Important Climate Fact That No One Knows." *The Atlantic*, May 8.

Michigan Public Service Commission. 2020. "About the MPSC." Retrieved October 6. https://www.michigan.gov/mpsc/0,9535,7-395-93218---,00.html

Mildenberger, Matto, and Leah Stokes. 2020. "North American Energy Politics." In *The Oxford Handbook of Energy Politics*, edited by Kathleen Hancock and Juliann Allison. New York: Oxford University Press.

Miller, Gary. 2005. "The Political Evolution of Principal-Agent Models." *Annual Review of Political Science* 8: 203–25.

Miller, Gary, and Norman Schofield. 2008. "The Transformation of the Republican and Democratic Party Coalitions in the United States." *Perspectives on Politics* 6 (3): 433–50.

Minnesota Legislature. Senate File 1706 (1994). Retrieved September 22, 2020 from a scan of 1994 Minnesota Session Laws.

Mooney, Christopher. 1999. "The Politics of Morality Policy: Symposium Editor's Introduction." *Policy Studies Journal* 27 (4): 675–80.

Mooney, Christopher. 2020. *The Study of U.S. State Policy Diffusion: What Hath Walker Wrought?* New York: Cambridge University Press.

Mooney, Christopher, and Mei-Hsien Lee. 1995. "Legislating Morality in the American States: The Case of Pre-*Roe* Abortion Regulation Reform." *American Journal of Political Science* 39 (3): 599–627.

Mooney, Christopher, and Mei-Hsien Lee. 1999. "Morality Policy Reinvention: State Death Penalties." *Annals of the American Academy of Political and Social Science* 556: 80–92.

Morris, Jackson, Andrea Cerbin, Jordan Stutt, and Adam Cohn. 2013. "New York's Renewable Portfolio Standard: Where to from Here?" Pace Energy and Climate Center. https://peccpubs.pace.edu/getFileContents.php?resourceid=58e2e2d4eca26f0

Nahai, David. 2011. "California's SB X 1–2 Law Walks Renewable Energy Tightrope." *Renewable Energy World*, June 10.

Nanavati, Payal, and Justin Gundlach. 2016. "Legal Tools for Climate Adaptation Advocacy: The Electric Grid and Its Regulators—FERC and State Public Utility Commissions." Columbia Law School Sabin Center for Climate Change Law.

Nangeroni, Erica. 2014. "Ohio Becomes the First State to Freeze Its Renewable Portfolio Standard." *Solsystems*, June 19.

National Alliance for Model State Drug Laws. http://www.namsdl.org

National Association for the Advancement of Colored People v. Federal Power Commission 425 U.S. 662 (1976).

National Association of Insurance Commissioners. 2019. "About." https://content.naic.org/index_about.htm

National Corn Growers Association. 2018. "World of Corn 2018." http://www.worldofcorn.com/#/

National Federation of Independent Business. 2017. "Cap and Trade Deal Will Raise Costs, Hurt Small Businesses." July 11.

National Mining Association. 2014. "Coal Production by State and by Rank." Retrieved 18 May 2021. http://www.nma.org/pdf/c_production_state_rank.pdf

National Public Radio. 2013. "Root Canals Are More Popular Than Congress." *Morning Edition*, 9 January. https://www.npr.org/2013/01/09/168937450/root-canals-are-more-popular-than-congress

Neufeld, John. 2008. "Corruption, Quasi-Rents, and the Regulation of Electric Utilities." *Journal of Economic History* 68 (4): 1059–97.

Neumayer, Eric. 2004. "The Environment and Left-Wing Political Orientation." *Ecological Economics* 51 (3–4): 167–75.

Nevada Legislature. Assembly Bill 366 (1997). Retrieved 10 October 2018, accessed via the Nevada Legislative Research Library at https://www.leg.state.nv.us/Division/Research/Library/index.html

New Hampshire General Court. House Bill 873 (2007). Retrieved 11 January 2019, accessed via the General Court website at http://gencourt.state.nh.us/bill_Status/

New Mexico Public Regulation Commission. 2021. Retrieved 20 January 2021. http://www.nmprc.state.nm.us/#gsc.tab=0

Newport, Frank. 2013. "Dysfunctional Government Surpasses Economy as Top U.S. Problem." *Gallup News*, October 9.

New York City Public Advocate. 2021. "Municipalizing New York City's Electric Grid." https://www.pubadvocate.nyc.gov/reports/municipalizing-new-york-citys-electric-grid/

New York Department of Public Service. 2022. "Meet the Commissioners." Retrieved 3 February 2022. https://www3.dps.ny.gov/W/PSCWeb.nsf/All/553FBA3F3EEF7FBD85257687006F3A6D

New York Public Service Commission. Order for Case 03-E-0188, September 24, 2004 (2004). Retrieved 17 October 2018, accessed via New York Department of Public Service Website at https://www.dps.ny.gov/

New York Public Service Commission. Order for Case 03-E-0188, April 2, 2010 (2010). Retrieved 16 May 2013, accessed via New York Department of Public Service Website at https://www.dps.ny.gov/

New York State Energy and Research Development Agency. 2020. "History of NYSERDA." https://www.nyserda.ny.gov/About/History-of-NYSERDA

Nordlander, Gerald. 2002. "Electricity Deregulation in New York State, 1996–2002." Public Utility Law Project of New York Brief.

Norrander, Barbara, and Clyde Wilcox. 1999. "Public Opinion and Policy-Making in the States: The Case of Post-Roe Abortion Policy." *Policy Studies Journal* 27 (4): 707–722.

North Carolina Clean Energy Technology Center. 2016. "Database on State Incentives for Renewables and Efficiency." http://programs.dsireusa.org

North Carolina Clean Energy Technology Center. 2020. "Database on State Incentives for Renewables and Efficiency." http://programs.dsireusa.org

North Carolina Legislature. Senate Bill 3/Session Law 2007–397 (2007). Retrieved September 23, 2020 from a scan of 2007 North Carolina Session Laws.

North Dakota Legislature. House Bill 1305 (2013). https://www.legis.nd.gov/assembly/63-2013/bill-actions/ba1305.html

Nye, Glenn. 2019. "How to Fix Political Dysfunction." *The Hill*, September 30.

Ohio General Assembly. Substitute Senate Bill 221 (2008). Retrieved 28 May 2013 from the Ohio general assembly archives website, available at http://archives.legislature.state.oh.us/

Olson, Mancur. 1965. *The Logic of Collective Action: Public Goods and the Theory of Groups*. Cambridge, MA: Harvard University Press.

Oosting, Jonathan. 2014. "Michigan Road Funding: Proposal to Cut Truck Weight Limits Falls in State Senate." *Lansing News*, December 2, https://www.mlive.com/lansing-news/index.ssf/2014/12/michigan_roads_bill_to_reduce.html

Orren, Karen, and Stephen Skowronek. 2017. *The Policy State: An American Predicament*. Cambridge, MA: Harvard University Press.

Ostrom, Vincent. 2008. *The Political Theory of a Compound Republic*. Lanham, MD: Lexington Books.

Overpeck, Jonathan, and Bradley Udall. 2020. "Climate Change and the Aridification of North America." *Proceedings of the National Academy of Sciences of the United States of America* 117 (22): 11856–58.

Pacheco, Julianna. 2012. "The Social Contagion Model: Exploring the Role of Public Opinion on the Diffusion of Antismoking Legislation across the American States." *Journal of Politics* 74 (1): 187–212.

Pardo, Bryce. 2014. "Cannabis Policy Reforms in the Americas: A Comparative Analysis of Colorado, Washington, and Uruguay." *International Journal of Drug Policy* 25 (4): 727–35.

Parinandi, Srinivas. 2013. "Conditional Bureaucratic Discretion and State Welfare Diffusion under AFDC." *State Politics and Policy Quarterly* 13 (2): 244–61.

Parinandi, Srinivas. 2020. "Policy Inventing and Borrowing among State Legislatures." *American Journal of Political Science* 64 (4): 852–68.

Parinandi, Srinivas, and Matthew Hitt. 2018. "How Politics Influences the Energy Pricing Decisions of Elected Public Utilities Commissioners." *Energy Policy* 118C: 77–87.

Parinandi, Srinivas, Stefani Langehennig, and Mark Trautmann. 2020. "Which Legis-lators Pay Attention to Other States' Policies? Comparing Cosponsorship to Floor Voting in the Diffusion of Renewable Portfolio Policy." *Policy Studies Journal* 49 (3).

Pennsylvania Legislature. Senate Bill 1030/Public Law 1672, Number 213 (2004). Retrieved September 23, 2020 from a scan of 2004 Pennsylvania Acts.

Perdana, Andrian, and Andres Lopez. 2020. "Solar Energy Potential: How We Can Help Arizona's Pollution Problem by Converting to Solar Energy." ArcGIS Brief. https://storymaps.arcgis.com/stories/7a5850caaac84b54b3e1abdb324f1cfe

Peterson, Paul. 1995. *The Price of Federalism*. Washington, DC: Brookings Institution.

Pierce, Patrick, and Donald Miller. 1999. "Variations in the Diffusion of State Lottery Adoptions: How Revenue Dedication Changes Morality Policies." *Policy Studies Journal* 27 (4): 696–706.

Pitkin, Hanna. 1967. *The Concept of Representation*. Berkeley: University of California Press.

Potrafke, Niklas. 2010. "Does Government Ideology Influence Deregulation of Prod-uct Markets? Evidence from OECD Countries." *Public Choice* 4 (1): 135–55.

Potter, Rachel. 2019. *Bending the Rules: Procedural Politicking in the Bureaucracy*. Chi-cago: University of Chicago Press.

PowerGrid International. 2002. "Arizona Ushers in Changes in Direction of Electric Competition." August 29.

Primeaux, Walter, and Patrick Mann. 1986. "Regulator Selection Methods and Elec-tricity Prices." *Land Economics* 62: 1–13.

Pyper, Julia. 2018. "The Battle over Arizona's Clean Energy Mix." *Greentech Media*, September 23.

Rabe, Barry. 1999. "Federalism and Entrepreneurship: Explaining American and Canadian Innovation in Pollution Prevention and Regulatory Integration." *Policy Studies Journal* 28: 288–306.

Rabe, Barry. 2004. *Statehouse and Greenhouse: The Emerging Politics of American Cli-mate Change Policy*. Washington, DC: Brookings Institution.

Rabe, Barry. 2007. "Race to the Top: The Expanding Role of U.S. State Renewable Portfolio Standards." *Sustainable Development Law and Policy* 7 (3): 10–17.

Rabe, Barry. 2008. "States on Steroids: The Intergovernmental Odyssey of American Climate Policy." *Review of Policy Research* 25 (2): 105–28.

Rainey, James. 2019. "More Americans Believe in Global Warming—but They Won't Pay Much for It." *NBC News*, January 24.

Ram, Manish, Michael Child, Arman Aghahosseini, Dmitrii Bogdanov, Alena Lohrmann, and Christian Breyer. 2018. "A Comparative Analysis of Electric-ity Generation Costs from Renewable, Fossil Fuel, and Nuclear Sources in G20 Countries for the Period 2015–2030." *Journal of Cleaner Production* 199: 687–704.

Renewable Energy World. 2007. "Illinois Approves Clean Energy and Efficiency Standards." *Renewable Energy World*, August 6. https://www.renewableenergy-world.com/baseload/illinois-approves-clean-energy-and-efficiency-standards-49544/#gref

Riker, William. 1964. *Federalism: Origin, Operation, Significance.* Boston: Little, Brown.

Rogers, Everett. 1962. *The Diffusion of Innovations.* New York: Free Press.

Rosenberg, Gerald. 1991. *The Hollow Hope: Can Courts Bring about Social Change?* Chicago: University of Chicago Press.

Ryan, Timothy. 2017. "No Compromise: Political Consequences of Moralized Attitudes." *American Journal of Political Science* 61 (2): 409–23.

Sarkisian, David. 2016. "Alternative Energy Law: Iowa Program Overview." North Carolina Clean Energy Technology Center. Database for State Incentives on Renewables and Efficiency. http://programs.dsireusa.org/system/program/detail/265

Schattschneider, Elmer. 1975. *The Semi-Sovereign People: A Realist's View of Democracy in America.* New York: Harcourt.

Scott, Mark, Mick Lennon, Daniel Turbidy, Patrick Marchman, A. R. Siders, Kelly Leilani Main, Victoria Hermann, Debra Butler, Kathryn Frank, Karyn Bosomworth, Raphaele Blanchi, and Cassidy Johnson. 2020. "Climate Disruption and Planning: Resistance or Retreat?" *Planning Theory and Practice* 1: 125–54.

Shane, Peter. 2009. *Madison's Nightmare: How Executive Power Threatens American Democracy.* Chicago: University of Chicago Press.

Shepsle, Kenneth, and Barry Weingast. 1987. "The Institutional Foundations of Committee Power." *American Political Science Review* 81 (1): 85–104.

Shipan, Charles, and Craig Volden. 2006. "Bottom-Up Federalism: The Diffusion of Anti-Smoking Policies from U.S. Cities to States." *American Journal of Political Science* 50 (4): 825–43.

Shipan, Charles, and Craig Volden. 2008. "The Mechanisms of Policy Diffusion." *American Journal of Political Science* 52 (4): 840–57.

Shipan, Charles, and Craig Volden. 2012. "Policy Diffusion: Seven Lessons for Scholars and Practitioners." *Public Administration Review* 72 (6): 788–96.

Shipan, Charles, and Craig Volden. 2014. "When the Smoke Clears: Expertise, Learning, and Policy Diffusion." *Journal of Public Policy* 34 (3): 357–87.

Shor, Boris, and Nolan McCarty. 2011. "The Ideological Mapping of American Legislatures." *American Political Science Review* 105 (3): 530–51.

Sickinger, Ted. 2019. "Cap and Trade: What Could Oregon's Carbon Policy Cost You?" *Oregonian/Oregon Live,* June 19.

Smith, Michael. 2002. "Lessons to Be Learned from California and Enron for Restructuring Electricity Markets." *Electricity Journal* 15 (7): 23–32.

South Dakota Legislature. House Bill 1123 (2008). Retrieved 30 May 2013 from the South Dakota legislative website, available at https://sdlegislature.gov/Session/Archived

Squire, Peverill. 2007. "Measuring State Legislative Professionalism: The Squire Index Revisited." *State Politics and Policy Quarterly* 7 (2): 211–27.

Squire, Peverill. 2017. *The Rise of the Representative: Lawmakers and Constituents in Colonial America.* Ann Arbor: University of Michigan Press.

Staley, Samuel. 2010. "States' Rights versus Obamacare." *Reason,* March 26.

State of Georgia Public Service Commission. 2020. "FAQs." Retrieved 6 October

2020 and accessed via Georgia Public Service Commission website at https://psc. ga.gov/faqs/

State of New York. 2002. "2002 New York State Energy Plan and the 2005 Update Memorandum." Retrieved 7 February 2022, available at https://energyplan. ny.gov/Plans/2002

Status of State Electric Industry Restructuring Activity. 2003. Accessed June 2, 2021, http://large.stanford.edu/publications/coal/references/docs/restructure.pdf

Stavins, Robert. 2006. "Vintage-Differentiated Environmental Regulation." *Stanford Environmental Law Journal* 25 (1): 29–63.

Stigler, George. 1971. "The Theory of Economic Regulation." *Bell Journal of Economics and Management Science* 2: 3–21.

Stigler, George, and Claire Friedland. 1962. "What Can Regulators Regulate? The Case of Electricity." *Journal of Law and Economics* 5: 1–16.

Stokes, Leah. 2020. *Short Circuiting Policy: Interest Groups and the Battle over Clean Energy and Climate Policy in the American States.* New York: Oxford University Press.

Stokes, Leah, and Christopher Warshaw. 2017. "Renewable Energy Policy Design and Framing Influence Public Policy Support in the United States." *Nature Energy* 2: 1–6.

Strumpf, Koleman. 2002. "Does Government Decentralization Increase Policy Innovation?" *Journal of Public Economic Theory* 4: 207–41.

Swank, Duane. 2006. "Tax Policy in an Era of Internationalization: Explaining the Spread of Neoliberalism." *International Organization* 60 (4): 847–82.

Teske, Paul. 2003. "State Regulation: Captured Victorian-Era Anachronism or 'Re-Enforcing' Autonomous Structure?" *Perspectives on Politics* 1 (2): 291–306.

Thornton, Dorothy, Robert Kagan, and Neil Gunningham. 2008. "Compliance Costs, Regulation, and Environmental Performance: Controlling Truck Emissions in the US." *Regulation and Governance* 2 (3): 275–92.

Troeksen, Werner. 1996. *Why Regulate Utilities? The New Institutional Economics and the Chicago Gas Industry, 1849–1924.* Ann Arbor: University of Michigan Press.

Troesken, Werner. 2006. "Regime Change and Corruption: A History of Public Utility Regulation." In *Corruption and Reform: Lessons from America's Economic History,* edited by Edward Glaeser and Claudia Goldin. Chicago: University of Chicago Press.

Tsebelis, George. 2002. *Veto Players: How Political Institutions Work.* Princeton: Princeton University Press.

Tulis, Jeffrey. 2017. *The Rhetorical Presidency.* Princeton: Princeton University Press.

Turner, Kris. 2016. "Indiana's Manufacturing History Also Is Key to the State's Economic Future." *Indianapolis Star,* March 18. https://www.indystar.com/story/money/2016/03/18/indianas-manufacturing-history-also-key-states-economic-future/81540742/

Union of Concerned Scientists. Various years. State Renewable Energy Portfolio Standard Summaries (Various States).

United Nations. 2021. "Climate Change." https://www.un.org/en/sections/issues-depth/climate-change/

United States Constitution. Article I. https://constitutioncenter.org/interactive-con-stitution/article/article-i#article-section-7

United States Department of Agriculture Economic Research Service. 2018. "Cash Receipts by Commodity State Ranking, 2017." https://data.ers.usda.gov/reports. aspx?ID=17844

United States Energy Information Administration. 2013. "State Energy Data System (Price and Production) Estimates." https://www.eia.gov/state/data.php

United States Energy Information Administration. 2018. "Coal Data Browser." https://www.eia.gov/coal/data/browser/

United States Energy Information Administration. 2021. "Coal Data Browser." https://www.eia.gov/coal/data/browser/

United States Environmental Protection Agency. 2014. "Sources of Greenhouse Gas Emissions." https://climatechange.chicago.gov/ghgemissions/sources-greenhouse-gas-emissions

United States Environmental Protection Agency. 2015. "Final Clean Power Plan Rule." *Federal Register* 80 (205), October 23.

Van Riper, Paul. 1983. "The American Administrative State: Wilson and the Found-ers—an Unorthodox View." *Public Administration Review* 43 (6): 477–90.

Vigilone, Giuliana. 2020. "Climate Lawsuits Are Breaking New Legal Ground to Pro-tect the Planet." *Nature* 579: 184–85.

Volden, Craig. 2002a. "Delegating Power to Bureaucracies: Evidence from the States." *Journal of Law, Economics, and Organization* 18 (1): 187–220.

Volden, Craig. 2002b. "The Politics of Competitive Federalism: A Race to the Bottom in Welfare Benefits?" *American Journal of Political Science* 46 (2): 352–63.

Volden, Craig. 2006. "States as Policy Laboratories: Emulating Success in the Chil-dren's Health Insurance Program." *American Journal of Political Science* 50 (2): 294–312.

Volden, Craig. 2015. "Failures: Diffusion, Learning, and Policy Abandonment." *State Politics and Policy Quarterly* 16 (1): 44–77.

Volden, Craig, Michael Ting, and Daniel Carpenter. 2008. "A Formal Model of Learn-ing and Policy Diffusion." *American Political Science Review* 102 (3): 319–32.

Volden, Craig, and Alan Wiseman. 2014. *Legislative Effectiveness in the United States Congress: The Lawmakers.* New York: Cambridge University Press.

Votesmart. 2021. Multiple legislators searched. https://justfacts.votesmart.org/

Wagner, John, and Scott Clement. 2017. "It's Just Messed Up: Most Think Political Divisions as Bad as Vietnam Era, New Poll Shows." *Washington Post*, October 28.

Walker, Jack. 1969. "The Diffusion of Innovations among the American States." *Amer-ican Political Science Review* 63 (3): 880–99.

Walton, Eric. 2005. "The Persistence of Bureaucracy: A Meta-Analysis of Weber's Model of Bureaucratic Control." *Organization Studies* 26 (4): 569–600.

Warf, Barney. 2008. "The U.S. Electoral College and Spatial Biases in Voter Power." *Annals of the Association of American Geographers* 99 (1): 184–204.

Weber, Max. 1978. *Economy and Society: An Outline of Interpretive Sociology, Volume 2.* Berkeley: University of California Press.

Weingast, Barry. 1984. "The Congressional-Bureaucratic System: A Principal Agent Perspective (with Applications to the SEC)." *Public Choice* 44: 147–91.

Welch, Eric, and Darold Barnum. 2009. "Joint Environmental and Cost Efficiency Analysis of Electricity Generation." *Ecological Economics* 68 (8–9): 2336–43.

West, William. 2005. "Neutral Competence and Political Responsiveness: An Uneasy Relationship." *Policy Studies Journal* 33 (2): 147–60.

White, Greg. 2018. Phone interview with White, executive director of the National Association of Regulatory Utility Commissioners, March 8.

Williams, Richard. 2011. "Using Stata's Margins Command to Estimate and Interpret Adjusted Predictions and Marginal Effects." Retrieved November 20, 2020, https://www3.nd.edu/~rwilliam/stats/Margins01.pdf

Wilson, Reid. 2014. "State Legislatures Are Very Very Busy." *Washington Post*, September 29.

Wilson, Woodrow. 1887. "The Study of Administration." *Political Science Quarterly* 2 (2): 197–222.

Wiser, Ryan, Christopher Namovicz, Mark Gielecki, and Robert Smith. 2007. "Renewable Portfolio Standards: A Factual Introduction to Experience from the United States." Berkeley National Laboratories Paper LBNL-62569.

Zero Waste Europe. 2019. "The Impact of Waste-to-Energy Incineration on Climate." https://zerowasteeurope.eu/wp-content/uploads/edd/2019/09/ZWE_Policy-briefing_The-impact-of-Waste-to-Energy-incineration-on-Climate.pdf

Ziegler, Mary. 2020. *Abortion and the Law in America: Roe v. Wade to the Present*. New York: Cambridge University Press.

Index